[No caption required.] New Jersey, circa 1990. Photo courtesy of Eddie Malluk.

Bahamas and California, 1968–1972. I don't often go back to Freeport, but when I do, I go in through the returning resident line. All photos by David Bierk.

Toronto. Maple Leaf Gardens. Parking Lot. 1979. Before people stared down at their cell phones, we checked out each other's Gene Simmons impersonations. Photo by David Bierk.

**KID
WIKKID**

Kid Wikkid seemingly popped
out of the ground this year to
conjure up one of the most
dedicated followings around for
any band without a record deal.
Originally formed as Herrenvolk,
the group went through a line-up
and name change to emerge in
their present form. Which is,
Sebastian 'Baz' Bach (vocals), Bill
Sax and Dave Aplin (guitars),
Kenny Fox (bass) and drummer
Brian Williams.

Kid Wikkid can be heard on the
Maple Metal compilation album
with a track called *Take A Look At
Me* and are in negotiations with
Heavy Metal U.K. for an album
expected in the spring.

Peterborough, Ontario, Canada, circa 1984. *Metallion* magazine. Thanks to Ron Boudreau and Lenny
Stoute for making this into the first ever button of my face. Photo courtesy of Ron Boudreau.

Tour of Hell, 1989. Shorts from Hell. Bon Jovi Tour. This was our home, and the leader of the house was a man by the name of Kenny Barnes. Photo courtesy of the author.

Live, circa 1987–1988. Perhaps at the Cat Club in New York City, where we got signed by the dude who signed Led Zeppelin. Photo by David Bierk.

Lake Geneva, Wisconsin. 1987–2015. We had the end of recording the first album party right here. I got locked out of my room and onto the roof, after a corporate gig, right behind where we are standing, almost thirty years later. Photo courtesy of the author.

Playing football with Jon Bon Jovi. New Jersey, 1987. Some people say Skid Row made it too fast. But it took at least two weeks. Photo courtesy of Mark Weiss.

To Hell & Bach. Bach on Broadway, 2000. © Eduardo Patino, NYC.

To my love Suzanne. Thank you for being by my side. Forever & Ever. Amen! Rock 'n' Roll? It's been very, very good to me! S.W.A.K. T.L.F. I love you. Photo courtesy of the author.

18 AND
LIFE
ON SKID ROW

18 AND LIFE ON SKID ROW

SEBASTIAN BACH

DEY ST.

An Imprint of WILLIAM MORROW

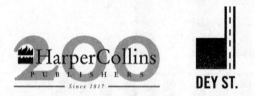

18 AND LIFE ON SKID ROW. Copyright © 2016 by Sebastian Bach. All rights reserved. Printed in the United States of America. No part of this book may be used or reproduced in any manner whatsoever without written permission except in the case of brief quotations embodied in critical articles and reviews. For information address HarperCollins Publishers, 195 Broadway, New York, NY 10007.

HarperCollins books may be purchased for educational, business, or sales promotional use. For information please email the Special Markets Department at SPsales@harpercollins.com.

A hardcover edition of this book was published in 2016 by Dey Street Books, an imprint of William Morrow.

FIRST DEY STREET BOOKS PAPERBACK EDITION PUBLISHED 2017.

Library of Congress Cataloging-in-Publication Data has been applied for.

ISBN 978-0-06-226540-1

21   OV/LSC   10 9 8 7 6

To my Mom Kathleen
for Inspiring me to Live
To my Wife Suzanne
for Inspiring me to Love
To all my Kids
for Inspiring me to Laugh
To Rick & his Team
for Inspiring me to Rule
To Dad
for Inspiring me to Dare
to Dream

CONTENTS

18 AND LIFE ON SKID ROW

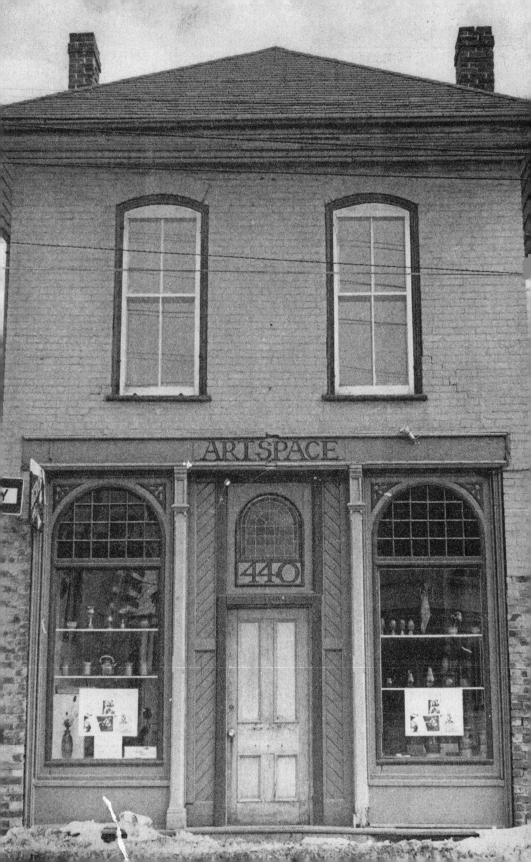

YOUTH GONE WILD

December 27, 1989
Springfield, Massachusetts

I touch my fingers to my lips. I stand. Bathed in sweat. In the center of the stage. The taste is salty to the tongue. I look at the ground.

I see a glass bottle under my gaze. Lying askew atop the metal grid. I feel the red liquid all over my hand. I touch the crimson substance to my mouth.

Why is there red liquid all over me?

I wipe my brow. I discover that my face is completely covered in what I am assuming is tomato juice.

Why would somebody throw a glass bottle of tomato juice at me while I'm on stage?

To my shock, horror, and amazement, my face is not covered in tomato juice. My face is completely covered in my own blood. In front of 20,000 people. Opening up for my heroes, Aerosmith.

I am standing on stage in front of a packed arena with my face and hands covered in my own blood.

I see red. Not from the blood in my eyes, but from the anger in my heart.

General admission crowds are by nature, crazy.

When there are no chairs at a concert, and thousands of people crush together into one sweaty, rocking crowd, things can get out of control all too easily. I look into the seething mass of highly charged rock 'n' rollers on the arena floor in front of me. I start to utter the infamous rap, as viewed millions of times now on YouTube.

"Who in the fuck threw that?"

About ten guys circle around one guy. They're all pointing at him. They're all shouting at me.

"It was him, it was him!!"

"Was it you, *cocksucker*?"

The man in the middle of the other ten says nothing. He looks straight at me, and extends his middle finger, in the gesture commonly known as "Fuck You."

What happens next is the first chink in the armor. Of Skid Row. Of stardom. This is the exact moment when my childhood dream shows the first sign of an adult nightmare.

I had spent at least seven or eight years previous to this moment playing in clubs. Bars. *Saloons*. Playing three sets a night. Cover tunes. To drunk rock 'n' rollers in Quebec and Northern Ontario. Fighting was just a part of the scene that I had been in for years now. I did not know any other way to respond.

But this was not a club.

This was a packed arena. Full of approximately 20,000 people. Not a place where I could act in the only way I had known how to act previously. My life had changed. But I was not mature enough at the time to realize that I had to change with it.

I say into the mic, "Everybody, get the fuck back."

I motion with my hands for everybody to move out of the way of this guy. Whose ass, I most certainly intend to kick.

I pick the glass bottle up off the stage. I walk as far back to the drum riser as I can, to get a good run at my nemesis. The song we are about to play is called "Piece of Me." Never could I have realized that the song would be taken literally. By a deranged fan. By me. By myself.

I stare into the man's face as he tells me again to *fuck off*. I am completely enraged and am not about to let him win this fight.

I then do the unthinkable.

I throw the glass bottle back into the crowd at the man with his middle finger raised in the air. Problem is, this is a general admission crowd, and although I did not know this at the time, I would later learn that the bottle . . . did not . . . hit its intended target.

I run with all of my power toward the lip of the stage. I jump off the stage, flying through the air, and plant my Cuban-heeled Beatle boot straight into the man's jaw. Breaking it immediately.

I start flailing my fists at the man whose jaw I just broke. I am standing on an arena floor, packed with 10,000 people, and I am literally trying to fight *all of them*.

After a minute or two, I am dragged off the man by security, back onto the stage, to the incredulous stares of my fellow bandmates. We once again attempt to launch into the song "Piece of Me."

> *Sleazin' in the city*
> *Well, I'm lookin' for a fight*
> *I'm on my heels and lookin' pretty*
> *On a Saturday night night night*

I wail into the microphone, in my heels, in the city, *lookin' for a fight*. Some may even have called me "pretty." I headbang and spray blood and sweat all over the front row. We finish the show, with my face covered in blood, pouring from the open wound in my head.

Convinced that all is well, happy with our literally *ass-kicking* performance, the band proceeds with our nightly ritual of drinking and smoking. But tonight will prove to be different than the other nights.

We make a hasty retreat to the bus as soon as the show is over. Management wants us out of the building as soon as possible. More precisely, they want us out of the *state* as soon as possible. We know why, but dude, that dude *deserved it*, dude.

I sit in the front lounge, and continue to bleed all over myself. The gash in my scalp is far bigger than I realized while onstage. It's a good inch or more long on top of my head. On the top of my scalp. My hair and face are caked in blood. Dave "The Snake" Sabo sits across from me. He pours us both a drink. He tries to cheer me up. I begin to cry.

The bus driver, a great man by the name of Kenny Barnes, is under instructions from our managers Doc and Scott McGhee to get us over state lines as quick as possible. We speed through town, sipping our drinks and ready to do it all again in the next town, on the next night. We try to tell ourselves, *Hey man!! This is rock 'n' roll!*

We don't make it too far.

We suddenly realize we are being followed by several Massachusetts State Troopers. Silently. Behind our bus. Many of them. Kenny the bus driver is freaking out. As are we all. Especially me.

Our bus ride comes to an abrupt end. The State Troopers put on their cherry lights and sound the sirens. We are pulled over into the parking lot of a strip mall. Just short of the State Line, if I recall correctly.

The bus is in the middle of a parking lot. The State Troopers have us completely surrounded. They are spread out in a wide circle, equidistant between one another. Each cruiser has its high beams on, sirens flashing, with all of the headlights pointed directly at us. The lights are shining through the tour bus, making the interior of the bus bright white, not unlike the scene with the little boy in the house from the movie *Close Encounters of the Third Kind*.

This, however, was a close encounter of the worst kind.

After about an hour or so, the Law comes onto the bus. For me. I am handcuffed and led off of my plush leather couch into the harsh glare of ten or so Massachusetts State Trooper cruisers.

I am completely unaware of the full weight of what had happened tonight. I get into the back of the police car, joking around with the State Troopers. I remain handcuffed, bleeding, and slightly buzzed.

The Troopers are not amused.

"Why'd you do it?" they ask me.

"Do what?" I reply. Surely these cops were like other policemen I have known. Most of them are rock 'n' roll fans, like everyone else I seem to meet. Surely these boys in blue would have my back, dude. How could I *not* go *whoop sum ass* on the guy who pitched a glass bottle at me? Couldn't they see the blood in my hair? The open wound on the top of my head?

"What's the problem, Officers?" I say, not ready for their answer.

"How could you do it, man?"

"What?"

"She's hurt. The girl in the crowd. The girl whose nose you broke."

"Huh?"

"Yeah, you fucking asshole. You whipped a bottle off the stage, and hit her in the face. You broke her nose. You broke a guy's jaw, too. How in the fuck could you do that? Hurt a girl?"

I slumped into the back of the police car. I could not believe what I was hearing.

I could not believe what I had done. The damage I had caused.

I had hurt an innocent girl in the melee. A fan of rock 'n' roll. The thing I held most dear to my heart.

Rock 'n' roll is supposed to be fun. The most fun you ever had. Rock 'n' roll is what you listen to, *to get away from all of the bad stuff*. It's not supposed to *be* the bad stuff. All this pain, all of this destruction, was because of *my fucked-up behavior.* Yeah, there is no doubt, I was indeed a total asshole that night.

As I thought of a bottle crushing into a fan's face, thrown by me, I hung my bloody head in shame in the back of the police car. And wept.

All I have ever wanted to do is entertain people with music. With singing. With my voice. I have never in my life, ever tried to be a "bad boy." All I have ever tried to be, is *good.*

The doors on my jail cell clinked shut that night, with a resounding thud. I sat in my cell and pondered the severity of my actions. The irony of my circumstance.

We Are the Youth Gone Wild. Indeed.

But at what cost?

1
LET'S BEGIN
AT THE BEGINNING

ca. 1970
Freeport, Bahamas

It's hot. The sun is shining brightly in my eyes, behind my father's head. I squint from the bright light of the Freeport, Bahamas, sun, but when I stare into my father's eyes, my own eyes relax. If I just look into my dad's smiling face, I realize, I don't have to squint.

This is the first ever memory of my whole life.

I figured I would start at the very beginning.

My bare feet are almost burning from the heat. We are in our backyard. I am beyond puzzled. I just cannot figure it out. There is a large star on the ground. I do not understand what it is. I remember pointing at it, saying, "Dad, what is that?" He explained to me that it was, in fact, a fish. That it was breathing. That it came from the ocean. It had somehow gotten into our backyard, onto our blazing patio. He said that it belonged in the water, because that is where its starfish home was. I was wide-eyed and wondrous. How could

a starfish become so out of its element, a fish out of water, out of breath, out of time? *Would it die if it got too hot?*

Or could we return it, to where it belonged, and save its starfish life?

What the hell is this thing doing in our backyard?

This is my first ever memory.

Second memory:

I am asleep.

The warm, sultry Bahamian air breezes through our screen porch. I remember the screened-in veranda of our home in Free-port. It ran along the side of the house. The screen was there to keep the island bugs and critters out.

Or so we thought.

I am on my side. My arm hangs down over the mattress, toward the floor below. I doze off to sleep with my mom and dad across the room, in the dining area of the simple island abode. An open floor plan, my bed (crib?) was in the corner of the house, right next to the screened-in porch.

I remember dreaming that something was tickling my hand. I slowly open my eyes out of my slumber and see my parents sitting around the dining room table, laughing and talking. There is a single light on above them, while the rest of the room, where I slept, was dark.

The dream continued on for a long time. It seemed so real. I remember thinking, Wow, this really feels like something is tickling my hand. I open my eyes again. I look under the bed.

The whole side of the bed, and the floor below, is covered in bright red blood. My hand had been dangling over the bed, and at the end of my wrist, where my hand started, is a gigantic rat.

The rat was eating my hand.

I froze. I was slowly realizing that this was not a dream. This was actually happening. A rat was chewing on my flesh.

I was fascinated. I did not scream right away. I just looked at all of the blood and watched the rat gnaw on me. I remember thinking, Wow, this doesn't even really hurt. I couldn't believe how much blood there was. The rat's face had my blood all over it. The creature kept on nibbling at the open wound on my bloody arm.

Then, I screamed. My mom jumped up from the table and screamed too, while rushing over to me and picking me up into her arms. Mom and Dad rushed me to hospital.

That's where the memory ends.

In my third memory, it is still hot. We are still in the Bahamas.

We are now living in an apartment complex, with a pool in the middle of the courtyard. My father and I are swimming. It is raining. It feels amazing, swimming in the cool water, in the tropical heat of the early evening, with the rain coming down, creating rivulets of water on the pool's surface.

Dad says, "We have to go in now."

"Why?" I say.

"Because if lightning strikes the pool, we will both get electrocuted and die." Umm, okay, Dad! Time to go inside.

This next, fourth memory I can recall of my life, was told by my father, to all assembled, at my first wedding. To the shock of many friends and family who were present that day.

My mom and dad had gone out for the evening. They had left me in the care of an elderly Bahamian woman. I only have flashes of memory of this particular night.

I can remember being in a crib. After my mom and dad left, the

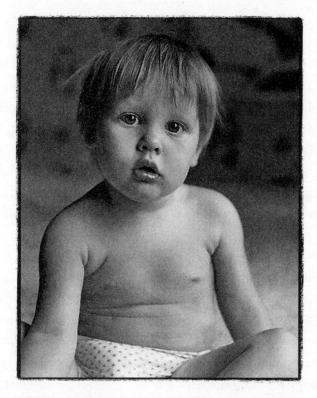

lady had brought over some of her friends, unbeknownst to my parents. I can remember them looking down at me in the crib.

My dad remembered the story in detail.

Upon my parents' return to the apartment, Dad looked through the window into a shocking scene inside our home.

He opened the door, and what he saw can only be described as disturbing.

The elderly Bahamian babysitter had brought over two other women to our house. The three of them did not notice my parents returning home. When Mom and Dad entered the room, the three ladies were dancing around my crib. Chanting some sort of unknown incantation, in unison. When my parents looked at me, their baby child, in my crib, they were horrified at what they saw.

The babysitter had taped two long wooden sticks to my forehead. An infant child, with, artificial "horns" affixed to my innocent skull. Some sort of symbol. Of what, no one knows but the women there that night. They were performing a ritual of unknown origin. Of unknown intent. The women were chanting, who knows what exactly, but evidently the two sticks were taped on my head as some sort of antennae. To another world, perhaps? What exactly was going on in that room that night, so long ago, is still a mystery, to this day. Why these Bahamian women would do this, to me, is also completely unknown.

These are the first memories I have.

One thing that has been constant throughout my career is that my art has always, without exception, imitated life. Or vice versa. From *Youth Gone Wild* to *Jekyll & Hyde* to *Jesus Christ Superstar* on to *Angel Down, Kicking & Screaming*, and *Give 'Em Hell*, I have always been amazed, and more than a little spooked out, about how the lyrics that I sing seem to come true after I sing them.

Just like dreams.

I have had all my dreams come true . . . and much, much more.

I have had nightmares come true, as well.

My father, in telling this last story to everyone present at my first wedding, explained to us all that he, too, had always wondered why his eldest son's *life experience* had been so *extreme* in nature. Why had all these amazing (and some not so amazing) occurrences and experiences happened around me, because of, or in spite of me? Why is it that my dreams came true, when so many others' did not? Why so many others dreamed the same impossible dreams, but had to settle for a life less than ordinary? If there is anything you will learn reading this book, it's that life can be anything but *ordinary*.

My dad believed that something supernatural happened that night in the Bahamas. Something that changed the course of my life. He believed that these island women had cast some sort of a spell on me.

It's just a theory, of course. Maybe it was just a meaningless game of sorts.

But maybe, just maybe, they did cast a spell on me that night. A spell on me . . . that would see me cast a spell of my own.

Upon the whole world.

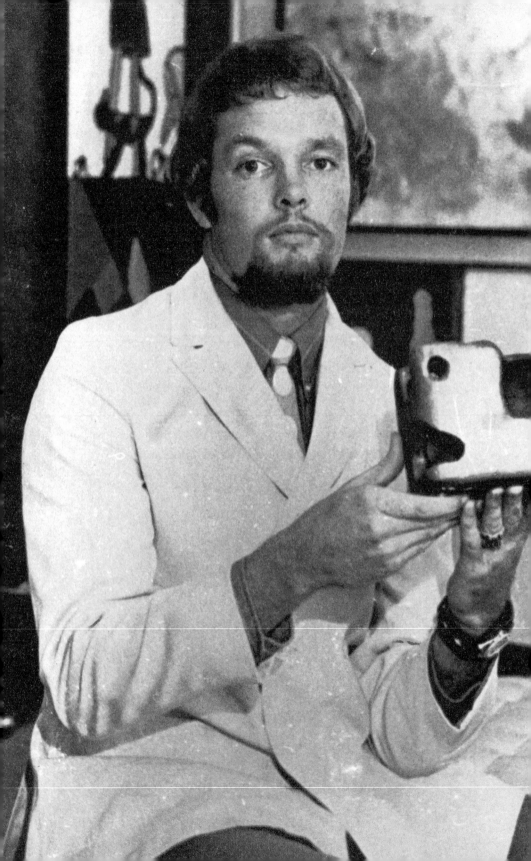

2
GROWING UP SEBASTIAN

1967–1968
Freeport, Bahamas

Dad was an art teacher. Mom was a nurse. The story of how my parents met each other is bizarre and somewhat hilarious.

As the story goes, Dad was having quite the wild night out the evening he met my mom. His nickname, at the time, was Hondo.

Hondo and his friends had decided that it would be most prudent to take a car out onto the back roads of Freeport and have a little fun. I don't know if they were drinking or not. But hey, this is 1967 we're talking about. So maybe, they were tuning in, or tuning out, as the case may be.

They were taking turns standing on the roof of the car, while racing down the gravel roads. Some kind of pre-*Jackass* Bam Margera shit. So you can see where this is going.

Hondo took his turn "surfing" on the top of the car. He stood on the roof of the speeding vehicle . . . until it slammed on the brakes. Dad went flying off the roof, face-first, into the pebbles, rocks, dirt, and gravel of the road below. *Cut to hospital.*

Where my mom was on duty that night.

My mother met my father that night. On his back, on the hospital gurney. Wincing in pain, as my mother picked the pieces of rock and gravel out of his fucked-up face.

Ah, the sheer *romance* of it all!

A little more than nine months later, I was born.

Bach in America: Pancratius on Tour

1800s
Germany
America

My father never knew his father before him. Grandpa left Dad when Dad was a little boy. We were forbidden to ever, never speak of him or his family. *Our* family. This was my introduction to ghosting. My

16

dad was real good at it. He tried to find his own dad in 1977, only to discover the man had died mere months before the reconciliation was attempted.

When Dad died in 2002, I researched his family for him. I suppose it was a way of not letting go. With the advent of the Internet, I was able to research our history in no way he would ever have been able to in the 1970s. It gave me great solace to look at the screen and discover names, pictures, stories, of my ancestry that my father never lived to see. He would've loved it. I have since reconciled with my father's side of the family, and y'know what? They love rock 'n' roll just as much as we do. Guess it's in the blood.

We never knew that we were from German descent. My grandma's family were from Norway. But I don't think that my father could have ever known that his dad's family came here from Baden

Wurzburg, Germany. I wish my dad could've known how his family got here in the first place.

In the mid-1800s, there was a priest in Germany named Martin Stephan, who told his congregation that America was the promised land. The German government found out about this, they excommunicated Martin Stephan from the clergy. So, he assembled his congregation on separate brigantine boats to go from Baden Wurzburg all the way to America. During their journey, one of the boats capsized, and all aboard perished into the ocean. The other boat made it to the Port of New Orleans, Louisiana. On this boat was the very first member of my family to come to North America. His name was Pancratius Bürk.

The boat then went from New Orleans up to Perryville, Missouri, where my grandfather's family first settled. I can hear my detractors out there right now. *Dammit!! Wrong boat!* Well, as you will learn in this book, we've always been a lucky bunch!

My dad was a wild dude. When people tell me, all the time, "Oh Sebastian, you are so hyper!" I just have to laugh. Dad had more energy, more excitement, more verve and zest for life than anyone I

have ever known. He lived for his art, which was painting. This was his most valuable lesson to me. Choose something you love to do with your life, and do it. If you work at something you truly love, you are never really working at all.

He liked to paint. I like to rock.

Most of my memories of him are with his shirtsleeves rolled up, with all of his skin from the end of his fingertips all the way up to his elbows, completely covered in layers of multicolored acrylic paint. Years later, he would die from leukemia and bone marrow cancer. I always thought that these lead-based paints from the 1960s and '70s could not have been too good for his health.

A lot of his friends, including his very best friend, Dennis Tourbin, were painters who died in their early fifties. Dad left us at the age of fifty-seven. Same age as his father before him. Believe me, if I make it to fifty-eight it will be one hell of a party.

Lifelong Obsessions

My mother and father influenced me in so many ways, it's hard to put into words.

Dad taught art at Humboldt State University while we lived in Arcata, California. There is still a mural on the wall today at the university, that he did of me as a baby, when he was a professor there. Mike Patton of the band Faith No More attended Humboldt and recalls walking past this painting every day on his way to class. He did not realize that he was, in fact, walking past the first-ever Sebastian Bach poster, as a student on his way to study hall.

We lived in California after I was born in the Bahamas, and then after we lived in California, we moved back to the Bahamas. Must have been an early '70s thing. After a brief return to Freeport in 1972 or so, Dad started looking for an actual permanent job with which

to support his wife and two children. Mom's family sent him the classified section from the *Toronto Star*. In the back pages was an ad for an art teacher at Kenner Collegiate in the town of Peterborough, Ontario, Canada. My dad applied for the job and got it. And so, we packed up the car and drove all the way across the country. From Arcata, California, to Peterborough, Canada. To our new life.

To say that we were "out of the norm" for the city of Peterborough would be an understatement.

My mom and dad were very much hippies of the day. With long hair, a Volvo station wagon was our family's mode of transportation. Dad, bespectacled in John Lennon glasses, with Mom in Frye boots by his side. Even our dog, a cute little Scottish terrier, was named Lennon. My sister was named Heather Dylan, after Bob. I was named Sebastian, not after Mr. French on the show *Family Affair*, like I thought. No, I was not named after the actor Sebastian Cabot, even though I liked to think I was. I loved that show. With Buffy and Jody. Still do. Got the DVD. I was, in fact, named after John Sebastian, singer/songwriter of the band The Lovin' Spoonful.

While attending Berkeley College in California in the early 1960s, my father was influenced by the artists, poets, and writers of the day. Michael McClure and Lawrence Ferlinghetti were two of his favorites. Michael McClure taught my father some classes at Berkeley and made a huge impression on him. I still have the book *Rebel Lions*, autographed by Michael McClure to my father, that remains one of my prized possessions to this day.

One of Dad's favorite bands was The Lovin' Spoonful, fronted by John Sebastian. The two actually got to meet. Dad told me the story like this: John and my dad went up onto a grassy hill overlooking the Berkeley campus. As my father told me, John Sebastian smoked a joint with him, after which Dad told him that he was going to name his first son after him. And here I am, now. Smoking a joint. Writing this book. "Hello, my name is Sebastian. Thank you, John. Please pass to your left!"

In Peterborough, my parents together created an art gallery, which they named ArtSpace. Some of my earliest memories include hanging out in this gallery. Helping Dad and Mom clean up after exhibition openings. Meeting important artists such as Christo, who came and had dinner with us at our house with his wife. Once, when I was around eleven or twelve, Dad paid me and my friend to sell beer at one of the art openings in his gallery. As the night wore

REGISTER
OF
ATTENDANCE · OFFERING

ATTENDANCE
TODAY

ATTENDANCE
LAST SUNDAY

OFFERING
TODAY

OFFERING
LAST SUNDAY

MISSIONARY

on, people got drunker. An inebriated gentleman ended up hassling me because he didn't have any more money to buy any more beer and I wouldn't give him free beer. Even at my young age, I could tell that this was a crazy night. Dad told us we could stop bartending.

It was a different time.

1973
Markham, Ontario, Canada

I am five years old. We are at my aunt Leslie's house. My father walks down the stairs, into the basement. I am goofing off with my cousins Kevin and Alyson on the beanbag chairs, listening to Phoebe Snow's "Poetry Man." As Dad enters the basement, I notice something in his hands, behind his back. He has a smile on his face. Like he knows what he is about to put into my hands will change my life forever. Which it does.

He stretches out his arm, and proceeds to put the first *comic book* into my hands that I have ever seen.

It's a Batman comic. I can see the cover in my brain still to this day. The Dark Knight, and Gotham, the mysterious city, lurking in the shadows behind decrepit buildings and various sundry characters. The vivid imagery made an everlasting impression on me. I held the comic and stared into the cover, and back up into my dad's beaming visage.

"*What is this?*" I ask of my dad, my eyes as bright and full of wonder as his were.

I couldn't figure out what I was looking at. I remember being fascinated, even just by the logo itself. Everything just popped right out of my hands at me. I couldn't wait to get into this book. I didn't know if it was fantasy or reality I was looking at. Which might explain the blurry line between fantasy and reality that I have indeed carried with me into my adult life. I have always been very good at making big *dreams* come true. For myself. For others. Yet some of life's more mundane realities remain a challenge for me. I truly believe that the parables of right and wrong, learned in comic books at an early age, have something to do with turning fantasies into reality, over and over again, throughout my life and career. When I entered adulthood, Dad and I would get into this discussion over a

couple of cold Canadian brewskis. I would ask, "How do you think this all happened, Dad?"

Hondo would just look at me and smile. "Sebastian. It's because you *believe*."

I look up at my dad and smile. He smiles down back at me.

I run into the next room and jump into the beanbag chair, where I *devour* every nuance, every iota, of that Batman comic. This starts a lifelong love obsession I will come back to, over and over again. Time after time. With comic books. With superheroes. With Pop. With Art.

With *reading*.

My days as a diligent comic collector began when I was a boy. Joining book clubs, racing down to the local variety store with a handful of quarters. There every Tuesday to pick up the latest issues of *The Incredible Hulk*, *Fantastic Four*, *Inhumans*, *Ghost Rider*, anything Jack Kirby, Neil Adams, Mike Ploog, Herb Trimpe. We had a fort in our garage where we started our own comic club, with hundreds, if not thousands, of comics between us. My friend Andrew

Springer lived across the street. We would go through the comics and alphabetize, categorize each book. Discuss the artists, writers, and stories. Even the story arcs themselves.

I try to explain to my children today how, back then, all we had was our imagination. With no Internet, cable TV, video games, IMAX, or other virtual bullshit, we had nothing but *still images* and our own *minds* to do the rest. Same goes for rock 'n' roll. All we had in those days were magazines, pictures, and posters to look at while we listened to the records. This is why the album cover imagery then played such an important role, and conversely in the gray and bland days of iTunes, that album cover art seems like a quaint thing of the past. What a true fucking shame that is.

The world of Marvel Comics, and DC Comics as well, became a real cornerstone of my imagination. Living in Cavan, Ontario, in our house we got only three black-and-white TV channels through the bunny ears. A lot of the Canadian TV programming seemed to be shows on curling, lawn bowling, field hockey, maybe even an exciting afternoon special on ice fishing. Not exactly *captivating* tele-

The Hulk

Emerald green like St. Patrick's
day
Roaring like thunder on a stormy
day
Tall as a mountain
strong as the wind
The Hulk is my favorite
I really like him.

vision for an active child's mind. The Marvel Universe was infinitely more interesting to me than television was. I could read about the Incredible Hulk and Spider-Man, and really *believe* the stories that I was getting into. They all had a basic premise. Good over evil. In my adult life, I have made enemies as well as friends from this black-and-white way of thinking. In my mind, I am always trying to *do the right thing*. I may fail in that task. I may, at times, be misguided. But that is always my intention.

> With great power
> comes great responsibility

and

> Don't make me angry
> you wouldn't like me when I'm angry

When I was in the second grade, the principal of my school and my teacher called in my mom and dad for a parent-teacher confer-

ence about me. They told my mom and dad that "we don't know what's wrong with Sebastian. Whenever he gets even just one thing wrong on a test, he beats himself up to the point of misery. We've never seen any kid like this." They explained to my mom and dad that I could not handle making a mistake. If I got one thing wrong on the test, I would punish myself.

I think this goes back to the time when my dad threw me out of the van and made me walk home in the Cavan swamp. In the dark. Because I got a B on a test.

Summer 1975
Santa Cruz Beach Boardwalk

I am holding my dad's hand.

We are walking along the boardwalk from the Giant Dipper on down the amusement park row. It is hot. I am eating cotton candy. I am seven.

It is a magical place. Today, I rode a roller coaster for the first time! We went on the Giant Dipper. I cried and threw up my hot dog all over my aunt, who was downwind in the car behind us. Oooops!

My dad and I walk toward the promenade far in the distance. There is a glass enclosure running vertically from the ground to the sky, featuring items that you could win in the arcade located below in the promenade.

Something at the very top of the display catches my seven-year-old eyes. From a far distance my gaze is fixed upon an image that I do not know how to process in my young mind.

I clutch my father's hand as we approach the promenade display. We get closer. To what, I am not sure of.

The noise of the amusement park boardwalk rides and laughter of the children enjoying the summer with their families recedes in my mind. My eyes are fixated upon this image in the display promenade, which is getting closer with each step.

For the first time in my life, I feel a sensation of excitement and fright at the same

time. It is confusing to me. I am completely fascinated by these figures that look scary but I cannot turn away from them, either.

"Dad? What is that?" I clearly remember looking up at my father for protection and some sort of explanation of what I was seeing.

"That, son . . ." my father said to me with a bemused look on his grinning face, ". . . is KISS."

"Gloria In Excelsis Deo": I Fell in Love with Singing at an Early Age

1976
Peterborough, Ontario, Canada

Age eight, to be exact.

Before the moment when I joined the All Saints' Anglican Church Choir, my earliest memories of singing always have to do with my mom, Kathleen. Her love of singing, and more specifically vocal harmonies, affected me from an early age. My mom, along with her sister Leslie, would harmonize all day around the house, singing the Everly Brothers, and other songs of their day such as this one by The Bird and the Bee:

I know, I know
that Tonight
You belong to me

They sang in perfect harmony, along to Linda Ronstadt, Elton John, Neil Young, The Beatles, Valdy, Murray McLaughlan, Rough Trade, Bob Marley, Joan Armatrading. We listened to the incredible Phoebe Snow on the family stereo, all the time. One of the most talented, and perhaps underrated singers, ever. Later on in life I would

meet Phoebe Snow on the set of a VH1 show that I did. She was so nice to me. We vocalized backstage on set.

"Hi Phoebe! I'm Sebastian! I love your voice! Hey, do you think you can sing as high as I can?"

"Hi Sebastian! I'm Phoebe! Do *you* think you can sing as high as *I* can?" was how our discussion started. Phoebe and I would even talk on the phone about hanging out and having dinner. I was drinking heavily at this time, and it still haunts me to this day that I took my friendship with Phoebe Snow for granted. She died a year or so after I met her, and we never did get to have that dinner like we talked about. I still listen to "Poetry Man" and her other songs, especially on airplanes, on the road. Her voice soothes me. Whenever I listen to her sing now, I regret not taking her up on her invitation.

My mom and her sister would make french fries and dance and sing to Jimi Hendrix's "Fire" while I would be standing there, at knee height. Taking it all in. The joy. The laughter. The excitement. Music was always about *fun* to me.

Perhaps my very first memory of singing involves Donny Osmond's song "Puppy Love." Mom would call her friends over from around the block, make me stand on the kitchen table, and have me sing this song. One day as I was singing "Puppy Love," we looked out the window and saw a fire blazing down the street in a distant house. We all flipped out, ran out of the house to watch the fire, and then came back, where I got back up on the kitchen table and started singing again. My mom would cry when I sang this song to her.

Then there was the song "Emotional Rescue" by The Rolling Stones. In the backseat of Mom's car, I would vamp out on Mick Jagger's breakdown:

I will be your knight in shining armor
Coming to your emotional rescue
You will be mine, you will be mine, all mine

Driving down the street, Mom and her friends would turn around and say, "Sebastian!! Sing it again! Sing it again! Sing it *again!*"

Laughing and carrying on, as if I were Mick Jagger himself in the backseat of the car. That's the way they made me feel.

But what really made me fall in love with singing?

The *church*.

I know. Go figure.

I was eight years old, living on Donegal Street in Peterborough. I would spend my days after school playing with my friends, or more likely riding my bicycle around the suburban streets, popping wheelies and doing skids.

I was on the road in front of my house when my friend Dickson Davidson peeled up to me on his bicycle.

"Hey!! I'm in the church choir!! And if I get you to join, I get an extra three bucks! PLUS they will pay YOU a monthly *stipend*!! If you pass the audition!!"

What the fuck is a stipend?

One of my vivid memories occurred right then. I turned to my left. Looked up at the sky. Around the street. Thought to myself exactly this:

Whaaaaat? Someone is going to pay me?? To sing?!?

Dickson was like, "Yeah!! Come on!! Let's go!! *Right now!!*"

Incredulous, I followed Dickson as we took off down the street on our bicycles. Baseball cards affixed to the spokes. So it sounded like we had real engines.

In a very real way, I was now on my way.

We raced down the blocks of the suburban Canadian town to All Saints' Anglican Church. Dickson took me down the steps from the parking lot, into the basement of the church, where the choir rehearsed. An all-male choir. Soprano, Alto, Tenor, and Baritone sections.

Dickson took me over to the piano, where the choirmaster was playing, auditioning other young boys to sing in the choir. When it came to my turn, I walked up to the right of the piano. The choirmaster was intrigued.

"Okay Sebastian, let's go up the keys and see how far we get. *Let's see if you can sing.*"

I remembered Mom's kitchen table, and Donny Osmond. I remembered the backseat of the car, where I would sing Rolling Stones songs to her and her friends.

Dear Grandma,
Thank you! For the piano. I am so excited! When you said the piano wold helpme play lots of instuments I thout about it and...WOW! I'll be a regulaur musishon! David Neely came up and we went to Mr. Bests house ~~and too~~ to give him a piese of cake and we saw a calf that was only born a few hours ago. We brout him a piese of cake because it waunt Jeanines bithday. I am writing this letter with a pen that Grandpa Bill gave me. Dinner time now, gotta go.

Grandpa gave me a case of stuff for school.

Enclosesed is a picture of me paying the piano.

LOVE,

Sebastian.

The choirmaster proceeded to take me up the keys of the piano. We kept going. And going.

We didn't stop.

As my voice travelled up the scale, higher and higher, the choirmaster looked at me. My voice was not slowing down. We got almost to the top of the piano before he smiled and said the words.

"Yes, Sebastian. *You are in the choir.*"

I was not ready to stop singing.

I couldn't believe it. I was to be paid a monthly stipend of over *three dollars.* For an eight-year-old boy in 1976, this was quite a sum to receive each and every month. At the time, KISS posters were about $1.75. It was my mission in life to collect KISS posters and put them on my wall. I calculated that I could buy two brand-new KISS posters a month if I joined the church choir now. Oh, hell yeah.

Where do I sign up for this?

This was a real gig.

I had committed to being at choir practice after school every Tuesday and Thursday night. On Sunday mornings, I would report to the church at 7:30 in my white cassock, blue gown, dress shoes, and gray slacks. Ready for the show. In the choir, we all depended on each other, just like I learned later that a real rock band does. We were all professionals. We took what we did very seriously. Singing psalms, in Latin, and classic English hymns is not exactly like singing Christmas carols you hear at the mall. It was challenging vocal music, and the choirmasters were taskmasters, to be sure. We were expected to never miss a rehearsal, or a church service. We were expected to sing, and sing well. Which we did.

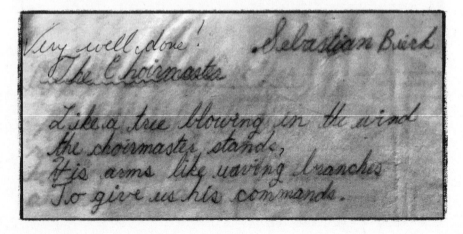

CHOIR

Back Row: K. Leonard, D. MacNicol, J Ketchum, S. Dawson, E. Beliczynski, S. Ramsey J MacGregor G. Russel, A. Trass, A. Grieve, H. McEwan, P Sanford, J Barker H. MacDonnell, Mrs. Smith, M. Peet, D. Pennock, S. Bierk, L. Greaves, A. Sibbald, F Ossenberg, A. Weatherill, Mr Smith.
Front Row: D. Baines. T Girling, J Murray

I first went on the road when I was eight years old with this church choir. More than once. We would travel to distant churches in Ontario. Sing on Sunday morning for congregations in other towns. We even took the bus all the way into upper New York. Mom

helped me pack my bag; I got on the bus, and traveled a day or so from Canada into *another country*. Went over the border and everything. We stayed at the house of a pastor in upstate New York. I slept in a sleeping bag in the pastor's attic, with other choir members. Then, on Sunday morning, with the sun blasting through the church windows, we were up early. Singing our hearts out for the Lord. Afterwards, a nice big lunch. Then, back onto the bus, headed north, for the return journey home. Seems hard to believe now. But it's no wonder I am used to being on the road at this point.

The exact single moment that I really fell in love with singing will forever remain permanently etched upon my mind. It was Christmas Eve, circa 1976. For our Christmas midnight mass, we were singing all of the classic English hymns such as "Land of Hope and Glory," Latin psalms with verses "Requiem In Eternat," and the like. The congregation was packed for the midnight mass. It was very rare for me at the age of eight to stay up past midnight, and I remember the service starting at 11:30 p.m. It seemed as if the whole city had shown up to celebrate with us. Outside the church, the snow was falling. All I could see were Christmas lights, snow, and a full congregation of excited and jubilant Christmas revelers.

We sang to the heavens that night. Mom was there, along with other members of my family, to sing along with me. As I hit the high harmony in the hymn "Gloria In Excelsis Deo," the whole soprano section reached a musical *crescendo* that I experienced in every part of my body, mind, and soul. The simple elation of hitting those high harmonies, in the soprano section of that song, was a feeling of exultation that I had never felt before in my young life. I looked around at the choir, the choirmaster, and the congregation. We were all *one*. Everyone was in such a state of musical and spiritual joy that it was mind-blowing for me to process at that early age.

I only knew one thing. And I knew it for certain.

I love to sing.

I am going to sing for the rest of my life.

This leads me to another lifelong obsession.

Ladies and gentlemen, the hottest band in the world: KISS!!!!

KISS were comic books, horror movies, Saturday morning cartoons, *and* rock 'n' roll, all rolled up into one. Much has been written about the influence of this band on people of my generation. Particularly, boys my age. As a loyal card-carrying member of the KISS Army, let me tell you how it was to be ten years old in 1978.

At the crux of the matter, it cannot be overstated today what it was like to have four masked men marauding around the planet belching blood and fire. Who kept their identities a complete secret. It may not seem like a big deal to you, reading in this day and age. But to a kid my age, in the mid to late 1970s, it was com-

pletely fantastic in every way. A complete *mind-fuck* to not know what these guys actually looked like. In many ways, their commitment to mystery really did make them seem like true-to-life superheroes.

We would try to draw pictures of what KISS might look like behind the makeup. It was the stuff of pure imagination. When the album *Double Platinum* came out, the inner gatefold sleeve contained embossed silver Mylar pictures of the four band members. We went and got trace paper and pencils, tracing only their eyes, nose, and mouth. Not the makeup. We were desperate to see what Bruce Wayne looked like behind the Batman cowl.

My father did everything to foster my immersion in the fantasy world of comic books and rock 'n' roll. He even took me to the Marvel Comics *offices*, in Manhattan, when I was no more than eight or

nine years old. We were staying at my cousins David and Michelle Neely's house, with Uncle Bob and Aunt Janine, in Madison, Connecticut. My dad had business in New York City. As he would oftentimes do in Canada, he asked me to come with him.

As Dad would drive, he would hand me a stack of art magazines—*Art in America, Art Magazine,* and the like. He would then have me read articles to him, on subjects such as the Duchampian Philosophy, which he had me memorize and dictate to his college classroom in Peterborough one day, much to the hilarity of his students. While he would drive, he always told me I was a *great reader.* This only made me want to read more.

On this day in New York City, he surprised me, as he loved to do. We went to the Marvel Comics headquarters. Took the elevator up to the main floor. Marched over to the reception area. Behind the desk were wall-sized murals of The Hulk, Spider-Man, Fantastic Four, all of my heroes. The secretary was so kind to us. She gave us a tour of the whole Marvel Comics offices, introducing us to artists and writers. I will never forget how nice they all were to me and Dad. They comped us Marvel swag—notebooks, T-shirts, pens. Looking back, it's astonishing a dad would do that for his nine-year-old son.

After we were done at Marvel, on the way back to Connecticut, we stopped at a variety store. The very first KISS Marvel comic had just come out. Right there on the newsstand, next to the first *Creem* magazine KISS special. I remember holding the KISS comic in one hand and a chocolate milk in the other. On the front, said the immortal words:

Printed in real KISS blood.

I stared at the red ink. In my nine-year-old mind, I 100 percent believed that the red ink I was holding in my hands was actually the *blood of the members of the rock band KISS.*

What other band does that?

You wonder why this band had such an influence on a whole generation? Can you imagine reading stories about your favorite band beating the shit out of Dr. Doom?

Printed in real blood?

Now, that kicks ass.

My world up to 1978 was consumed by comic books and music. And then my world was forever altered. In a way that many children's worlds were altered in the late '70s, and continue to be to this day. My own children included.

In 1978, my mom and dad decided to get a divorce.

Breaking Up Is Hard to Do

For the last couple of weeks, I couldn't help but notice. Dad just *wasn't around*.

I didn't really think much of it. A couple of months before this, my aunt Leslie had gotten divorced. It seemed unfathomable, unimaginable, to me at the time. Riding in my aunt's car, I asked her, "Why? How could that happen?"

"Your uncle told me that he doesn't really like me anymore, Sebastian. Can you imagine how that feels?"

Although I was only ten years old, I could not help but feel my aunt Leslie's pain.

I was about to learn what pain was all about.

"Where is Dad?"

One night, Mom told my sister Heather and I that we were going to have a family meeting. This was the first time we had ever had anything we needed to call a *family meeting*. *This can't be good,* I thought. As dinnertime approached, Dad showed up at the house, for the first time in weeks. Although this made Heather and I both very happy, it seemed to make each of our parents squirm. We sat down to dinner, as we had done many times before. Up until recently.

An uncomfortable quiet filled the dining room. Years before, when we had lived in Cavan, Dad would bound through the door. Sit down at the dinner table, with his arms covered in paint and turpentine. The acrid smell of turpentine will always remind me of Dad. He would literally *explode* with enthusiasm, over the daily events of Artspace. The paintings to be painted. The places he had driven. The people he had met. The art shows, by the artists he admired with such passion. I looked up to him from the dinner table one night.

"Dad? Can we please talk about *anything*?? Other than art???"

My parents laughed.

On this night, however, I would have given *anything* to hear Dad talk about art.

To see Mom laugh.

"Well, kids, we have to tell you something."

"What's that, Mom?"

The words hit us like a nuclear bomb.

"Your father and I have decided to *get a divorce*."

Next, an unexpected, strange thing occurred. An early sign of my behavior, in coming years, that could be disconcerting at times. I was only ten years old, but for some reason, what followed next seemed to be a great idea at the time.

I stood up from the dinner table. Not saying a word, I walked into the kitchen. Opened up the drawer containing tools. Retrieving a ball-peen hammer, I proceed to walk up the stairs. To my bedroom.

I am having an out-of-body experience. For the first time in my life, it seems as if my actions are not my own. This would not be the last time.

Once in my bedroom, I take the hammer, raise it above my head, and slowly, methodically, precisely start to *bash in the walls of my bedroom*. I wield the hammer, like Thor's Mjolnir, and Hulk smash!! the drywall into pieces. As hard as I can. Something is telling me that I must *make holes. In walls.*

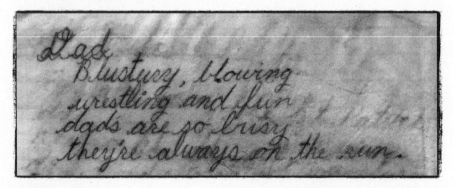

By Asgaard
Odin, My Father
Please
Don't leave us

This was my reaction to the news that my father was leaving my mother, my sister, and me.

He was leaving us.

He was leaving *me*.

I smashed the drywall into dust. A few months before, Dad had painstakingly painted a giant mural of the Incredible Hulk onto one of my walls. I did not smash that wall. I was not about to let anyone take the Hulk away from me too.

I stood in the rubble of the destruction of my childhood. I turned and looked into the doorway.

My dad had opened the door. He had been standing there, watching me do all of this.

He did not get mad at me.

He did not say a word.

The Demons of Rock

My world after 1978 was *consumed* by rock 'n' roll.

My world after 1978 was consumed by KISS.

After my parents' divorce, after the breakup of my family, I made a single, visceral commitment to myself. For the rest of my life. I would never, ever let *anybody* take rock 'n' roll away from me.

I would not let anybody destroy *my* world . . . of KISS. My family had been taken away. Dad was gone now. So, at the age of ten, I created a brand-new *world* for *myself*. A world which I would never want to leave.

My world consisted of fire belching, blood drooling, guitars shooting out of the sky, levitating drum kits, dry ice, volume, pyro, and smoke. I loved lots of other music too. But KISS was my band. KISS was my life. And nothing, or nobody, would ever come between me and my love for KISS and rock 'n' roll.

I began saving up money from choir and my paper route. Started working for Dad whenever I could, to get money to buy *CREEM*, *Rock Scene*, *Circus*, *Rocket*, *Rock*, *SuperRock*, *16*, *Teen Machine*, *SuperTeen*, all the cool magazines of the day. Like lots of other kids, I cut out pictures, tore out posters, and covered the walls of my bedroom with KISS. Mom moved us into a townhouse at the corner of Charlotte and Rubidge Streets in Peterborough. I would come home from school, escape into my bedroom, where my world was complete. Drop the needle on my favorite record. Fall asleep with the headphones on. Memorize every note. Read every interview. Study every picture. Learn every pose.

My world excited me.

Made me feel not alone. Made me feel like there was so much *fun* to be had. I will forever be thankful to the band KISS for being there when I needed them most. When I needed *fun* desperately. When I was a little boy searching for a coin that didn't roll away.

I loved other bands as well. Cheap Trick, Van Halen, and Rush came after KISS. But there simply never was, and never will be, another band that *captured the imagination*, quite like KISS. My relationship with this band, their music, and the impact they have had on my family, and career, is nothing short of a lifelong obsession. That continues. Even to this day.

My parents had been divorced for around a year when we got the earth-shattering news.

KISS is coming to town.

To Maple Leaf Gardens. In Toronto.

This was not to be my first concert. The first show I ever attended was by a band called The Stampeders, who had a hit song called "Sweet City Woman." My next-door neighbor's babysitter Carolanne Heath's older brother took me to see them at PCVS high school in Peterborough when I was probably eight or something.

Then, the band Boston came to Maple Leaf Gardens in 1978, when I was ten years old.

Winning a Ticket to the
Rock 'n' Roll Lottery

Sammy Hagar opened the show. My dad and his new girlfriend Liz took me to the concert. I could not believe my ears as Sammy Hagar bellowed into the microphone.

"TORONTO!!!!! We are gonna get FUCKING WILD tonight, motherFUCKERS!!!! ARE YOU READY?????"

Sammy dropping that F-bomb felt more like an *atomic* bomb to my brain. Over and over again, into the cavernous halls of the revered Maple Leaf Gardens' sanctified, conservative Canadian air. Which just so happened to be consumed by a heavy cloud of marijuana smoke that permeated my nostrils as much as the swear words that were coming out of the PA system. Well, since we're talking about lifelong obsessions . . . I digress . . . *(cough cough)*.

I held my dad's hand, slightly alarmed at the situation, and looked up to him for reassurance.

"Daddy! Is that man up on the stage *allowed* to say that????"

Pops just looked down at me and laughed.

Hearing bad words through a large PA system. Lifelong obsession, check number three.

August 4, 1979
Toronto, Ontario, Canada

Having KISS come to Toronto, on the Dynasty Tour, changed my life. Forever.

Mom, my sister, and myself had moved out of our house we shared with Dad on Donegal Street. Into a multi-family town-house on Rubidge Street. This place was far different than any-where we had lived before. I had not seen Dad and Mom in the

same room together since the night they told us Dad was moving out. The night I trashed my bedroom with a ball-peen hammer.

My parents fully understood how much KISS meant to me since they had divorced. The band had given me a very real psychological outlet for my frustrations. My fears, my uncertainty, my longing. For my dad. For fun times. KISS, in a very real way, countered the very real pain of divorce I felt in my heart. So, Dad made an incredible decision, that looking back, meant so much to me that it never fails to put a tear into my eye when I tell the story.

My father decided that he would reunite with my mother. One last time.

For one night only.

To take me, my mother, and my sister, to go see KISS. Live in concert.

I repeat. My mom and dad were going to *reunite our family*. They were about to give me a memory that would change my personality. Alter my life. Forever.

It is hard to describe what it meant to me, to see Dad walk down that sidewalk, back into our lives. He showed up at our townhouse that day in the *de rigueur* "Canadian Tuxedo." Blue jeans, jean jacket, white cutoff T-shirt. Red bandana tied to his head. As he strode down Rubidge Street with the biggest smile on his face I had ever seen, he exclaimed to me, "Heyyyyyy BASS!!!!!"

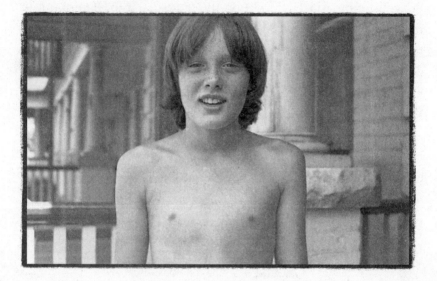

As he used to call me.

I ran down the steps, off the porch, and jumped back up into my dad's arms. We laughed. He gave me a big hug. I turned around. Saw my sister laughing, through tears of joy. With Mom behind her. Ready to rock. Our family was *back together*!!!!!

We are going to see KISS!!!!!! TONIGHT!!!!!!!!!!!

What this correlation of events did to my eleven-year-old mind is the very essence of who I am. How *I* became to *be*. This night explains the origins of my deep, unending love for rock 'n' roll. Combined with bittersweet loss. Of love. Of family.

Escapism. Fantasy. Theatrics. I have told this story to a few therapists over the years. They always look at me with an expression that says, "Well, *that* explains *that*. It's really *no wonder* why you do *this* for a living." Well, they are right.

We all piled into Dad's car together, for the first time any of us could recall. It was a beautiful summer day. To Toronto from Peterborough is about a two-hour journey, that we had each made many times. But never to go see *the hottest band in the land*. In the middle of the drive, listening to CHUM FM on the radio dial, the DJ announced that Gene Simmons would be coming on for an interview after the next commercial. I was so excited I was going to vomit out the window as Gene came on the air and hyped the show. I listened to his low, serious voice, describing to our reunited family, in our car, how KISS were going to blow the whole *town* apart in only a couple hours' time. *I will be there,* I thought to myself. *I cannot believe this is happening to me.*

We got closer and closer to the hallowed halls of Maple Leaf Gardens. Parked the car. Getting out, we were surrounded by fans dressed up as KISS. Complete, elaborate look-alikes, with boots, makeup, costumes, everything. I was in complete heaven.

Up the street to the McDonald's at College and Yonge for dinner. As we waited in line for the ultimate pre-KISS Happy Meal, we were surrounded by more KISS look-alikes. Faux-Ace had stopped by for a McShake and Peter Pseudo-Criss was sporting a CAT Diesel Power trucker cap. This was going to be the best night of my life.

As we made it into the arena, it became evident that our seats were not all that great. We were kind of in the rafters, near the back of the hall, up pretty high. *We're quite far away from the stage,* I thought. It didn't much matter to me. As we watched the opening band, New England, I was happy just looking at the crowd. My surroundings. This was *my* world. The feeling of excitement was palpable. As the saying goes, I was more than happy to just *be* there. Little did I know . . . my father had other plans.

Dad then did the most unexpected thing. After New England's set, we sat in our shitty seats, laughing, looking around, as a family, together again. We had hot dogs and Cokes from the concession stand. My dad never uttered a word about what he was planning to do. I realize now that he just didn't want security to spot him where we were sitting. Because only Dad knew the truth. We were not going to be in the cheap seats much longer.

The lights go dark. After the intermission.

KISS were about to destroy the city.

My father grabs me. Picks me up in his arms. In the black of the arena, all eyes are focused on the stage. The intro music, a low, demonic bass rumble, erupts from the speakers as the screaming of the crowd reaches unparalleled decibels.

"We're not sitting HERE!!!" my dad shouts at me over the din of mayhem. I had no idea what was going on.

Then, carrying his eleven-year-old child, my dad springs over the railing of the hockey rink seats, and onto the concert floor itself. He holds me just like he used to tell me how to hold a football. Like a loaf of bread. Under his arm. We are near the back of the concert hall. Dad sprints toward the front of the stage as fast as he can. Ducking

and weaving, out of the view of the security guards, who were all too busy watching KISS explode upon the stage anyhow.

We reach the very front of the 10,000-plus throng on the floor, into the first row of the concert. I could not believe what was happening. Crushed into other fans, Dad picks me up from under his right arm. Hoists me up onto his shoulders. I was now level with, and only feet away from, my heroes. KISS!!!!!!!

We were so close to the stage, that when the flame pods shot out molten fire into the Canadian night, I could actually feel the waves of heat bake my skin. It was *hot*. It made me sweat. Mine was literally a rock 'n' roll baptism *by fire*.

By the time KISS got to the song "Calling Dr. Love," I was crying on top of my dad's shoulders. Much like the footage of girls weeping at early Beatles concerts, I was experiencing a mix of many different emotions. Excitement, wonder, fright, elation, terror. All rolled up into one blubbering mess. I had never experienced anything remotely like this before.

Dad, armed with his omnipresent Leica-lensed camera, took picture after picture. Thank God he did. KISS had some new stunts on the Dynasty tour that they did not have before. Our collective jaws hit the floor when Gene Simmons lifted up his bat-wings and flew into the sky, up through the air, onto the rafters above. Ace did his solo, shooting flaming rockets out of his guitar, exploding the smoking sunburst Les Paul he had played only moments before. Near the end of the show, Ace took a drink out of a Styrofoam cup, and threw the cup right to *me*, which I caught, brought home from the show, and treasured for years to come. During my own concerts, decades later, I still remember the impact that had. If I myself ever see a little kid near the front of the stage, I always try to give him a bottle of water. I never forgot how special that made me feel, to receive something straight from Ace Frehley himself.

These concerts captured my imagination, as well as many others' my age. It's hard for me to understand when the members of KISS themselves sometimes talk about how the Dynasty tour was somehow disappointing for them, because there were so many "kids" in the audience. I was one of those kids. Along with my friends Vinnie Paul and Dimebag Darrel (RIP) of Pantera, Tom Morello of Rage Against the Machine, and so many others. Even though some of us may have been "kids" coming to see this tour, KISS was like a gateway drug to all other kinds of rock 'n' roll music. Some of us even grew up to be rock stars ourselves. I thank the band KISS for giving my generation such a passion, and appreciation, for showmanship. For fun. Attitude. Most importantly, for cool songs. That made you wanna "Rock and Roll All Nite." And party every day.

As the last strains of "Black Diamond" rang out, into the confetti storm blizzard inside the whole of Maple Leaf Gardens, I was changed. Forever. We packed up the car and drove straight back home after the concert. It was late. It was time for us to go to bed.

I never saw my family alone together ever again.

Mens Sana in Corpore Insane-O

1980–1982
Lakefield, Ontario, Canada

After Dad remarried, I was thrust into a completely new situation entirely. Sent away, to live at Lakefield College School for the next three years. At the all-boys' private boarding school, I roomed in a dormitory with four other boys. Dad leaving Mom was enough of a change. But now, leaving all of my family put together, to go and live with complete strangers, really blew my mind.

Being a total heavy metal freak, coming into a prestigious preparatory facility was like feeding a square peg into a round hole. Unlike Dad and Mom, being hippies of the age, my new stepfamily was conservative in nature and this meant that private schools were the norm for them. Dad got me an application, and I went and took a series of tests. There were only seven or eight students in my seventh-grade class when I started there in September 1980. An exclusive and expensive school. I took the entrance exams and was accepted on a scholarship based on my test scores. To all of our surprise, I was accepted into the student body.

It meant something in those days to attend LCS. Just three years before Sebastian Bach was enrolled, none other than Prince Andrew, the Duke of York, spent a year there, as an exchange student from Gordonstoun, in the UK. Now there is some trivia for you. Us two? At the same school? Who knew?

Lakefield was a great school. It helped shaped me into the man I became, for better or worse. The school motto was *Mens Sana in Corpore Sano,* which translated from Latin means *"Sound Mind, Sound Body."* This meant each student taking a sport every single season, every single day. Each morning we would be up at 7:00 a.m., showered and changed into our green-crested lapeled suit, tie, gray flannel pants with black dress shoes. Any variations on this wardrobe would be grounds for punishment. By 7:50 a.m. we would all be in chapel, sing-

THIRD
CRICKET

Standing: ▮▮▮▮▮▮▮
Sitting: ▮▮▮▮ S. Bierk, ▮▮▮
Missing: ▮▮▮▮

ing church hymns, every single morning, every single day. Again, all of this church singing was joyous to me. I looked forward to it.

There is a book out recently whose thesis states that all boys who ever even *attended* an all-boys' private school were, emotionally if not physically, abused in some way. What I witnessed firsthand was a situation of all males where the older males would prey upon the young. Walking down the hallways to the next class, when there was no teacher present, older students would grab a younger student, pushing him against the lockers, and punch his arms till they were black and blue. Everybody else laughed and cheered. This is the way it was at an all-boys private school in the early 1980s. Lakefield went co-ed decades after I attended.

FIFTH SOCCER

Left to Right, Standing: Stephen Meinhardt, Tim Bachelder Sebastian Bierk. **Sitting:** Doug Baines, John Lederman, Alan Fullerton, John Stapleford, Peers Barker **Kneeling:** Brian Phillips.

Fifth Soccer lead faithfully by Hugh McBride, had a mediocre season

After playing victoriously in our first game against St. Georges, we had confidence in our ability to win again and we were right! St. Georges played us again this time at home, and again we beat them We were now over confident in our game and it was hard to lose 4-2 and 8-0 to Cresent. We ended our season with an even record of two wins and two losses.

In spite of the season we all had a good time thanks Hugh

Sebastian Bierk

I received plenty of punches and charley horses myself. After dinner, some kids would be assigned to Study Hall at night, before bed. Yes, it was a full day. A senior prefect I thought was so cool was in charge that night. I said something I thought was funny to try and get his attention. He came over, grabbed me by the hair, and started smashing my forehead into the desk cubicle to which I was assigned. Everybody laughed.

But I was always a big boy for my age. So many received it far worse than I. For me, the stress came in the form of being away from my recently divorced family. I continued to escape into my music. When I moved into Upper Colebrook House, I brought along my full stereo system that I had worked all summer for previously. The vinyl I brought included Cheap Trick and Rush. The very first second I came in the dorm I put KISS posters on the wall around my upper bunk. The other guys walked in and dug it. This was the way I made friends when I was in grade seven. I liked to make people laugh.

Perhaps due to the fact that I had been put in kindergarten twice, once to be babysat in the Bahamas and then again two years later in Peterborough, school up to this point had always been easy. I was a straight-A student and taller than the other kids. About halfway through the seventh grade, the decision was made by the school to skip me up a grade. So, in the middle of the seventh grade, I was put directly into the middle of the eighth grade. Leaving all the friends I had just made only months before. But I was used to that kind of scene now.

At the time, I was the first and only student at Lakefield College School to ever skip. I don't know if that has changed, but immediately upon my arrival into the next grade, I sensed that this was somehow a *mistake*. The first day I walked into the eighth grade, I sat down in my assigned seat. A couple of minutes later, the teacher left the room for a minute or two. When she shut the door, I was alone with the rest of my new classmates. They turned around and stared at me. This one kid ripped into me.

"Oh Sebastian, you're so fucking smart, oh my God, you're so smart, oh wow, we can't believe how *smart* you are, oh wow, how did you get so *smart*." The rest of the class guffawed. As I harrumphed.

Lakefield College School

Name   Sebastian Bierk   Form   7

Term   Fall   Year   1980

House   Colebrook

Average = 80% Scholar

Housemaster's Comment: and Tutor's Report.

This has been a splendid term for Sebastian. He has handled his adjustment to his new school well and is getting along well with his peers. He has accepted cautions about carrying pranks to an extreme without difficulty and I now find him to be a very cooperative enjoyable member of the house.

I feel that Sebastian is capable of handling work at a more challenging level, and would welcome the chance to discuss the possibility of him tackling Grade 8 work in the second term. Socially, he is quite mature for the present Grade 7 class, although he is not out of place.

Headmaster

A fine start. Well done.

The teacher came back in the room. Class resumed.

Oh wow. This is really gonna suck.

LCS instilled certain values upon me that thankfully remain to this day. There was a disciplinary system in place. If a student ever broke any rules, they would be assigned Penalty Drill. PD consisted of being up on Monday mornings at 5:30 a.m., with the rest of the losers, and running up and down a hill for however many demerits we received. Fifteen points equaled fifteen minutes, thirty loser points would have you running thirty minutes, etcetera. I was on this list many times. In Canada, it snows a lot. Many was the morning I would be up before dawn, in my winter ski clothes and boots, running up and down an ice-filled hill outside the cafeteria, in repentance for all the terrible deeds I had done that week.

In retrospect, PD did an amazing thing. It actually made me *enjoy* running. I would go on an early-morning penalty drill run, sign some piece of paper on some tree a mile or two away, and then run back. All before the sun came up. This is just when cassette Walkmans had come out. I would listen to Jimi Hendrix's *Are You Experienced?*

> *not necessarily stoned*
> *but*
> *beautiful*

I had never smoked anything yet. But it sure sounded like fun.

It was at Lakefield that I had my first taste of alcohol. My buddy who lived in Peterborough worked at the local record store. I told my buddies from Toronto this, the rich kids that were in my new grade. I was younger than them and was eager to impress. They told me that if I got them booze, they would dig that. So that's what I did.

We would have parties in Toronto at their incredible houses. Far from anything where I had ever lived, or seen. This is where I first saw dudes drinking tons of beer who were having a ton of fun doing it.

The very first alcohol I ever tasted was Kahlúa. Somehow, we had gotten a bottle. With my buddy Scott Carter, we drank the whole thing. Then proceeded to vomit all over the backyard. I have never wanted a sip of Kahlúa ever again.

Second time was a bottle of gin. My friend Rick asked me if I needed anything at the liquor store and I didn't really know what to say. So he came back with a bottle of gin. Which we drank, and once again, puked all over some other person's backyard. Have

Lakefield College School

Name Sebastian Bierk   Subject Mathematics

Mark 81 B   Class Average 70.9

Master's Comment:

After some minor altercations at the beginning of term, I think Sebastian and I are seeing eye to eye. He is a good student, and with a little less hostile approach, could add much to his classmates.

SJG.

never had a sip of gin ever again in my life. The smell and taste of it reminds me of wood.

But most of the time at Lakefield was indeed spent in pursuit of a sound mind and sound body. We spent a majority of the days outdoors, in canoes, on portage from park to park, sleeping, camping, cooking outside. Learning to live off the land of the countryside of Northern Ontario was a unique way to spend one's preteen years. The breathtaking beauty of the Canadian landscape is something that will always soothe me. Canada will always have a precious place in my heart.

I played lots of sports at Lakefield. Quarterback on the football team, left defensive end. Downhill skiing in the wintertime. A slalom racer, I developed a lifelong love of skiing. We would get in the school bus after school and get to Devil's Elbow Ski Slopes for an hour or two every single day. Pretty amazing when you think about it. The lead bowler on the cricket team, I found it very funny that we would play in the rain and mud while wearing completely all-white attire. Which would be black and green after rolling around in a field all day.

We trained to ski even when there was no snow. We would get to the top of the mountain with prototype tread-skis that have long been taken off the market. For obvious, painful reasons. We would strap our ski boots onto these little tank treads, and zoom down the hill.

Falling into a rock is a lot harder than falling into snow.

On the night that John Lennon died, December 8, 1980, I was asleep in my dorm at Upper Colebrook House. Our seventh-grade teacher was an amazing man by the name of Mike Chellew, who I looked up to in every way. Mr. Chellew came and knocked on our door. He stood there in the doorway, in silhouette as we wondered what was going on.

"Hey guys, sorry to wake you up. But I just have to tell you some bad news. John Lennon, the singer of the Beatles, has just been shot. He died an hour or so ago."

And then he shut the door.

I was absolutely inconsolable. I fell apart. Burst into tears and wailed, as if one of my own family members had died.

My dad worshiped John Lennon. He even wanted to look like him. The round glasses and everything. Our family dog growing up was a beautiful little Scottish terrier named *Lennon*. I had grown up listening to John Lennon sing and I was just becoming a genuine fan myself. I loved the record *Double Fantasy*. "(Just Like) Starting Over," which he lovingly dedicated to his wife. That inspired me. Not to do what people expected of him. I could feel his love even at my young age. This inspired me many years later, when I met the love of my life, Suzanne, and we got married. She has made my life so much better in every way. I would love to inspire others that yes, indeed it's true. *All you need is love.*

Anyway, back to the night he got shot. Even I didn't quite understand my *physical* reaction to this news. I could not stop crying. I was away from my family. John Lennon *felt* like family to me. After a considerable amount of time, Mr. Chellew came back into the room.

"Sebastian. I had no idea this would affect you in this way. Come with me."

He brought me into the TV room and switched on the news. I was the only student in there. He had compassion. He could see how this was killing me.

As I watched the late-night news, what I saw was completely heart-wrenching to a little boy. How someone could just take away someone else, who had touched so many. How someone could silence the voice and music of generations. It was unfathomable that John Lennon was no longer on this earth. This is maybe my first real experience with death.

There was an amazing part of the school curriculum called Playfair/Pathfinder, which entailed all grade-ten students spending two weeks on a real brigantine ship, sailing around all five Great Lakes, from Ontario to Michigan and beyond. Together, living at sea (actually, lake), embarking upon a true *expedition* before the school year started. Very much a *Lord of the Flies*, separate-the-strong-from-the-weak kind of deal. Kids heaved up their guts into the pristine Canadian waters on a daily basis. This was an incredible experience for an average tenth-grade student to go through. I was a year younger than all the other kids, but I had a great time.

We would spend some days on the calm waters of Lake Huron. I can see it now. No other humans, no land in sight. Just us, cracking jokes, having fun. Cooking food in the galley below, where we also slept. In tiny bunks. We sailed all five Great Lakes and lived to tell the tale.

Not all nights were easy, or even remotely safe. One night we all thought we were going to die. A class of tenth-grade students, sailing Lake Superior, caught in the midst of a Noreaster. If the keel leaned any more to the right of the dial, it would mean we capsize. Sent up on the deck to change the jib sheet, required us to fasten ourselves to the railing, with wire attached to our bodies, lest we be jettisoned into the raging waters below. I am not making this up. When I write this down, for this book, I can't believe what I'm reading.

We would get shore leave every couple of days, where we would pull up to a dock somewhere in a Canadian or American town. Walking around the streets for an hour or two, before we would be required back to the brigantine. A funny sight to see, kids standing in line at a Harvey's Restaurant with sea legs. Standing in line and just falling over, for no apparent reason, not being used to a stationary horizontal plane for days.

One morning, on top of the crow's nest, I heard an amazing sound. Coming up out of the galley quarters, I climbed up the ladder and onto the deck. Looking up the rope netting, where we would climb up high above the waters below. Looking out at the horizon, upon the still, reflective lake, was a beautiful sight to behold.

On this day, a guy by the name of Tony Vineberg was sitting by himself high up in the crow's nest. With an acoustic guitar. I could not believe the music he was playing.

Tony was playing the lead guitar solo to "Runnin' with the Devil" by Van Halen. I flipped out immediately, and scaled the heights of the poop deck to the crow's nest above. Where Tony was sitting cross-legged and playing the guitar. It was the first time I had ever heard an actual human being play a Van Halen song on the guitar, in front of my *naked steaming eyes*, as David Lee Roth himself would say.

Immediately Tony and I became best friends. I was in the church choir, and he was the only guitar player I knew of in the school. We decided to form a band.

A couple of days later we found out that we had been assigned to the exact same dorm. Tony and me would be living with each other for the whole next year. This was good news for two nascent rockers who had just formed a band.

We collected albums and played them constantly, getting ready for football, falling asleep at night, whenever we could. Which wasn't all that much, because of our insane school schedule. He turned me on to guitar music such as Al Di Meola, John McLaughlin, Paco de Lucía. We even went to see those three play live in Toronto with opener Steve Morse. My dad's friend Bill Kimball took us to the show.

We went to other shows as well. When Van Halen played the Carrier Dome in Syracuse, New York, on the *Diver Down* Tour, my dad was cool enough to take me and my friend George Jeffery all the way from Lakefield to Syracuse, six hours, to see the mighty Van Halen. What an incredible experience. We turned into Syracuse, and the area of the Carrier Dome, being completely surrounded by dudes in spandex pants, with bandanas going from their knees down to their ankles. Just like fans dressed up for a KISS show, there were so many David Lee Roth clones walking around I couldn't believe my eyes. This was a considerable influence on the young Sebastian Bach.

We went to the concert and had the shittiest seats imaginable. We sat at the very top of the back row, on the side. We could barely even see the stage. It was still fun to be there, though. After the show we met Dad in the parking lot. He had an insane story to tell. As usual.

"Hey guys!! Did you have fun????"

"Yes."

"Do you know where *I* watched the show from???"

"What do you mean, you watched the show, Dad??? You didn't even have a ticket!"

"Well, check this out, fellas!! I went to the backstage and told them that my son was missing! Could they *please* let me come in and find him? At first they wouldn't let me in, but after I begged and pleaded, they said 'Okay, come on in!' And then I found myself on the side of the stage watching the show. That is until David Lee Roth walked *right past me*! In a pair of *assless chaps*!" Which we couldn't see, because we were sitting five miles from the stage.

I could not believe that my dad was standing side stage at Van Halen, while we were up in the rafters. I made a note to myself that would have to change in the future at some point.

The singing continued on at Lakefield. I sang in the church choir the whole time I was in the school, and was picked by the choirmaster Mr. Thompson, to sing the lead at Christmas mass. A song called "Once in Royal David's City," at the Lakefield Town Church, on an assembly day. I shut my eyes on a Sunday morning and for about six hundred people sang the song myself with Mr. Thompson on piano. We did it again in chapel for the school the next day.

The older kids congratulated me and told me I was a good singer. I couldn't believe I was picked to do this.

Back in our dorm room, Tony and I played our albums. This was around the time when my voice started to change. Due to my newfound status as a singer, I did not want to get kicked out of the choir. So I did something that I don't know if anybody else ever did. Feeling my voice change from a higher pitch to a lower pitch, I locked myself in my dorm and sang along to the highest music I could find. Rush. The Police. Anything that would keep my voice in the soprano register. I don't know if this worked or not. But I like to think that it did.

One day I was singing along to a Police song called "Roxanne." There was a knock at the door. An older prefect, Dave Kitchen, sat down and said, "Who was singing that?" Tony pointed at me. David, from grade thirteen, said, "Sing it again." I sang the Police hit. He told me to do it again. And again. He called his friend Louis Paget into the room. And other older kids. Then they asked me and Tony an incredible thing.

"Hey, we want you guys to join *our* band." We were blown away. They were all so much older than us. Then of course we said, "Okay." Thus, the band Anthem was born!

We rehearsed in one of the classrooms whenever we were allotted the time. An eclectic mixture of songs, including "Red Barchetta" by Rush, "Message in a Bottle" by The Police, "The Weight" by The Band, "Under My Thumb" by The Rolling Stones, "Freebird," and perhaps most incredibly, we even covered the song "Wino" by Lynyrd Skynyrd. Yes, I repeat. I covered the song "Wino" in my first-ever band! The mind boggles. Life imitates art? More on this later!

We were asked by Head Boy Michael Hope to play at the upcoming school dance. For this we needed girls. The girls were bused in from our sister school, Bethany. Imagine that. An all-boys school having girls shipped in from an all-girls school. Neither of us having seen boys or girls in months. The pressure was on the band to deliver the goods.

I was so nervous, I really didn't think it would even go down. Somehow I had obtained a red driver's one-piece racing suit, an all-body red outfit that I thought looked really cool. For totally badass effect I tied a bandana around my thigh. I was thinking David Lee Roth. But I looked more like Chachi from *Happy Days*.

I took a bunch more bandanas and tied them around my ankles, up to my knee. Like I had seen the guys do at the Van Halen concert at Carrier Dome. But with my short hair, I wasn't quite pulling off the look yet.

The night of the dance, we walked to the makeshift stage, which was put together in front of the fireplace. The full school cafeteria, cleared of tables and chairs, was now packed with the whole student body. Plus the girls from Bethany. It was time for my first ever show to begin.

There was no way this was going to happen. I wanted to puke, and die. We went through the kitchen of the cafeteria so we could make our entrance unseen by the crowd. In the kitchen, near the ovens, I said, "I can't do this." I sat down and told them, "There's no way."

The older guys in the band literally grabbed my racing suit by the scruff of the neck and dragged me to the stage, which they proceeded to throw me onto. I had no choice. I grabbed the microphone, closed my eyes, and begin to sing.

After the show, an amazing thing happened to me. For the first time.

Girls wanted to talk to me.

Michael Hope ran up.

"Oh my God Sebastian. You're not going to believe this. Every single girl here wants to say hello to you. I have a lineup of girls who want to say 'Hi' to you and get a picture." This was in 1980, before smartphones, folks. Some things never change.

As I stood there, Michael introduced girl after girl to me. They all looked at me in a way I had never been looked at before. Whereas before, my way of making friends was to be the class clown, to make people laugh, now my whole perception, to others, had changed. After I did that show, people looked at me with *respect*. Older kids in the school came up and shook my hand. Kids that had never spoken to me before all looked at me with that same weird look in their eye. It was that very moment I decided. This is what I want to do for the rest of my life.

Moons Over My Hammy:
Suspended Animation

On our way to after-school sports, at nearby Trent University. Today was a day of swimming. We were all put in a yellow school bus to make the short drive to the nearby school. As we bounced on down the road, boys will be boys and we're joking around. Having some fun. As boys tend to do.

It was fun back in those days to *moon* complete strangers. Pull your pants down, grab your ankles, and flash your ass to some stranger, unbeknownst of the mooning assault about to occur. This was one of those times.

Guys were mooning the cars that were following the bus. We made a barricade of students so the bus driver couldn't see. Cars would be following our asses, pressed to the windows, as they honked on in utter dismay, behind the bus.

Okay, so it was my turn. I went to the back of the bus. Made sure the driver couldn't see me behind the other guys. Pulled my pants down to my knees, and pressed my ass up to the window. Everybody laughed. Until they stopped. I turned around and looked behind me.

The car directly behind my behind passed us, and the car behind that one took its place. Behind my ass.

Behind the wheel of this car was now our English teacher, Mrs. Brown. Staring at my ass.

Katie Brown was the only teacher in school that had tits. We would sit in her class and stare at her bountiful bosom, a bunch of boys with no girls except for the teacher in front of the blackboard. Now here she was in her car, driving home after a day teaching school. Staring at her student's ass, above her. The student's ass was mine, dear reader.

The look on Mrs. Brown's face was a look I will never forget, or want to ever see again.

She stared up at me, as I pulled up my pants in terror. She glared at me with a look that said, "You are going to be completely destroyed for doing this."

We all shot to our seats in horror, completely aware of what was about to happen next. Someone was going to get an insane amount of penalty drill for *this*. And we all knew who that someone was.

As a result, I did not get PD only for mooning the teacher. I got suspended from school. Summoned into the Headmaster's Office, he ripped into a vicious personal attack that really showed how much he considered me to be a waste of flesh. I ran out of his office and across the soccer field back to Wadsworth House. Crying all the way, confused as to why I was being *suspended* for doing what all the other guys were doing too.

Dad came and picked me up. Took me back home for a couple of days. Great. On the way home, he said, "Maybe you shouldn't be going here anymore." I was relieved. As much as I loved going to Lakefield, after three years the thought of going to a *normal* school very much appealed to me. Now that I had played in a rock band, my mind was consumed by music, and the prospect of kicking some ass. That's what I knew I had to do. And I couldn't do it here.

I finished up that school year and went home for the summer. Then started a new life at Peterborough Collegiate Vocational School. The new kids I met would not be from private schools. The new kids I was hanging out with hung out at the arcade, and did purple microdot acid.

Let the video games begin.

3

BACH FORMATIONS

Acid, Arcades, and Aerosmith

1982–1985

The transition from private school back to public could not have been more marked. Gone were the gray flannel slacks and green suit jackets. The cassock and gown had now been replaced by Accept Balls to the Wall and Twisted Sister You Can't Stop Rock 'n' Roll concert T-shirts. I had a jean jacket, on the back of which I painstakingly detailed the Twisted Sister and Queensrÿche logos. In white Liquid Paper. I was nothing if not resourceful.

I could now go to every single show I could afford. From the dormitory at Lakefield back to Mom's house in Peterborough, I started rocking immediately. The alienation and frustration I felt from being suspended from LCS worked wonderfully in my pursuit of singing heavy metal rock 'n' roll. I released my frustrations vocally in my bedroom every single day, practicing my voice. Much to the chagrin of my mother. I would attempt to sing Queensrÿche's "Queen of the Reich" and Judas Priest's *Unleashed in the East*, attempting to hit supersonic high notes that were possible only in my wildest dreams. I sang hours upon hours behind my locked bedroom door. The music absolutely consumed me.

When my buddy showed me the album *Unleashed in the East*, it changed my life. He dropped the needle on the song "Victim of Changes." "Listen to this." When Rob Halford hit the high note in the second verse, I told my friend, "That's not a human voice." I thought it was, in fact, a guitar. It sounded that foreign to me. I could not believe anyone's vocal cords could be capable of such a sound.

One day my buddy Rick came over. We were both trying to sing Rob Halford songs to my stereo. All of a sudden we saw the most incredible sight. Of my mother kicking down my bedroom door.

A huge crashing sound startled us as we turned around. There was my mom's tanned leather Frye boot heel, destroying my bedroom door as she flattened it to the floor.

"Turn that shit down right now!!"

Mom stood on top of the dust and debris of the wreckage she had just hooved in. She looked like a character from the Robert Crumb comic my dad had given me a week earlier.

Right around this time, video games were invented. On high school lunch hour we would go down to Western World arcade and play Asteroids, Pole Position, Galaga, Centipede, Robotron, Scramble, and the like. The exact same time these video games were brought into the world, someone gave me a hit of purple microdot LSD. Some of my more adventurous friends and I would drop acid and destroy aliens in that little Canadian town north of Toronto. None of us knew there was anything wrong with it.

But the suburbs have no charms to soothe
the restless dreams of youth.
Subdivisions.
Be cool or be cast out.

It's amazing how the Rush song "Subdivisions" captured the restlessness I was feeling back then, and the video completely looks like my time at Peterborough Collegiate Vocational School. I had the same exact haircut as that dude. And I swear that was me on Yonge Street in those shots from the video.

*Lit up like a fire fly
just to feel the living night.*

On hot summer nights we would go swimming. The balmy, thick, humid air of the Canadian early morning. Inverlea Park. Hours after the arcades closed, coming down from acid. As the sun came up. Up the top of the bridge, over Lake Otonabee, we jump off. Hit the water forty feet below. Seems a lot higher when you're flying on LSD. Swim around, laugh and marvel at the incredible beauty. The cool mist rising off the placid waters up into the new day's sun. The feeling of being immersed in the fresh water as we walked around and felt the riverbed beneath our feet.

There was nothing in us that would give us a *bad trip* at that point. We were just kids goofing off at the beach.

My most vivid memory of doing acid is laughter, to the point of paralysis. Me and a buddy were at Mac's Milk, across the street from Kenner Collegiate, where my dad used to teach art. We were high on 'sids, as we used to call acid back then. Roaming the aisles of the variety store, the drug hit us hard. *Overwhelmingly* hard. We picked up magazines, bottles of ketchup, loaves of bread, what have you. Staring at these ordinary household items, feeling them, touching them, we would laugh to the point of being on our backs, in the middle of the aisle, kicking our feet up into the air and holding our stomachs. We would look at a bottle of mayonnaise and laugh so hard that tears streamed out of our eyes. We could not breathe. I remember being in that variety store for an insane amount of time, hours. Our friends even came over to hang out with us in the store and see what we were laughing about. It seemed like we were there all night.

Although, in reality, it could have been only a minute or two.

Kingswood Music Theatre
Canada's Wonderland
July 9, 1984

Aerosmith played Canada's Wonderland, an amusement park out-side of Toronto, on the *Back in the Saddle* tour. Me and another buddy decided this would be a great time to take a bunch of acid, go ride the roller coasters, and then see our heroes in concert. The perfect night out!

My memories of this day are obviously somewhat hazy. I do recall ripping up the blotter page, and dropping more than one hit onto my tongue sometime in the afternoon. We hit every roller coaster and laughed the whole time. Aerosmith went on early. We had pretty good seats, close to the stage. Under the shed roof, as opposed to being on the lawn. Somewhere near the soundboard. I can remember a couple things about the concert. How wild Steven Tyler seemed that night. The roof over where we were sitting . . . was *moving*. Undulating, back and forth, up and down. I listened to the concert and let the lights swathe over me. Stared at the roof of the shed. Marveled at how it seemed to be almost liquid-like in its texture. At the end of the concert, Steven Tyler got into it with the local police. Having us all shout, "Hell no, we won't go!! Aero-smith Rocks!!!! Kingswood SUCKS!!"

Or something along those lines. Don't quote me on that. I was high at the time.

We got back home about six in the morning. We made a bunch of noise stumbling up the porch. I opened the front door.

My mother stood at the top of the stairs. She was decidedly not amused. Understandably, Mom had had enough of this.

"Where in the HELL were you?"

Perhaps I had not even *told* her I was going to Toronto that night.

It was two hours away from Peterborough, with traffic. No son should treat his mother like this.

I think I told her that I had been to Canada's Wonderland to see Aerosmith, but I have no idea what I actually said. I might have told her I was from the planet Xenon for all I know.

"Well, I've had enough, mister!! Get to your room RIGHT NOW. We will talk about this in the morning!! This bullshit has GOT TO STOP."

I didn't mean to hurt Mom at all. I was just being a goofy teenager. I guess being a teenager in 1984 was not exactly *Leave It to Beaver* anymore.

The next day Dad came over, unexpectedly. I had started to grow my hair long at this point. Dad glared up at me, outside on the lawn. I stood on the porch.

"YOU, young man, will cut your hair NOW!"

Of course this was hilarious, coming from a man who had long hair most of his adult life. I laughed, shut the door, and vowed to myself that I would grow my hair down to my ass. I would have long hair for the rest of my life. I am still working on that, sitting here, as we speak.

My buddy Curtis came over to crank tunes and hang out. He told me there was a band near him, in Toronto, that was trying out lead singers. As we rocked out to the heavy metal records in my room, he said, "Hey! You should go try out!"

There was only one problem. I was so young, there was no way this was going to work. Even if I got the gig, that would mean I would have to move to Toronto. At my young age? That would be impossible. Besides, I wouldn't get the gig anyway. They were all at least five or ten years older than me. So what the hell? I might as well go give it a shot. Besides, it was something to do, other than jumping off a bridge, high on LSD.

I took the bus up to Toronto on a Saturday morning. Met up with Curtis. Went over to this rehearsal room. In the back alley of a strip mall. I went downstairs and the room was filled with hopeful lead vocalists, all far older than I was. One guy was the lead singer of a well-known band called Moxy that was influential in the '70s. I couldn't believe I was sitting there about to sing in front of all these old dudes.

The drummer sized me up.

"Hey kid. Think you can sing, huh? How many *octaves* do you have?"

"Oh, I don't know, about eight I think."

The older guys in the room chuckled and laughed. I had no clue what I was talking about.

Everyone took a turn at the mike. Next it was time for me to step up and sing. Curtis was friends with Ande Ryche, the guitar player, who said to the other guys, "Come on, give the kid a chance. Let's at least check him out." I took a deep breath and stood behind the mic. I

asked them to do a song by Judas Priest called "Bloodstone."

The riff kicked in. I started up on the verse. Everything was go-

ing well. When it came time to hit the chorus note "BLOOOOOOD-Stoooooone," I turned to my left and looked at Ande. He was looking at drummer Brian Williams and the other guitar players in the band. They were all laughing. After the song was over, everybody seemed to be in a good mood.

The older guy, from the band Moxy, was also an accomplished session musician. He stood up in exasperation and started out the door.

"Hey Sebastian, you be careful with those *eight octaves*, okay?" he snidely remarked as he walked out the door. Well, how did that work out for you?

I got the gig.

I had a meeting with my father at our favorite restaurant, Mother's Pizzeria in downtown Peterborough. The conversation went something like this.

"Hey, Dad. I'm moving to Toronto. To become a rock star."

"Hey, Sebastian. No, you're not."

After I explained to Dad that this was actually going to happen, he finally relented. He realized there was no changing my mind. He said to me, "Sebastian. You can go to Toronto, with my blessing, under one condition. That you take vocal lessons once a week, in order to learn how to sing *properly*, and also how to protect your voice. I will pay for these lessons, as long as you show up to every single one."

Dad made good on his promise. Every Wednesday I would show up on Eglinton Avenue, a little west of Yonge Street. Gwenlynn Little Vocal Studios. She would work with me on my singing. Taught me a lot. Like, to bend my knees really quick if there was a note I couldn't get. She told me it would take my mind off not hitting the note, and would allow me to hit it correctly. I tried it and it worked. One day she said, "You know what, Sebastian? You

sound a lot like Neil Diamond." That was the first and only time I ever heard that. I thank my dad for looking out for my pipes at such an early age.

   Playing in this band was actually a great opportunity. We were

out to get signed to a talent agency, and do some real gigs. *Paying gigs.* Or at least that was the plan.

Someone came up with the ridiculous name of Herrenvolk. I was told it was German for *men who look like women.* I'm serious. It was that silly of a scene at that time.

On the subway, on the way to Safor Rehearsal Studios, south of Jane and Finch in Northern Toronto, I saw a wall of graffiti out the window as I zoomed past. It was signed *Kid Wicked.* I said that to myself a couple times. Being in my mid-teens, I thought it might be a cool name for a rock band.

I told the guys and they thought it was a good name as well. I changed the spelling to *Kid Wikkid* since I was a kid. See what I did there? And so, Kid Wikkid was born. I moved into a room at my aunt Leslie's boyfriend Jay's house, who owned a printing press. We printed up fliers for each show and plastered them all over town. I played my very first Headline Rock Show at Larry's Hideaway, in November 1984. Several years under the legal drinking age, I should've been arrested for even being in the place. But I was six foot seven with my hair teased to the roof, and had on more makeup than Tammy Faye Bakker. So nobody was the wiser.

We went on tour. Got crabs in Sudbury. Drank beers in Brock-ville. Smoked hash in Québec. Playing three sets a night, at places such as Sainte-Anselme. Sherbrooke. Le Papillon, outside Ottawa, in Hull. Drinking age was eighteen at the time. I was still under-age, headlining these clubs. Standing on the tables, careful not to kick off the lines of cocaine the Montréal bikers laid out, rocking all night long to Kid Wikkid.

This is where I started to learn to do what I do. Touring Québec and Ontario, in the back of a station wagon, set the standard for many decades to come.

Around this time I met a guy by the name of Rich Chycki. Rich-ard has since gone on to be the producer of many Rush albums. He is now regarded as one of the industry's top sound technicians. Producer of countless albums, 5.1 surround sound, he has even re-mixed and remastered some of the world's favorite Rush records. He is one of the best in the world at what he does.

One day we were lying on the beach in Toronto. It was hot. My friends and I went to the corner beer store, at Woodbine and Queen, and bought a two-four. *Two-four* is Canadian for a case of beer that contains twenty-four beers. That should do, for the

Entertainment

Peterborough Kid Gets Wikkid
by: Ron Boudreau

"Sebastian Bach — What kind of name is that?" The name that's got Toronto's music scene talking. Much Music, Maxell Tapes, Metallion Magazine, Attic, WEA Records and anyone else who's involved in the fast-paced Heavy Metal scene.

Bass is the front man for the wild Toronto based Glamor Rock Band Kid Wikkid. Everyone is asking, how old is this "Kid Wikkid" Bass, and how far can be take the band? For those who are not familiar with Bass, he is a sixteen-year-old Peterborough boy born in the Bahamas, with a tall flashy image, looks, style, stage charisma, an amazing voice and most of all ambition that just won't quit. Bass says "I know my destiny and I'll be damned if fate is

gets a chance. He loves Toronto's fast-paced life, and he only fears of burning out before his time. Bass feels that Peterborough is a "bubble" where it is very hard to maintain individuality and the only way for him to expand was to break the "bubble" and get to work on his career. He said "I'm not going to sit around and wait for things to happen, I'm going to make them happen."

With quite a few credited shows behind them at Larry's Hideaway, the Gas Works and El Mocombo, they are now looking for bigger and better things. They just completed in Maxell/Metallion Metal Marathon last month. They placed a strong third ahead of Canada's more seasoned metal bands like Harlott, Rue Morgue, Tittan and Jade. With two of us this afternoon. Of course we were underage. I don't remember how we even got it. We hoisted the two-four up onto our shoulders. All we had, other than beer, was a Frisbee. That was all we needed.

Immediately upon finding our spot on the beach, we dug a hole in the sand. Buried the case of beer. Besides being not of legal drinking age, it was completely illegal to drink alcohol on the beach. Not that we gave a shit. We took our shirts off, grabbed a couple of brews, poured them into cups, and started firing the Frisbee around.

All of a sudden this Adonis dude with crazy blond hair came up to me. "Hey, how are you guys???" he asked me.

"Hi, my name is Sebastian." I proceeded to tell him I was a singer. We exchanged numbers after having a ton of laughs that afternoon. He invited me over to his place to check out his tunes.

After I sang for him, he played me some songs. I liked what I heard and agreed to meet him in the studio. We cut a song called "You Should Know Me." A plaintive ballad that had my voice in a register kind of around the song "Sara" by Jefferson Starship. I had never been recorded this professionally before. This was the first time I ever heard my voice played back through the speakers the way it was to sound on the Skid Row records, years later.

I played the tape for a concert promoter in Toronto named Shawn Pilot. He was a guy responsible for bringing Hanoi Rocks to the El Mocambo, and other glam rock shows. Loving what he heard, he sent the tape to a band he had booked called Madam X, out of Detroit, Michigan. Along with a picture from *Metallion* magazine, which was being made into buttons and being sold on Yonge Street now, much to my amazement.

Madam X liked what they heard. They wanted me to come down to Detroit and try out for their band. I could not believe this was happening. I was so happy in Kid Wikkid. They were my friends. We had even built up somewhat of a following in Ontario and were working somewhat steadily. But I knew that making it in America was where it was at. If you made it big in Canada, that was one thing. But if you made it in the USA, you would have an *international career* as well. I had to take a shot at this, at least.

The phone call I had to make to Brian of Kid Wikkid to let him know I was quitting the band was the saddest moment I'd had in music yet. Our voices choked up as I told him the news. We had been through a lot. I really liked these guys. We were both crying. As I hung up on my friend, I grabbed a pillow, buried my head in it, and cried some more. But this was the path I had to take.

On the day I had to go to Detroit, I knew what I had to do. I showed up at the border in my full stage gear. Hair teased up to the sky. A pinstriped suit jacket. Snakeskin boots, makeup, shades. This would *definitely* get me in the band, I was convinced.

This *definitely* ensured I did not make it across the border.

The bass player, named Godzilla, and the guitar player, Maxine Petrucci, had showed up at the Windsor/Detroit border to pick me up from my six-hour bus ride from Toronto. I was seven feet tall and my hair look like a pineapple. U.S. Border Patrol took one look

at me and laughed. "Turn around, son. Go back home. You're not getting into the States today."

For fuck's sake.

Godzilla came up with a brilliant idea. Since we were about the same height, same hair, we looked not dissimilar. He came up with the plan that we were cousins. He was coming to pick me up to go to an amusement park. He was going to take me back home afterwards—honest, officer.

Sounded good to me.

He drove up to Toronto, from Detroit. I was under strict orders to dress as conservatively as possible. Which I did. Hair tied back. No guyliner.

We drove the car to Sarnia. Surely they would not catch on to our plan. To become huge rock stars and take over the planet. "Hey, this is my cousin Sebastian. We're going to go on a roller coaster ride."

I'll say.

My time in Madam X was a trial by fire. They were ten years older. We played paying gigs across the United States. After forming the band in Detroit, we packed it up and moved to Phoenix, Arizona. The band had been signed to Jet Records and released an album called *We Reserve the Right (to Rock)*. A friend in Phoenix would let us rehearse at his bar Rockers, on Indian School Road, for free. The stipulation being, we could only rehearse when there was nothing else going on in the bar. Which meant our rehearsal hours were from 7:00 to 9:00 in the morning. Not the ideal time for a singer to vocalize. Especially a singer who was seventeen years old.

I was not in any way ready for this gig. Although I had a pleasant-sounding voice, I did not have the muscles built up in my throat to sing a two-hour show every night, night after night. This

takes years to develop. I simply did not have throat muscles to be a professional vocalist at this time. I had a *falsetto* scream that could split glass. And it actually did, at a place called The Network in Baltimore, Maryland. But every time I hit this high falsetto, it would blow my pipes out for the rest of the set. Once I learned how to sing properly, from the diaphragm, I lost that high freak squeal that was louder than the PA itself.

To support myself in Detroit, I took a job as a telemarketer. We would pretend to be photocopy ink salesmen and call some poor elderly woman in New Orleans or somewhere, at churches and monasteries across America.

"Hi, Mrs. Chadsworth! This is Ace Johnson! From the photocopy store, up the street! I see it's time for another shipment!"

"Of what, dear?"

"Well, I see that your maintenance sheet calls for some more blue ink toner cartridges! Don't worry! I'll have them delivered by next week!"

"Why, thank you, son!" The lady would warble on down the line, perplexed. Confused. We would get their credit card numbers and charge them money for printer ink. They probably didn't even own a printer.

One of the guys at this telemarketer place told me that I would sell more ink if I did cocaine at lunchtime with him. I thought this to be a good idea at the time. We would snort lines and drink coffee in the Michigan winter, behind snowbanks and minus-10 temperatures.

Those weren't the only snowbanks in town.

One night we were eating dinner at Maxine's mom's kitchen. She made incredible homemade pasta, along with homemade wine. I looked forward to having dinner there every single night. Maxine would sometimes talk to Steve Stevens, guitar player for Billy Idol, on the phone in the kitchen. I couldn't believe it. He was one of

my guitar gods. I would never be allowed to speak to him myself, however. I was just a nobody, so that was appropriate. Years later, when I started working with Steve myself, he told me the real reason he was calling Maxine was to get a hold of me. He had seen my picture on a flyer for a Madam X gig. "Who's the singer? Can I get his info?" We just did an album together, for the first time, called *Give 'Em Hell*. Who knows what would've happened if we had gotten together back in 1985?

But I digress.

We played Shreveport, Louisiana, at a place called Circle in the Square. I was discovering around this time that it was necessary to warm up my voice before the show. But I had no idea what this meant. I just thought it meant screaming as loud as I could or something. I couldn't really do that in my hotel room without getting kicked out. So, I went out into the median in the middle of the highway and sang heavy metal songs at the top of my lungs. Surrounded by the traffic on either side of the road, I thought this was the only place one could do such a thing.

We played at a place called the Sports Page in Baton Rouge, Louisiana. These are the days way before in-ear monitors. Standing on a postage-stamp-size stage right next to the drum kit, manned by my buddy Bam Bam McConnell? There was no possible way I could hear myself perfectly every night. Such venues are not exactly designed for their acoustics. *In the middle of one song, I am standing in front of the drum riser, trying to rock as hard as I can. Godzilla is staring me in the face. I think I'm doing great. Obviously he thinks otherwise, as he backs up and proceeds to hock a gigantic loogie straight into my face.* Onstage. In front of the band, crew, and crowd. Humiliated, not understanding why. Godzilla had to *spit in my face* to make me stop? Well, he certainly did. As soon as we got back to Detroit I said, "Fuck this shit," and quit the band.

Headed back to Toronto and formed a cover band, with the biggest hair in town, called Vo5. Heated up a bottle of VO5 shampoo, peeled off the label, took it to Kinko's. Made fliers for our shows. It was a cool logo. Got back with Rich Chicki. Recorded some more great music. One of the songs was called "Saved by Love Again." This was the song I sent to Dave Feld in New Jersey. There was a new band that wanted to check out my pipes.

The band was called Skid Row.

I Lost My Virginity at the Age of Thirteen

On the floor of my aunt's boyfriend Jay's apartment, where I was living at the time. I had invited this girl over, and we got a large bottle of Kressmann white wine that I either bought somehow, or more likely stole from my aunt. I remember downing most of the bottle of wine together, then lying down on the floor and putting my thingy in her thingy. This would be the first of many, many times that I would get drunk and fuck.

One time at a Kid Wikkid show, two strippers from Montréal named Bunny and Manon came to see us. They had heavy French Canadian accents and I really dug them a lot. I brought them both back to Uncle Jay's place and I proceeded to have my first threesome. It's pretty cool when you are fifteen years old to have two women doing each other in your bed, and doing you at the same time. It's like Twister. Only different.

I remember Uncle Jay opening the door to my room the next morning and seeing the three of us nude, our limbs entwined and the most visceral look of shock on his face. I sure was a lucky boy!

When I was in Kid Wikkid, I was with some girls. Not too many, because I didn't really want any of them. I remember being fourteen or fifteen and meeting this thirty-year-old woman who took me back to her place. I fucked her for literally hours. I was hard as a rock, but I couldn't cum. I remember looking down at her and saying to myself, this is great . . . but I don't have any feelings for this person. After hours of sex with no ejaculation, she looked at me and said, "I am amazed at your stamina." I was like, *"Thanks."* I did not want to hurt her feelings with the truth, which was, I wasn't really into her scene.

I lived with a stripper known to most as Crazy Sue, who was much older than me. She took me into her apartment, at the corner of Yonge and Eglinton in Toronto, when my aunt broke up with Jay and I had nowhere else to go. It seems crazy to me now, when I look back, that I moved in with a stripper when I was fourteen or fifteen years old. Hey, it was the '80s.

Crazy Sue had one or more "sugar daddies." When these men would come over, she would kick me out of the place and I would go hang out in the stairwell of the building. I would sit there, by myself, not knowing what to do. One time I snuck back to the apartment and put my ear up to the door. I could hear Sue and some strange man having sex, laughing, having fun. While I sat in the hallway hurt, jealous, and confused. Sue was my friend, and although we weren't boyfriend and girlfriend, I lived with her and felt protective of her because she gave me a place to stay when no one else would. I listened to her have sex with another man and felt betrayed.

I met my first wife, Maria, around this time. I was fifteen years old. She was twenty-one.

We met at a concert by a band called Harlot at a bar called Studio 21. I had my hair teased up to the rafters and was wearing more makeup than Caitlyn Jenner at a Kanye West concert. When Maria first saw me, she thought I was . . . a girl. An extremely tall, lanky, girl.

I was wearing a black T-shirt with the sleeves cut off, which showed my bare shoulders. On my right shoulder, I have a black mole. Maria told me later that she and all her friends were saying to each other, "Oh my God, look at that poor, tall girl! She is so tall and she has a MOLE on her SHOULDER! How can she walk around in that T-shirt! She has NO TITS!!!!" When I walked towards them in the club, they all exclaimed to each other, "Oh my God! *It's a BOY!*" Hey, it was the '80s.

I had a weird dream about Maria the other night. She had fixed up our master bedroom's bathroom. In the house that was lost to Hurricane Irene. The countertop and drawers are all gone. In its place is a brand-new counter, new mirrors, ornate lighting. The bathroom looks completely beautiful and brand-new. I try to thank her. But she ignores my thanks. She ignores me completely.

"*Why won't you let me thank you? Why can't I thank you?*" I begin shouting at her. She will not acknowledge me at all. We finally wind up on the floor together. "*I just want to thank you! I just want to say thank you for making the room so nice! Why won't you let me thank you? Why?*"

She just shakes her head in fear.

No, no, no, her eyes say.

4
FROM PARK AVENUE
TO SKID ROW

I joined the band Skid Row in 1987, through a series of events. The story has been told many times.

I had met Mötley Crüe in Toronto on the *Girls Girls Girls* tour, in Toronto. I gave Nikki Sixx a cassette tape and a picture, which he then passed on to Doc McGhee, who also managed Bon Jovi. I was the one with the most blow at Rock 'n' Roll Heaven, the club we were partying at that night. This was a great way for me to meet Tommy and Nikki. They liked me right away!

We closed the bar together that night. Mötley Crüe got us backstage at the show at Maple Leaf Gardens the next night. Their security guard, Fred Saunders, was awesome, telling me to "please *not smoke hash*" backstage at the Garden. I ignored him, and then he ignored me smoking. Fred is a wonderful dude.

I was *nineteen* years old.

After I spent a year in the band Madam X, the photographer Mark Weiss invited us to his wedding. He had shot Madam X in Phoenix at Rockers, on Indian School Road, when we were rehearsing there. It was an awkward trip because Madam X had already broken up at that point. But we decided to drive together from Detroit to New Jersey to attend Mark's wedding. I can remember right before we left for New Jersey, Maxine from Madam X was on her porch screaming at me and Mark McConnell, our drummer. "Everything was great for us until we got you guys in the band!!!" Little did we realize that this trip would not only see me out of her band, but into one of the biggest bands of our time.

I remember driving to New Jersey that summer of 1986. Coming down the Garden State Parkway for the very first time, and feeling the breeze. The *Bruce Springsteen/Southside Johnny/Little Steven/Clarence Clemons* vibe of the whole state. Bon Jovi was absolutely massive at this time. *Slippery When Wet* became one of the biggest-selling albums of that year and we were headed straight to the promised land off of Route 9. The New Jersey "rock 'n' roll pride" feeling was palpable. I wanted some of that.

Mark's wedding was held at the Molly Pitcher Inn, Red Bank, New Jersey. The day of the wedding was sunny. I went to the pool in my blue jean cutoff shorts and took my shirt off. I started getting a tan.

A girl named Sydney Masters, a publicist, started taking pictures of me. I cracked open a bottle of Jack Daniel's and started drinking. In the afternoon. It was a beautiful day.

I remember Zakk Wylde was at the wedding. Known by his real name of *Jeff Wielandt* back then. He was a super nice guy. Very much a "pretty boy" of the times. I handed Zakk my bottle of Jack Daniel's.

"Come on, dude, swig some Jack with me!"

The future Mr. Zakk Wylde then turned to me and said, "Oh no thanks, dude, I don't drink." This is remarkable, considering

the amount of liquor Zakk would consume a couple of years down the road. But when I met him that night, he was sober, young, and pretty. Pretty damn talented, too.

There was a wedding band present at the reception. I remember Zakk and me talking about what songs we were going to do when we took over the stage. I had been screaming in Zakk's ear all afternoon. He thought my high-pitched scream was hilarious, which it really was. I had a scream when I was in the band Madam X that was absolutely earsplitting. It was so high it's hard to describe what it sounded like. Zakk kept saying to me, *"Do that scream! Do that scream!"*

Kevin DuBrow of the band Quiet Riot was at the wedding and whispered to me, "No matter what you do, please don't ask me to come onstage and jam. I sweat a lot when I sing. I'm wearing this blue suit. I don't want to sweat it out tonight." I said, "Okay." Of course, this meant I was going to get him up onstage no matter what!

Zakk and I took over the wedding. We did "Whole Lotta Love" by Led Zeppelin. I hit that scream for Zakk. I then asked Kevin Du-Brow to come up and sing a song, with him approaching the stage dripping in sweat, looking at me like "You little bastard." It was pretty funny.

Also present at the wedding were Jon Bon Jovi's parents. After I sang, I was summoned over to their table, where I was asked to sit down. It felt pretty amazing to meet them. I asked Jon's dad, what was his favorite Bon Jovi song? He responded, "Never Say Good-bye." I told him I liked that song too, but my favorite one was "Let It Rock." It was a fun night.

They explained to me that their son had a friend named Dave who had a band. They were looking for a singer. Bon Jovi's parents thought I would be a good fit for the band. There was a guy named Dave Feld at the wedding as well. He took my phone number and information, and promised to the Bongiovis he would get my tape to Dave. Dave's band was called Skid Row.

I drove back to Detroit with Mark. I remember him telling me in his green van, on the way home, that I was *going to be a star and that I was going to make it big.* It all seemed like a dream.

After we got back to Detroit, I quit Madam X. I had been in that band exactly one year, to the day, from 1985 to 1986. I went back to Toronto in a car that I bought in Troy, Michigan, for fifty dollars. It was my first car. A Grand Prix. That barely worked. I got it from some guy and drove it by myself from Detroit back to Toronto. The car died two blocks away from Maria's house. I pulled the car over onto the side of the road and left it there. She came and picked me up. We never saw the car again.

Hey, it was cheaper than a bus ride.

Me and Maria moved into an apartment on Roncesvalles in Toronto. This is where Skid Row sent me their demo tape. We then moved into a basement apartment right near the CNE (or for you Americans, the Canadian National Exhibition). It was one room, which would get flooded out sometimes. We would wake up in a puddle where our soaked futon lay. It was no big deal. As long as the stereo didn't get wrecked, we were happy.

There were around five songs on that original Skid Row demo.

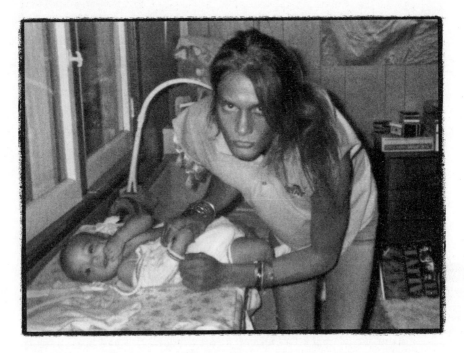

Two of the songs were "Youth Gone Wild" and "18 and Life." I kept listening to the tape, and at first, I did not like it. The singer they had at the time was a complete Jon Bon Jovi vocal sound-alike. I did not want to copy anybody. And my taste in vocals was much more heavy metal oriented. My main vocal influences were Rob Halford and Steve Perry. I wanted to hit high notes on my albums, and in these songs. Which there were none of. But I kept listening anyway, and the song "Youth Gone Wild," in particular, really stuck in my head. I began to love the song. I also liked "18 and Life," but I needed to figure out a way to rewrite the vocal melody to make it more intense. Which I did, by the time we got to recording it in studio.

I knew that "Youth Gone Wild" was a good song. I knew that the lyrics *fit my life*, and many other people could relate to it too, if I could. It turned out I was right. A whole generation completely got off on the track.

I loved the song but I didn't want to leave Toronto. After being unhappy in Detroit, I loved being back in Toronto with Maria in our little apartment. We had a baby on the way.

I had been singing jingles, including one for Schooner Beer that paid me a couple of thousand dollars. At the age of sixteen, this seemed like an incredible amount of money. I was very happy doing that, but I just couldn't get the song "Youth Gone Wild" out of my head. But I needed to sing it in my own way.

After a couple of letters from Dave Sabo and Rachel Bolan, I agreed to go down to New Jersey. They bought me a plane ticket for $180 from Toronto to New Jersey. I was quite impressed that they would fly me down, all expenses paid. Of course I got a shock, and had to laugh, a couple of years later, when I saw the $180 charge come back to me, from my accountant, to pay for myself, years after the fact. Gotta love showbiz.

Rachel Bolan picked me up at Newark airport. In order to not repeat the experience of getting turned away at the border, like what happened coming to audition for Madam X, I had a black Helloween baseball hat on. Rachel told me later that he thought my hat was very uncool. At least I got into the country this time. We got along immediately. I thought he was a cool guy, looked cool, played the bass cool, and he wrote cool tunes. I was excited to be in a band with him.

He took me to Dave the Snake's house. Straight off the plane. We immediately had a couple of beers and went off to a bar called Mingles, only hours after I landed from Toronto. There was nobody there, but we jumped onstage and did some sort of jamming, if I recall correctly. I remember we all got pretty drunk that night and we all had a great time. We got along very well, upon first meeting.

THE AIR COMPANY

Sept. 18/87

ACTRA
2239 Younge St.
Toronto, Ont.

Attn: Celia Hamilton

Dear Celia:

Last week singer, songwriter "Sebastian Bach" submitted a tape to us.

After listening to his tape, I decided to call him in to audition for
various commercials I will be producing this month.

His originality and voice perfection in his singing makes his voice
most suitable for many different rock tracks for commercials which
need a certain style to make them stand out.

After auditioning many singers, Sebastian turned out to be an excellent
choice for a "Schooner Beer" commercial I am producing Wednesday Sept. 23rd,
and we hope to use him on many jingles in the near future.

Sebastian his recently moved to Toronto from the States and has not become
an ACTRA member as of yet, but if you look at his experience in many albums
and singles produced, you will realize that he is a professional artist.

In light of the above, and again keeping in mind that Sebastian has come
to us with a voice of much originality and versatility, and a voice that
sounds like no other (ACTRA) singer in my opinion, I recommend you
accept his application into ACTRA.

Yours sincerely,

Robert Armes

Robert Armes
Partner/Producer - THE AIR COMPANY

One of my most treasured memories of the early days of Skid Row is of an all-out brawl that we got into, at the local White Castle, of all places. New Jersey was a culture shock to this Canadian boy, in many ways. I had never seen foods or towns with names like *Manalapan* or baked ziti. My first encounter with baked ziti was at a pizzeria with Dave the Snake. I looked up at the menu and I said to Dave, "What in the hell is *baked zit*?"

Going to White Castle was a similar culture shock. I had never experienced food quite like White Castle's. It was definitely unique.

This was not a brawl that we got into against each other. This was a real feeling that we were a gang. A team. Brothers. United. Against the same *jerks* that *held us down*. With the same goal. On this night, we would literally fight *for* each other.

We were coming from an Aerosmith show on Long Island at Nassau Coliseum. Dokken opened the show, if memory serves. We were driving back home and stopped at the Sayreville White Castle. Only blocks away from Snake's house.

It all started when this huge drunk guy came over to our table. This guy was bigger than me. He had to be at least six foot six. Burly. Wasted. Big. Fucked up.

He came over and started giving us shit about our clothes, the makeup we were all wearing. The standard *"you look like a girl"* kinda stuff. He was particularly mad at Scotti, our guitar player, and got in his face. "Why do you wear that shit?" I can remember him laughing. Scotti said something back to him, and this asshole grabbed the ketchup container on the table and squirted ketchup all over Scotti. Possibly even mustard, as well. Have it your way.

A switch then went off in my head that said, *"I'm going to knock this motherfucker out."*

Sebastian,

Well, here it is...finally! Most of the stuff was recorded on 8-track but it will give you a pretty clear idea of what we do. Please call me or Jimmy as soon as you recieve this so we can get an idea of what you think. In case you didn't have it, my home phone number is ████████ or you can reach me or Jimmy at the music store (███-███-████)

Hope you enjoy it. We're all looking forward to meeting you soon

Take it easy, Dude

Dave "The Snake"

SKID ROW

Don't fuck with my guitar player. Maybe I can say things about Skid Row. But fuck you if you say anything about old Skid Row. Nobody's a bigger fan of the Original Skid Row than I was. These were the days when if you're in a band, and somebody puts down your band, those are fighting words, for sure.

I was not about to let anybody fuck with my band.

I got over the table and told the dude to come outside. He was laughing and being a total idiot. I couldn't wait to jam my fist into his face. I was maybe nineteen years old at the time.

We walked outside the White Castle. The guys in the band went right behind me. Rachel was to my left.

I had had enough. This big jag-off walked out of the White Castle and straight into my outstretched right arm. I rifled my fist into his mouth and knocked him back with the force of the punch. He went flying backwards, and as I did this, I saw Rachel jump through the air and land on top of this guy. He commenced to punch him, in the face, as he was landing, from the air, onto his chest. It was an amazing moment in SkidStory. They kept fighting, and then Rachel got off the guy. He was a rumpled mass on the pavement. Then the cops came.

We peeled out of the parking lot in somebody's car as we could see the police cars heading towards the establishment of fine cuisine known as White Castle.

Got to Snake's house. Cracked open a couple more brews. Congratulated ourselves on kicking some ass. New Jersey style. All was well, until the next day. We got served with police notices to appear in court for fighting. I was very worried because I was not yet an American citizen, and certainly did not want to get deported. But on the day of court, we had a lawyer show up for us and the other guy didn't show up at all. So we won by default. It was an amazing moment in New Jersey White Castle parking lot

SAYREVILLE POLICE DEPARTMENT
OPERATIONS REPORT

TIME CALL RECEIVED	TIME CALL CLEARED	DIVISION	DATE	NUMBER
0133	0209	Uniform	11-9-87	87-17799

NATURE OF INCIDENT	Fight
LOCATION OF INCIDENT	White Castle, Rt. 9 NB
VICTIM, ADDRESS TELEPHONE NO.	
COMPLAINANT, ADDRESS TELEPHONE NO.	
ACCUSED, ADDRESS TELEPHONE NO.	

ACTION TAKEN:

Dispatched to White Castle on report of a fight taking place in the parking lot. Upon arrival all fighting had ceased but the parties involved were still present. In all a total of seven people were actively involved and admitted to physically fighting with each other. The fight was between a carload of two males and one female and a carload of five males. All seven males involved were issued summonses for fighting in public, borough ordinance summonses. Issued summonses were JAMES SOUTHWORTH, 1185 Bay Ave., Toms River, NJ, SCOTT MALVEHILL, 140 West Main St., Middletown, NY, ROBERT J. AFFUSO, 3 Kings Dr., Wall Kill, NY, DAVID SABO, 26 Robin Pl., Parlin, NJ; SEBASTIAN BIERK, 6026 W. Loma Lane, Glendale, Arizona. All the above parties were staying at Mr. Sabo's on Robin Pl. Also issued summonses were JOHN CASSIDY, 34 Druelle Ave., Spotswood, NJ and GARY TAYLOR, 45 Druelle Ave., Spotswood, NJ. All accounts of the incident from White Castle workers and patrons in the restaurant tend to indicate that the incident was provoked and started by Mr. Cassidy. GREG YLAGAN, 4501 Wells Dr., Parlin, NJ was one of the patrons witnessing the event. Mr. Ylagan stated that it was Mr. Cassidy and his friends who started the incident and that the other parties did not want any trouble. Mr. Taylor had his glasses broken during the scuffle and Mr. Cassidy had a bloody lip and facial cuts. Also with Mr. Cassidy and Mr. Taylor was DIANE M. WOODAN, age 17, 101 Ashmill Ave., Spotswood, NJ. Ms. Woodan claims to have been assaulted but there is no proof of this and all reports indicate that she too was provoking the incident. .

OFFICER Ptl. A. Donnamaria	BADGE # 76	DATE OF REPORT 11-9-87		

history. And one of my favorite memories of hanging out with Rachel and the band.

We had a lot of good times. In those days.

The thing that was different about Skid Row than other bands I had been in was that it was all about the *music*. We rehearsed every single day. Without talking about it. We rehearsed in Rachel Bolan's parents' garage. Rachel played the bass. Whereas the focus on my previous bands was more about the *look* than the sound, Skid Row was first and foremost about the sound. The songs.

After I had joined the band, and we had played around the tri-state area, Doc McGhee came into the picture. He already managed Bon Jovi, so he knew what was happening. He remembered my cassette and picture that I had given Nikki Sixx at Rock 'n' Roll Heaven back on the Mötley Crüe tour. Doc agreed to sign the band to a management deal.

Next up, an accountant was chosen for us. Although a red flag should have been raised in my head, I was far too young to understand the music business even remotely. Bruce Kolbrenner was Bon Jovi's accountant at the time. He would become Skid Row's accountant as well. We were each given a check to celebrate at the signing.

Doc also signed an assistant manager to help us on the road. His name was Steve Pritchitt. He traveled with us to a couple of shows, but then had a falling-out with McGhee Entertainment. Apparently Steve wanted to own more of Skid Row than Doc wanted him to. So after Steve left Doc assigned his little brother, Scott McGhee, to co-manage the band.

Scott and I would have many, many laughs together, and he would become a great friend to all of us in the following years.

The next piece of the puzzle was an entertainment lawyer.

U.S. deal lifts band up from Skid Row

Two years ago, **Sebastian Bach** was the tall and cocky frontman for **Kid Wikked**, a local glam band that was lucky to scrounge the occasional gig at the Gasworks.

Now, the 20-year-old Toronto native's new group has just been signed to Atlantic Records, in a deal personally handled by legendary label chief **Ahmet Erte-**

CRAIG MacINNIS

Pop notes

band had toiled in relative ob-

Scott found a guy named Michael Guido who would handle our legal affairs. Michael was a great guy. I partied with the man, and became great friends with him as well, in the Skid Row years. Michael Guido kept me out of jail more than once, and got me through the insanity detailed in the prologue of this book. He has since gone on to an incredibly successful career being Jay Z's long-time lawyer.

We started playing live around the tristate area and attracted the attention of the record labels in New York City. We did a showcase at SIR Studios where Tom Zutaut came down, along with some other industry execs. It was nerve-racking to say the least.

I tried to say "Hello" to Tom Zutaut. I was nervous, because he was the guy who discovered Mötley Crüe and Guns N' Roses. Being a fan of those bands, I was wanting to be this guy's friend.

"How are you doing???" I said over the microphone.

He talked to his friend, then turned to me and said the immortal words, "*Just shut up and sing.*" I will never forget that. What an arrogant person!

I was nineteen years old. He would see me later in life, after we had sold millions of records, on the side stage of Guns N' Roses concerts. I had opened these shows, and *now* he would come over and try and be a cool guy. But I could never forget what a dick he was to me that day. He stayed a couple of minutes, and then split. He passed on signing the band.

Eventually Atlantic Records came on the scene. Jason Flom came to a lot of early shows, and turned us on to Doug Morris, who turned us on to the legendary Ahmet Ertegun. The man responsible for starting Atlantic Records, along with his brother Nesuhi, Ahmet had signed Led Zeppelin, The Rolling Stones, and Buffalo Springfield, to name a few. Maybe you've heard of them.

We played the Cat Club in New York City and Jason brought Ahmet. He also showed up at one of our shows in Allentown, Pennsylvania, in a helicopter, with twelve hot women flying with

him to see the show. After the show at dinner he regaled us with stories of Keith Richards wiping coke off his face at Mick Jagger's wedding to Bianca.

At the Cat Club, Jason came up to me after the show. He said, "Hey Sebastian, Ahmet's here. I want you to go up to him and shoot the shit with him!" I couldn't believe what I was hearing. This was the guy who signed The Rolling Stones. What was the scene?

I didn't know what he meant, but I went up to Ahmet and started talking to him. He started telling me some off-color jokes and I laughed. I guess this did something for the band. I went back to hang out with Jason, who was laughing, telling me "we did great." Atlantic Records signed us not too long after that show.

Maria came down to New Jersey with our son Paris shortly after he was born. They lived at Jon Bon Jovi's house for a couple weeks. It was extremely nice of him and Dorothea to open up their home to us in that way.

One day, Jon even brought me into his closet and gave me some of his stage clothes. He literally gave me the shirt off his back. Pretty heady stuff for a nineteen-year-old aspiring rock star! Of course, Jon would be heavily recompensed, many times over, for "helping out" our band. But he gave us a shot like very few other bands ever got in their career. Neither one of us ever expected us to actually *make* it.

Bon Jovi Tour, 1989
Tour Bus
Toilet

This was an exciting day for me.

For years, I had collected magazines such as *Metal Edge*. I loved it because it was so thick, I could spend literally weeks reading it.

There is a lady named Gerri Miller who loved heavy metal so much, her love of the music and the bands exploded off the magazine pages. I remember buying the very first issue across the street from my dad's studio in 1983. I read every single issue front to back that came out after that.

It was exciting for me, and the band, to start to be featured in these magazines. After our first photo session with Mark Weiss, they printed a full-page pinup of me in *Metal Edge* magazine next to the band's very first article. I couldn't believe it. Here we were, next to our heroes . . . and I have my own pinup in a national magazine. It certainly felt like we were "on our way."

Rachel and Snake lived very different than I lived when I met the guys. We shared a common vision of creating high-quality, high-energy rock 'n' roll and stopping at nothing to make our band succeed. We were all at the top of our game in our chosen field at the time. I liked the songs, and I dug the way they looked, and we got along great. In the beginning.

But these guys were indeed living a different life than I had been living. Both Rachel and Snake still lived with their parents when I met them. I had left home at the age of twelve, lived with a prostitute, already rented and moved from my own apartment two or three times. I had actually done the whole find a place, pay the bills and the rent kind of thing. I was also about five years younger than the guys in the band.

I had known and hung out with real punk rockers in Toronto. People like Steve Leckie of the Viletones, Teenage Head, and Carole Pope of Rough Trade. Metal stars like Anvil and Slayer. The punk rockers I knew did speed and coke. They lived on the streets of Toronto, went to some of the same rock clubs I went to, got in fights, went to jail, and were generally not nice people. I hung out with these people growing up in Toronto. We were very different people as far as our life experiences had been up to that point. My girl was

pregnant with our first child. That child would depend on me. That child would be my *responsibility*.

To me, at the time, rock 'n' roll was a real lifestyle. Living on "Skid Row," for me, was actually *living on Skid Row*. I would always cringe in interviews when Snake or Rachel would explain how they thought of the name. "Well, we were cruising down the Garden State Parkway in my parents' car," they would say, "and we thought, Skid Row! What a great name." Gee, isn't that cute.

Rock 'n' roll to me was always about being *authentic*. I probably took that whole belief way too far. I believed that rockers had to *live* the lyrics we sang in our songs. If the band was called "Skid Row," then the members should know what Skid Row is actually *like*.

Our parents were all very gracious helping their sons achieve their dreams. We practiced in Rachel's garage, and this is where the first Skid Row album was born. We had space heaters and drank coffee to keep warm. We practiced every day, and it was a lot of fun thinking nothing about anything else except for music. All we concentrated on was Skid Row, 24/7. This is what separated us from other bands. Our attention to the music. To the songs.

My personality started to rub some people the wrong way. I guess me really coming from Toronto's version of Skid Row to the suburbs' version of Skid Row perturbed some people in some way. I was not trying to make anybody upset. I was not trying to do anything bad. All I have ever tried to do was be *good*. A good front man. A good singer.

I spent a lot of time wondering what in the hell it was that I was doing wrong.

I remember the very first day Bon Jovi came to our rehearsal in Toms River. It freaked me out.

We were jamming in the garage. I looked through the little windows of the garage door. There was a red Ferrari. Snake said, "Jon's coming today."

He came in and watched us rehearse, offering input into the songs and such. I couldn't believe it when at the end of rehearsal he asked Snake for ten bucks for gas to fill up his Ferrari so he could get home. We all laughed.

We continued to butt heads creatively. Sometimes this led to us bonding unexpectedly. We were in Rachel's basement with him playing some of his old songs. I heard a riff that I thought was very cool, sort of a *Peter Gunn* meets *Batman* kind of feeling. Rachel said, "You like that?" and looked at me. "Yeah, I really love that." The song was called "Piece of Me."

I thought it would make a great song. Decades before Britney Spears's tour of the same name, it became our third single and video, and one of our big hits. The song was even cited as an influence to "Enter Sandman" by Metallica in *Kerrang!* magazine's review of the "Black" album. Lars played the song live with Axl Rose and me years before the Black album, at the *Rip* magazine party in Los Angeles.

One big example of my influence and direction on the first album is the song "I Remember You." Rachel and Snake first played me the verse of the song at rehearsal, almost as a joke. They were laughing, saying, "This is *definitely* not going to go on the record!" I couldn't believe my ears. I thought the song was beautiful. I knew that I could sing it straight from the heart. I loved the melody of "I Remember You," and the words. I knew I could write some incredible screams into the melody line because the emotion of the music was right there.

When I have that feeling, I just go with it.

Rachel thought the song was too soft and not in play with our image of Skid Row, super-duper tough guys. I ignored him and kept telling everybody about the song.

One day Doc McGhee came to our rehearsal in the garage. We ran through the set as usual. At the end of the set, I said, "Hey Doc. You have got to hear this song 'I Remember You.' You got to hear it, man!!! It's great."

Rachel shook his head and explained how the song was not a good fit on the record. We were punk. This was a ballad.

I said "Please, let's just play it for Doc." As we went into the first verse, "Woke up to the sound of pouring rain . . ." and built up into the chorus, I looked over at Doc. He was looking at me and laughing. After the song ended, I said, "Rachel does not want the song on the record." Doc burst into laughter. "That's funny. Because this song *will* be on the record."

It became our biggest single. "I Remember You" became 1990's "Prom Song of the Year" in *USA Today*, and has since been covered by Carrie Underwood, Zoe Kravitz, Corey Taylor, Disturbed, among others. The song has lasted the test of time.

It's an absolutely beautiful track, and I am honored, to this day, to sing it onstage.

5

PRETTY BAD BOYS

1987
New Jersey

People talk about bands. And their image. Whether they are "bad boys," or "pretty boys," or whatever. In this book I talk about touring with Bon Jovi, Aerosmith, Mötley Crüe, Pantera, Guns N' Roses, Nine Inch Nails, Soundgarden, and more. Surprise, surprise: no matter what you think of their image, or their music, guess what? Bon Jovi partied as hard as, or harder than, the rest of these bands. I know it's crazy. But it's true.

A couple of our early club shows in Skid Row were played at a place in New Jersey called the *Raritan Manor*. For one of the shows, Bon Jovi wanted to come and jam with us, as a mini warm-up for the upcoming *New Jersey* tour. Snake, for some reason, decided to tell them, "No." I can't remember why now, and I didn't understand then. I thought it would be really cool to have these big arena rock stars come up and jam with us at a little club. I think the reason why was Snake did not want Bon Jovi to overshadow our show. Jon was super pissed. I remember him yelling at Snake. Gives you a good insight to how close these guys were. We were very lucky to have a band as huge as Bon Jovi helping us out. Even to the point of us telling them to *go away*. But as we would learn later, you get what you pay for.

Finally, Snake said, "Fine. You guys come jam with us." I thought it was pretty crazy, a kid coming from Peterborough, Ontario, Canada, *allowing* Bon Jovi to share the stage with us at our show. In NEW JERSEY, no less.

Before the concert, we got ready in a hotel room across the street from the gig. Richie Sambora and I were just getting to know each other. I thought he was a hilarious dude. He loved to party, pretty much all of the time. Just like most of us did. I certainly did.

I was sitting on the bed in the hotel room. Richie had his shirt off. He was looking in the mirror, blow-drying his hair. I noticed that his body did not look much like the airbrushed version I saw in *Metal Edge*, or *Faces*, or *Circus* magazine. I could not help but notice that Richie had a gut hanging over his belt buckle that I had not seen before in any of the MTV videos. Being nineteen years old, I thought nothing whatsoever of saying to him, "Hey dude, what the hell is that?? Hanging over your belt buckle? What's up with that belly, man?" At the time, I was rail-thin and as androgynous as David Bowie, the Thin White Duke. I was like a human praying mantis, I was so skinny. But when you are nineteen years old that is easy. I didn't understand how the great Rock God did not have rock-hard abs of steel.

He looked at me with a giant grin on his face. "What, that?" He motioned to his expando-gut. He then said, and I'll never forget these words, "I'll just get an eight ball of blow and I'll look *great*!" He laughed that big Italian rock 'n' roll laugh of his.

I had done cocaine at this point, but not tons of it. The first time I ever did it was in Crazy Sue's bathroom, with a local music journalist. I was fifteen or sixteen when he gave me my first line of blow. I had done it a couple of times after that, such as with Mötley Crüe at Rock 'n' Roll Heaven. To be honest, cocaine was a bit beyond my budget, at that point. But things were about to change.

I don't think I knew what an "eight ball" was. In any case I asked the dude, "What do you mean?"

He explained to me, "I'll just get a couple of eight balls of coke, do that for a couple of days, and this'll be gone!!" He was serious. This is where I first learned of cocaine's dietary properties. Not that I needed to lose any weight. But I did like the way it smelled.

This was 1987 in New Jersey, USA.

Fast-forward a couple of months, to the Bon Jovi *New Jersey* tour. Doing blow here and there, but not too much because it could freeze your voice. But sometimes it didn't. Not very good for a singer. You could never tell what it was going to do. Same went for sex. Sometimes, I would do coke and freeze up and not be interested in sex. But then other times I would do it and have the most intense, hot, sweaty, craziest, longest sex sessions imaginable. But that was the exception to the norm.

Bon Jovi/Skid Row Tour 1989: Young, Dumb, and Fulla Cum

January 26, 1989
Dallas, Texas

The Bon Jovi *New Jersey* tour, in 1989, was the first time I ever played in an arena. Stepping on that huge stage, at that very first show, in Dallas, at Reunion Arena, was one of the most intense feelings of my life. We went up there in front of 15,000 or so people, and I was completely terrified. Just the same way I felt at Lakefield College School the first time I went onstage, when I tried to hide in the cafeteria kitchen. That band had to grab me by the scruff of my neck and literally throw me onstage behind the mic. Tonight was the exact same feeling . . . and I reacted the exact same way.

Again, I just grabbed the microphone, shut my eyes, and sang. It wasn't until near the end of the set that I allowed one of my eyes to crack open even partially. It was that scary to me. It was like I was somebody else. Finally, the moment I'd been dreaming of my whole life thus far had become reality.

The whole tour was definitely a learning experience. We were playing every single night, on the biggest stages across America. We got better and better as the tour went on. Living together on the "Moonglow" tour bus, we all learned quick what an extreme challenge it was to get one's self to go to sleep driving down the road at 70 miles an hour. Our solution was to get drunk and pass out in the bunk. Over time· it would become necessary to wear earplugs, a sleeping mask, and eventually take sleeping pills as well, to knock myself out on a tour bus. I've been touring so long that I even need earplugs and a sleeping mask when I am at home. Every time I go to sleep. My whole adult life has been spent trying to learn how to adapt to different environments, sometimes nightly, for months at a time.

We learned so much from Bon Jovi. Stagecraft. How to work the crowd. There's nothing like playing every single night to become good at, well, playing every single night. Bon Jovi were an incredible band to watch, and learn from.

Our first single, "Youth Gone Wild," came out and went straight to Number One on the *Dial MTV* music video countdown program, which was broadcast daily across the USA. All of our first seven videos, in a row, went to number one on *Dial MTV*. It was such an awesome show, and a magical time to be in a rock band. And to be a rock fan. Kids would race home from school and call up 1-800-DialMTV and vote for their favorite video. Then the show would air at 5 or 6 o'clock, and the whole country would tune in and watch. "Youth Gone Wild" hit the right chord . . . with the actual *youth gone wild*. The world over.

When it was time for our second single, "18 and Life," we decided to shoot the video in Los Angeles,

Graffiti mars park, school

by Betty S. Spaar

City and school officials were shocked Saturday morning when they learned that graffiti had marred public buildings and property sometime during the early morning hours.

The graffiti, which included the name of a rock band, *Skid Row*, was scrawled in six-foot letters on the beige brick at the front of Odessa High School, on the east side of the Community Center at Dyer Park, on the pillars at the park entrance and on a stop sign at the four-way stop in downtown Odessa. The high school message also says "youth gone wild".

again with Wayne Isham and Curt Marvis at the helm. The day of the "18 and Life" video shoot, we were staying at the infamous *Hyatt House* on the Sunset Strip, where Led Zeppelin had ridden their motorcycles down the hallway, or something like that. Maria had come out to visit. I rented a white Corvette, and zoomed around and across Southern California. It was glorious. My dad came down and loved the car. We were playing at the LA Forum for four nights with Bon Jovi. He saw the white Corvette, jumped in the driver's seat, and bellowed at me, "Give me the keys, dude!" We proceeded to speed up and down Laurel Canyon Boulevard with the top down. Living the California dream, with his son playing the LA Forum, thumbing his nose at the cognoscenti who had denied him artistic success in his native USA. Made him move to Canada. I could feel his triumphant attitude in the way he was driving. "Fuck you, America!" he seemed to say.

We shot my sequence for the "18 and Life" video in a studio in downtown LA. Maria came down. There was a workroom upstairs. With a mattress. Lying in the middle the floor. We were in love. It was springtime.

AM 980

CHEX TOP 40

VOL. 4
ISSUE 12
SEPT 22/89

Peterborough's 'HOT HITS'

TW	LW			WKS
1	4	SKID ROW	18 & LIFE	6
2	3	ROLLING STONES	MIXED EMOTIONS	4
3	1	NEW KIDS ON THE BLOCK	HANGIN TOUGH	7
4	6	GLORIA ESTEFAN	DON'T WANT TO LOSE YOU	7
5	2	PAULA ABDUL	COLD HEARTED	9
6	11	MILLI VANILLI	GIRL I'M GONNA MISS YOU	5
7	13	TEARS FOR FEARS	SOWING THE SEEDS OF LOVE	3
8	9	KATRINA & THE WAVES	THAT'S THE WAY	6
9	5	GREAT WHITE	ONCE BITTEN TWICE SHY	7
10	12	MADONNA	CHERISH	4
11	15	CHER	IF I COULD TURN BACK TIME	3
12	23	WARRANT	HEAVEN	4
13	8	KAREN WHYTE	SECRET RENDEZVOUS	5
14	7	RICHARD MARX	RIGHT HERE WAITING	10
15	24	JANET JACKSON	MISS YA MUCH	3
16	19	NENEH CHERRY	KISSES ON THE WIND	4
17	10	FINE YOUNG CANNIBALS	DON'T LOOK BACK	6
18	27	ALLANAH MYLES	BLACK VELVET	4
19	28	TINA TURNER	THE BEST	2
20	25	SOUL II SOUL	KEEP ON MOVIN'	5
21	26	BEE GEES	ONE	3
22	34	THE ALARM	SOLD ME DOWN THE RIVER	2
23	14	ROB BASE/ EZ ROCK	JOY AND PAIN	8
24	30	PARADOX	WATERLINE	3
25	32	ELTON JOHN	HEALING HANDS	3
26	31	THE GRACES	LAY DOWN YOUR ARMS	3
27	35	TOM PETTY	RUNNING DOWN A DREAM	2
28	22	JODY WATELY	FRIENDS	5
29	21	DONNY OSMOND	SACRED EMOTION	7
30	16	DON HENLEY	END OF INNOCENCE	9
31	18	JOHN MELLENCAMP	JACKIE BROWN	6
32	36	EDDIE MURPHY	PUT YOUR MOUTH ME	2
33	37	DOOBIE BROTHERS	NEED A LITTLE TASTE OF LOVE	2
34	38	ANDREW CASH	WHAT AM I GONNA DO	2
35	--	MARTIKA	I FEEL THE FARTH	--
36	--	THE CUBE	LOVE SONG	--
37	39	GRAPES OF WRAITH	ALL THE THINGS	2
38	--	AEROSMITH	LOVE IN AN ELEVATOR	--
39	40	BRIGHTON ROCK	CAN'T STOP THE EARTH...	2
40	--	RAY LYELL & STORM	ANOTHER MANS' GUN	--

Kawartha Broadcasting
Company Limited

We looked at each other, as I shut the door. We took our clothes off and lay down on the floor. She got on top of me. Or I got on top of her. Or vice versa. Or all of the above. There was a knock at the door.

"Sebastian! It's time for your scene!" I was like, "Wow." We finished our business, and I zipped up my pants. I walked down the stairs, sat on a stool, and commenced to sing the "18 and Life" video that we have all been watching on TV for decades. I remember being wet from my waist down to my knees, sitting there singing the song. No wonder the video turned out so good.

"18 and Life" changed all of our lives. Once that video came out on MTV, around the globe, we were bona fide superstars. We watched the video, for the first time, in the back of the bus on the road somewhere in Middle America. Nobody could believe how powerful it was. Fred Saunders looked at me after he watched it, and just said, "Baz, you are about to become very, very famous." "Youth Gone Wild" was big. But "18 and Life" became an actual top-five Gold Single on the *Billboard* chart, selling more than 500,000 copies in the USA alone. Just that song itself.

Record sales of the first album were, and continue to be, phenomenal. The album has sold over 6 million copies in the United States, as of this writing, and over 10 million copies worldwide. Someone at Atlantic Records once told me that the first Skid Row album went Gold in just Orange County, California, alone. Meaning that the album had sold over 500,000 copies in just one *county* in just one *state*. Those are days gone by, as much as I hate to use that term, but there is no way we will ever see music sales like that again. The album currently is in the top 10 selling albums in Atlantic Records' history, up there with Led Zeppelin's *IV*, AC/DC's *Back in Black*, and Foreigner's *4*.

1989
Johnstown, Pennsylvania

It was a day like any other on our first arena tour. Just years before, when I was in Kid Wikkid, I would watch soap operas like *Another World* before I would go to rehearsal, in the cold winter of Canada. I would wake up in the morning (afternoon) and have a grilled cheese and some tomato soup, perhaps, and a coffee. Just a few short years later, I would do the same. Only now I would have my tomato soup and coffee in a tour bus in the middle of an arena parking lot, surrounded by people straining for a glimpse of us through the tour bus window. I would turn on the TV and watch *Another World* at 2:00 p.m. (followed by *Santa Barbara* at 3:00 p.m., which was a place I always dreamed of going) after waking up from driving all night from the last show. I was still the same. But things were very different.

I remember this day just like all the other days on the tour. Like every time, before the show I locked myself in the back of the bus, as I do every single show night, doing my vocal warm-ups and drinking as much water as I possibly can, in order to sing properly and remain hydrated during the performance. I always have the biggest bottles of Evian water with me, all day. Literally drinking as much water as humanly possible. My bus driver Kenny Barnes used to say, "Where in the *Hell* do you put all that water, boy?" It was funny, because I was actually as skinny as the bottle of water itself. It really *did* look like I had nowhere to put it. I was literally a walking "tall drink of water."

As I finished my warm-up, I grabbed a half-empty bottle of Evian water and walked out of the bus door. My security guard, whom I had lovingly nicknamed "Shat," was with me, as we ventured out of the parking lot into thousands of Bon Jovi and Skid Row fans jammed into the adjacent street, teeming and overflowing into the surrounding city itself. It was another sold-out show. Twenty thousand fans a night or so, that tour, was typical. Shat cleared the way for me to get backstage as I clutched my water bottle and drank copious amounts in preparation for the vocal histrionics that were about to ensue. We rustled through the crowd. Everybody yelling and screaming, grabbing at us, as we made our way to the backstage gate. About ten cops, Johnstown's local Finest, were standing there at the gate with the security guards from the venue.

The policeman stopped us. Shat said to them, "Let us through. This is the lead singer!"

They said "Yeah, right. What you got in the bottle, boy?" I looked at them, incredulously. I told the police officer the truth. I told them, "It's water. I am the singer of the band about to play. We have to get onstage right now." It was true. My vocal warm-up is timed exactly one hour before the show. It ends exactly one half hour before I am due to sing. This is what was taught to me in the Bel Canto Vocal Method by vocal coach extraordinaire Don Lawrence.

I told the police officer again, "Please let us through right now . . . I have to get on the stage." As the opening band, you cannot be late or go over time. The headliner, crew, and local unions are all *depending* on the opener to be onstage, and off, precisely *on time* as to not affect the headline set.

The police officer said, "Yeah, sure. That's not water!! That's vodka!! That's vodka in your hands, boy!!" Without even checking what was in the bottle, all of a sudden, without warning, the policeman reached into his utility belt and pulled out a stun gun. Something I had never even seen in person before.

As I stood there in absolute disbelief, he jammed the stun gun, with as much force as he could muster, straight into my abdomen and pulled the trigger. The fans surrounding us let out a gasp of complete shock. Which was nothing compared to the electric shock that was coursing through my body. As I got zapped, down to the ground, in front of hundreds of fans, who were all paying to watch me sing. In about fifteen minutes.

Even my security guard could not believe the situation. From my vantage point on the ground, poor Shat looked like he had actually shat his pants.

The police all surrounded me, convinced that my bottle of Evian water was actually a bottle of Evian "vodka." I was being electrocuted in front of my fans in the middle of the street for drinking water during my vocal warm-up. I couldn't believe what was happening. The fans all yelled at the officers, "Stop it! You're killing him! *You're killing Sebastian Bach!*" I remember lying there on my back on the pavement hearing one fan specifically scream, "Quit shooting Sebastian! He is the singer of the band!"

I saw the fans freaking out and literally rushing the cops, as they proceeded to *stun* me a few minutes before I was to sing onstage in front of the whole city. "You're drinking vodka! You're drinking vodka!" the police kept on repeating. Isn't it ironic? Don't you think? I have never got drunk before the show in my career. I cannot believe they were so quick to use a stun gun without even checking if I was in fact drinking vodka or not. Which I was not. I actually hate the taste of vodka.

Bon Jovi's security crew ran over to the scene and verified to the police that I was in fact the singer of the opening band. "Let them through. Let him up. He's okay!" As the fans just stood there, still freaking out, I was helped up to my feet and escorted through the police, and into the backstage area. My head was in a daze from being stunned with the stun gun. I was trying to concentrate on my performance, which was going to happen very soon.

But soon I was dealing with a burning cauldron of rage inside me, which was just starting to surface. When I get mad, or actually even when I get happy, I'm like the Incredible Hulk. I get excited or enraged and I literally feel like Bruce Banner turning into *Ol' Green Skin*. Instead, it's not gamma rays for me. This time, anyway, it was a stun gun. Same principle.

As I entered my backstage dressing room, I was so pissed off at the cops that I was ready to let them know how I felt. Where it counted.

On the stage. In front of their city. In front of their coworkers. In front of the very people who pay their paycheck. Their peers. Their kids. Their friends.

My fans.

At this stage of my career, I loved to do "raps" to get the crowd going. I was in my early twenties, full of piss and vinegar, among other more nefarious substances. My friend Jon Bon Jovi knew this about me. All of a sudden there was Jon, standing in the doorway of the backstage dressing room. Just me and him in the room. He looked at me very clearly, straight into my eyes, and said, in a very succinct way, *"Sebastian. Don't do it."*

I knew what he was talking about. "Don't do it, dude," Jon said again. The room was quiet. I sat on the couch and held my head in my hands. I dropped my hands to my knees and shook my head. I said, "Fuck this, man! This is bullshit! How can they shoot me with a stun gun for drinking water??"

Jon reiterated, "Don't do it. The police are pissed off. They have told me that if you say anything, you will go to jail." In the tradition of my father's hero, Jim Morrison, I just thought about what garbage it was for a cop to use a stun gun, when all I was trying to do is make my voice work, for the thousands of people who were paying money to come hear me sing. I looked at Jon. I really did appreciate the opportunity to tour with him that he was giving us. His guidance.

I said, "Okay, I understand, man. You don't want any trouble. You don't want the opening act to cause a hassle. I totally get that. I will go do the show. Everything will be fine." But the fact is, sometimes I am *not* in control. Of myself. Sometimes things happen to me, or because of me, that are out of my control. Maybe it's that crazy whack-ass Bahama-mama voodoo shit. But I digress.

We hit the stage. It was an outdoor show. The sky was overcast. We always went on around 7:00 p.m. or 7:30 p.m., so the sun was setting. There was a feeling of tension in the air. No doubt fueled by what had just happened between me and the local boys in blue. I remember looking at the crowd and just feeling a sense of a *bad attitude*. I sensed that the crowd felt this way, too. Was it all just in my head?

I have been called a *visceral* performer. The first time I read that description, I had to look up what the word meant. Years later, one of my reviews of *Jekyll & Hyde* on Broadway would say, "Whatever Sebastian is feeling onstage, the crowd feels too." It was the same on this night, in Johnstown, Pennsylvania. Decades before.

As we got through the set, my anger only increased. I was feeling the inherent power of a general admission crowd pressed up against the stage. It started to rain. Rain, and sweat, that pressed the T-shirts the girls were wearing tightly against their teen tops. It was a sea of teenage Bon Jovi and Skid Row fans, teenage girls in wet T-shirts on the shoulders of their boyfriends, reaching off into the horizon, singing every word, with their fists in the air. As I strutted up and down the boards, in leather pants, with my shirt off, in high-heeled boots, like a heavy metal Peter Pan gone wild. But I have always felt more like Godzilla than Peter Pan.

I noticed the heavy police presence on the sides of the stage. This only made me rock harder. I was rocking in defiance of their authority. Yes, they were police officers. But this was my stage. And nobody was ever going to tell me what to do on my fucking stage. Not the police. Not Bon Jovi. Not anybody. We got to the last song, "Youth Gone Wild." I looked at the crowd. I looked at the police. Behind the police, I can see Jon Bon Jovi, his band, and his security team checking me out. Seeing what I would do.

After "I Remember You," I started into my rap, which prefaced "Youth Gone Wild." I just decided to tell the crowd what had happened to me. That was all. That was enough. This is rock 'n' roll.

"You wanna know what the FUCK just happened to me, Johnstown, Pennsylvania???" Now, all the crowd of 20,000 scream back at my every nuance. My every inflection. My every word. I loved it. I love the power.

Never fuck with the guy holding the microphone. "YEEEEAHH-HHHHH" shout back the 20,000 or so in attendance.

"Well, I was walking to the stage, and some fuckin' *boy in blue* here"—as I pointed to the police who were now extremely agitated on the side of the stage—"decides to reach in and fuckin' SHOOT me with a fuckin' STUN gun!!! Right before the show, mothertruckers!!!"

The crowd roars back in disbelief, and aggravation, towards the police on the side of the stage. The mood in the venue is becoming black. "Yeah, this motherfuckin' boy in blue, decides to use the *stun gun*! On me! Right before the show!! What you think of that shit, Johnstown, Pennsylvania???"

"Boooo," the crowd moans.

"And what is it that you want to say to these boys in blue, Johnstown, Pennsylvania???"

"FUCK YOU!!!"

I lead the crowd of 20,000 people in a chant of "FUCK YOU" aimed straight at the cops on the side of the stage. "Fuck *You*!!" We say it together again. "Fuck You!!" It was loud. It was dark. Simple. It was joyous. It was glorious.

Then comes "Youth Gone Wild." The crowd goes absolutely mental. *No harm, no foul*, I thought. *It's just a rock 'n' roll concert, after all. Just words.* I would soon find out that the local police felt differently.

I walked off the stage, and the police immediately grabbed my arms and put them behind my back. Slapped on the handcuffs and wound 'em tight. I was led through the backstage area. I looked into Jon's face as he shook his head in disappointment. I did feel bad for letting Jon down. But this wasn't about him. It was about the power of saying what I wanted to say, in front of the people who were there to hear me say it. If there is an injustice done, I should be able to say it on the stage. I was brought straight to the Johnstown, Pennsylvania jail.

The judge on duty that night was not impressed with me. "We don't like your kind here, boy." I can clearly remember him using those words. "We don't like what you say. We don't like what you look like. We don't like what you dress like." It was really like stories I had read about Jerry Lee Lewis, or Little Richard, or The Rolling Stones on tour in America in the '60s. This was 1989, but I was still pretty much an alien to this judge in Johnstown, Pennsylvania. I was arrested that night. For inciting a riot. But at my new job?

Just another day at the office.

I noticed things began to subtly change as the weeks rolled into months on the road. The very first time that we outsold Bon Jovi in T-shirts at a show, there was a vibe in the air like we had done something wrong, like people were mad at us. Again, this was completely out of control. The band was taking off. Nobody, especially us, expected things to get as big as they did, as quick as they did.

My swearing became an issue. One night we were summoned into Bon Jovi's dressing room. Dave Bryan, the keyboard player, was mad. As was Jon. Dave explained to us that the parents in the crowd were mad that I was swearing onstage, and that I needed to stop. I was then summoned into Jon's room, by myself, alone with him. He stared me down and said the words, "I'll fucking *own* you."

No Need for Speed

1989

One night on the Bon Jovi Tour, Dave Bryan, the keyboard player, asked me if I wanted to do a bump. I was like, "Sure." He cut out these tiny little lines. I was used to doing rails of coke the size of your forearm. But these were the smallest lines I had ever seen. I did one. Then another.

It burned my nose. Way more than any coke I had ever done. I knew it wasn't coke. I asked Bryan, "What is this shit, dude?" He said, "It's speed, bro! Bikers do this shit!" I had never done speed before. And I would never want to do it again.

As the drug began to course through my bloodstream, it hit me in the weirdest way. All I wanted to do was tell people how much I loved them. It doesn't sound bad, does it? But after an hour or two of me repeating "I love you" in your face, over and over again, *ad nau-*

seam, you would realize, too, that *speed* is a drug that Sebastian Bach should definitely not take.

I was once again in the bathroom in the front lounge of the bus. I had somehow cornered Snake in there while I was high on speed. And drunk on Jack at the same time. What a joy it must've been for all present.

For hours, I would not let Snake out of the bathroom. I kept explaining to him, over and over, and over again, "You are my Keith, dude. I am your Mick. You're my Keith! I'm your Mick. You don't understand, though!!!! *You're my Keith.* I am your MICK!!! We are meant to be together. I love you, man!!! You're my *brother*!!!"

At first, he just started laughing and agreed with me. Nodding his head, laughing, and saying, "I know, bro! I know, bro! I know, bro." But he was not high on speed. I was.

As we raced down the highway, Snake began to tire of my repetitive drug-induced rambling. He tried to get out of the bathroom, to

no avail. I would just grab the door and slam it shut so he could not escape. I would not stop telling him that he was my *Keith* and I was his *Mick*. After a while it just became boring. But I wouldn't stop. This is what speed does.

A couple of hours later, about 4:00 or 5:00 in the morning, I made Kenny Barnes, our bus driver, pull over onto the side of the road. This was the days before cell phones. I needed him to stop at a phone booth. And I needed him to do it *now*.

The sun was just about to come up.

I locked myself in the phone booth, as my teeth rattled from the amphetamine speeding through my body.

I needed to call my dad. *I didn't care what time it was—I needed to call my dad and tell him I loved him, that is all I needed to do and I needed to do it right now and that was what I was going to do.*

I dialed the number to my dad in Canada. We were somewhere in the middle of America. The sun was starting to rise. My step-mother, Liz, answered the phone, out of a deep sleep. "Hello?" she said.

"Hi Liz!!!!!!!!!!!!!! It's Sebastian!!!!!!!! Is Dad there?"

Silence on the other end of the line. Then Liz moans into the phone, "It's five in the morning. Oh my God, don't you know we are sleeping right now?"

"Please put Dad on the line I have to talk to him it's extremely important!" At least it was to me.

"Hey Dad! It's Bass. How are you doing, dude?"

Dad woke himself up from his sleep, and at first was excited to hear his son on the other end of the line. "Hey Bass! How are you doing? How's it going out there on the road, son?"

I addressed my dad in the same way I had cornered Snake in the bathroom earlier, for hours. Like a drug-crazed, rabid wolf. Who loves his dad. A lot. And he better let me tell him all about it.

"But you don't understand, Dad. I love you, man. I love you *so much*. I miss you and I love you and I really *want you to know* that I love you. You're my dad, man."

Dad put his hand over the phone and turned to his wife Liz, with pride. "He's just calling me to tell me he loves me, honey. He really loves me."

"I love you, Dad." I won't stop telling him this.

"I know," he says, again and again.

But I won't stop. The speed in my veins will not let me stop. I keep him on the phone and I will not let him get off. For a long time. The sun is coming up over the horizon. I just keep telling my dad how much I love him. Or the speed keeps telling him.

After a while, my dad could not help but tell that I was out of my mind. On something. His tone went from being appreciative of me calling and telling him that I loved him to being a sad dad concerned for his son, all that way away from home. When he first

answered the phone, he was happy to hear from me. After with-
standing me spout my gibberish, he was just worried about me.
Thinking back on it now it disgusts me.

I have put a lot of people through a lot of pain with my behavior.
No one more than my family and loved ones.

I really didn't like speed. It burned my nose and made me act
weird and I couldn't sleep. The only other time I can remember being aware of doing it, was once with Lemmy from Motörhead. We
were hanging out at the Rainbow. Across the street from his place.
We went back to his apartment and he laid out a couple of lines of
speed. There were a couple of girls in there with us, but not room
for much else, as it was a very small space crammed full of World

War II memorabilia. Knives, grenades, Nazi insignias next to dishes and Corning kitchenware.

After we did some speed, Lemmy got out one of his lyric books. I obsessed over one particular verse, in one particular song, that he had written. I read it out loud over and over again for an interminable amount of time. I could not stop telling him how much I loved it, and I loved the words he wrote, and the alliteration, and his attention to the rhyming and phrasing in his lyric writing. I would not shut the fuck up, and it went on for hours and hours. This is what speed did to me.

The next night I was at the Rainbow again. After sleeping a couple hours, maybe from noon till 5:00 p.m. or something, Lemmy was there as usual. I said, "Hey Lemmy! Thanks for last night!"

"You were out of your fucking *mind*," said Lemmy.

That was what speed did to me.

No Rings, No Strings

1989
MTV Awards
Los Angeles, California

We had a week or so off on the Bon Jovi tour, coinciding with the 1989 MTV Music Awards, which we were invited to. I went to the awards and sat in the third row as Jon Bon Jovi and Richie Sambora performed what many consider to be the prototype performance of what eventually became the *MTV Unplugged* format. As they did "Wanted Dead or Alive," Jon, in his black leather silver-fringed jacket, stared straight into my eyes and smiled. We had been through a lot together that year. At the time, bands playing acoustic seemed like kind of a new thing, after the bombast and spectacle of the '80s rock scene. As if for a little bit of reassurance, I smiled back and gave him the thumbs-up sign. It felt good to see my friends up there, without the band, singing and playing great. They set the standard that night for the plethora of *Unplugged* performances for years to come. Most people cite this night, this performance, as the very first *MTV Unplugged*.

That night was also memorable for another incident that occurred. Vince Neil was there, along with Izzy Stradlin from Guns N' Roses. Vince had heard that Izzy had either hit on his wife, or actually hit her. I can't exactly remember which, many decades later. Nevertheless, I was standing with Vince as he stood there waiting for Izzy to come off stage, after jamming with Tom Petty. As soon as Izzy stepped off the stage, Vince punched him, coldcocked him without warning. As Vince's fist landed contact into Izzy's face, Vince's solid gold bracelet flew off his wrist, onto the floor, at my feet. I bent over and picked it up, as Vince was being picked up himself by security and escorted out the door.

A couple of weeks later, I saw Vince. I brought his bracelet, to give it back to him. I told him the story that it flew off when he punched Izzy. Vince just laughed.

"Dude, because you did that? You picked up my bracelet and brought it back to me? You can have it, man!! That's your bracelet now, dude!" We high-fived each other, in exaltation.

Vince and I always got along great. Except for years later, when we didn't. And then, we did again.

After the MTV awards show, I took my fully stocked limousine to the after party, which was held at Universal Studios. Ian Astbury from The Cult came with me. I was drinking my drink of choice at the time, Jack Daniel's whiskey. As I stumbled out of the limousine, I poured the Jack with some Coke into the ubiquitous red cup that was always on standby, always near us, at all times. So we could swill our whiskey in public.

Ian and I walked around, amongst the music business elite gathered at Universal. I thought it was hilarious that he refused to do any pictures or sign any autographs. I had always been "Mr. Accommodating" in that respect, yet every time someone came up to Ian, he wouldn't stop. Almost as if he was going to walk right over people. I laughed and kept on guzzling booze.

Gene Simmons was there and I walked right into him. Back in 1989, out of makeup and stripped of codpieces, KISS was a bit uncool. Yet I never stopped singing their praises to the press, the fans, the public, anyone who would listen. I don't change who it is that I like depending on the mood of the critical mass. If anything, I find it to be fitting in the spirit of rock 'n' roll to *rebel* against what is usually currently popular. Gene, in particular, has always thanked me for this. Back on this night, way back in 1989, Skid Row was a much bigger band than KISS. Yet Gene is as unwavering in his character as am I.

"Hey Gene!"

"Sebastian. What is that in your cup? What is that that you are drinking?"

I said nothing as he snatched my cup out of my hands. He put it up to his face and took a sniff.

"This is Jack Daniel's. Alcohol?!?!" I was busted.

Gene has always been known as a teetotaler. Talk about a major buzz kill. Wandering around getting fucked up and running into Gene Simmons was like being sent drunk to the principal's office. It sucked.

He condemned me, admonished me, with no hesitation.

"How can you put this poison into your body? How can you do this to yourself? You are so talented, so gifted, such a *powerful and attractive man.*"

Yes, he used to say that all the time even back then.

"You have been given a *gift* and you are *throwing it away.* With this *garbage.*"

Zzzzzzz. Snore. At my age, I thought it was so uncool, so corny, that it was cringe worthy. Now, when I look back, I realize he was only looking out for my best interests. Gene Simmons genuinely seemed to *care* about me, and what path I would take in the crazy world I was now inhabiting.

I apologized to Gene and grabbed back my cup. Went back into the crowd.

Moments later, I turned and was immediately struck by the look of a beautiful girl. Her name was Christina Applegate. As the sixteen-year-old star of *Married . . . with Children,* she played the role of Kelly Bundy on one of the highest-rated TV shows in the country.

She was totally gorgeous.

"Hi. What's your name?" she said, with a twinkle in her eye.

"My name is Sebastian. What's your name?"

"Christina."

"Christina! How's it going? Hey, do you want to get the fuck out of here?"

Christina and I hit it off immediately. We exchanged numbers. I really liked her. She was very nice, very beautiful, and very famous. Part of me thought that it would be good for the band if I hooked up with her. I thought of Maria back in Toronto, but we were not married.

No rings? No strings.

Christina and I kept in touch, as I went back out on the road with Bon Jovi. We talked on the phone and planned on when we would see each other again. She organized a trip out to see me on the road with the band. It was somewhere in the Midwest, when at sound check, I turned to my right and there she was. On the side of the stage. Beautiful. Long, blonde, gorgeous hair. Tight jeans and black leather jacket. "Come fuck me" pumps. This was the girl on the biggest TV show in the USA. Flying out to see me. Watching my band from the side of the stage. I wasn't even aware of where I was. Somewhere in Middle America. Somewhere in my dreams. I was very happy to see her.

She was eighteen years old.

We spent the night together in my hotel room. The next day was a day off. We went to some outdoor restaurant that had all sorts of kitschy furniture, sculptures, bric-a-brac. It was about 1:00 or 2:00 in the afternoon, and we were eating lunch. I was drinking beer. Could not have been happier. Living the dream. I had a wonderful afternoon with her, and she was so nice. I really enjoyed her company. I liked her genuinely, for her personality . . . and the fact that we laughed a lot. She was a lot of fun to be around and a very sweet person.

As we got back to the hotel, we got noticed by some fans who took some pictures of us. I was worried about Maria back home seeing the pictures, with our newborn son, and how much it would hurt her. Even though we were not married, I was in love with Maria. I had just met Christina, and as much as I liked her, I was not in love with her.

I told Christina to wait at the elevators as I went back to the fan with the camera. He was freaking out to meet me, as I told him to give me the film in his camera, one of those "disc" negatives. I took it out and destroyed it. On that film were the only pictures I can think of, of me and Christina. We went back up to the room.

The next time I was in LA, I went to stay at her house. She lived in Jim Morrison's *actual apartment*, near Laurel Canyon Country Store. It was mind blowing to be lying in bed with Christina, as she explained to me the history of the apartment, and knowing that Jim Morrison himself slept exactly where I was sleeping that night.

We did not have crazy, wild sex. She was very young. We talked a lot, and had a lot of fun, cuddled and made out. But, sorry to say, dear reader, we did not make love. I was very attached to Maria back home and Christina was very young. I remember thinking it was somewhat unusual that a girl her age would have her own place. She was one of the most famous actresses in the world, but she was still only eighteen years old. She lived there alone. We had a fun night together, and then I was back out on the road.

Skid Row had just been informed that we were going to be touring Europe with Mötley Crüe in a couple of months' time. So, Christina and I agreed to rendezvous on the Crüe tour, in Paris. We were very excited to see each other again, only this time in French.

End-of-Tour High Jinx:
Sinister Turn

The Bon Jovi *New Jersey* tour ended in somewhat spectacular fashion. There was a whole stupid thing back then where bands were expected to play "end-of-tour hijinks" on one another. Maybe some musicians thought this was fun, but I always hated this, and thought it to be goofy. It seemed to be just something that bands did at the time.

Popular examples of this would be: dumping flour on the band, greasing up drum pedals and/or drumsticks for the drummer, dousing the lead singer's microphone in Tabasco, etcetera, etcetera. The audience rarely knew what was happening on the stage, but it was ridiculous trying to put on a performance with the other band dousing your microphone in Tabasco sauce or whatever (which actually did happen to me, thank you, NOT Pantera). More on that later.

The end-of-tour hijinks on the Bon Jovi/Skid Row tour took a more sinister turn than the antics I had read about in *Circus* or *Blast* magazine. Maybe it was some of the road crew's assumption that we had somehow made it only because of Bon Jovi helping us out. Or, because of Bon Jovi's friendship to Snake. Maybe the crew thought that Skid Row hadn't paid their dues enough. Which may or may not have been so, but the fact is people loved our music. People weren't buying our records and radio wasn't playing our songs just because we knew Bon Jovi. Maybe the following incident occurred because of the growing tension within the bands. But for one reason or the other, one night of presumed hilarity crossed over into the dark side, and was anything but fun.

1989
Rupp Arena
Lexington, Kentucky

I walked to the stage at 8:00 p.m. sharp, as I had done previously for months. It's always a long walk from the hockey/football-style dressing room into the cavernous arena crammed with tens of thousands of screaming fans. There is nothing I love more about playing live than the feeling I get when the house lights go to black, and the roar of the crowd erupts into the darkness of the arena. I get goose bumps every time.

But on this night? Umm, not so much. I walked down the ramp of Rupp Arena, in Lexington, Kentucky. Underneath the steel grid of the stage. As the house lights went down, I could not comprehend what was happening to me. Three of Bon Jovi's road crew grabbed me and held my hands behind my back. I could not see who it was. They were laughing the whole time, but also attempting to be quiet, as if they were trying to disguise their voices. As they proceeded to pull my head down, as I was held, one of them poured a vat of freezing-cold ice milk over my head, as the intro tape for our show began to reverberate through the packed arena.

Ha ha ha, this is really funny, I thought to myself. They let me go and I stood up and shook my head around. I had vertigo, like when you jump in the water when it's too cold. My skull was rattling along as I heard the guitar riff for the first verse of "Makin' a Mess" kick in on the stage above me. Without me on it. I was about to miss my cue, due to being held down and soaked with freezing-cold ice milk. This night was going to be *hilarious* for sure.

I looked around, trying to get my bearings, and then ran under the side and up the stairs onto the brightly lit stage. My band members stared at me with an expression that seem to say, "Where in the fuck *were* you, dude?" I grabbed the mic and started screaming.

I was pissed. Wouldn't you be? I was mad that somebody (other than the band) messed up the performance. I was not seeing the humor in the situation. I asked our roadies at the side of the stage, Chris Mohr and Ronzo, to go into catering and get me two cartons of eggs. Theirs was not to question why. They said "okay" and ran backstage to procure . . . retaliation.

A song or two later, Chris and Ronzo returned to the side of the stage. With two cartons of eggs. Twenty-four total. I ran over to the monitor console and picked up the food, leapt back to the drum riser, and carefully placed the eggs behind my glasses of water and Gatorade, which I drank every night during the show. The eggs weren't there to help out my voice, however.

Fred Saunders, my dear friend, was Bon Jovi's head of security on the *New Jersey* tour. He was standing in the pit in front of the stage with some other of Bon Jovi's roadies. Laughing. Gloating. They were elbowing each other in the side of the ribs and looking at my wet hair, doused with milk. But they would not be laughing much longer.

I pranced around the stage in my high-heeled boots, casually stopped at the drum riser, and reached into the carton of eggs, with a delightful feeling. With what can only be described as sheer glee, I did a quick, triumphant pirouette and rifled the egg, like a fast pitch in a baseball game, right at my buddy Fred Saunders. He couldn't believe his eyes as he saw an egg whizz by his head. I missed him that time, but I had twenty-three more shots. For him. And the whole Bon Jovi road crew. Eggs. It's what's for breakfast.

In between songs, I was a complete nightmare. I taunted Bon Jovi, on his own stage, and made fun of his name. At his own show. And what was wild was that the crowd was on my side while I was doing this. I really don't want to go into detail as to what I said exactly to the crowd that night in 1989, because I certainly do not feel that way today. I was young, dumb, and full of cum. In some ways, I felt that to be my job description.

We all had to laugh when we saw the Bon Jovi road crew disappear for half a verse, only to then come back wearing cut-out garbage bags over their heads. They *each* had a carton of eggs. The war was on.

When I write about this now, I am laughing. It is truly ridiculous. But I was mad as hell that night, for sure. And I was about to find out I was not the only one.

This ended up being the only show in history I can think of where an audience watches a band being splattered with eggs, as said band throws eggs back into the pit at the same time. You could've made a Denny's huevos rancheros with all of the food flying around at the gig that night. It was like a tennis game, with eggs. I would run, and get hit. *Splat.* I would throw eggs and pelt the crew members with breakfast à la carte. The show went on for another forty minutes or so.

Ha ha ha, that was hilarious, I thought as the show was over. The lights went back on and Terry Sasser, our tour manager, escorted me from the stage to the bottom of the ramp at the back of the arena. I thought, *the show's over, time to get my drink on.*

Wrong.

As we walked up the ramp, we laughed about all the crazy shit that had ensued on the stage that night. But, as we walked more and more up the ramp, Terry turned to me and said, "Hey Sebastian . . . I think we got a problem here." He looked up the ramp.

We saw about sixty people coming towards us. Leading the pack was Jon Bon Jovi himself. Flanking him, on side to side, was his dad and his brother Tony. Behind them was the full Bon Jovi road crew. Led by Head of Security Fred Saunders and his auxiliary contingent. It was like the movie *300*. Only there were three hundred of them. And two of us.

We kept walking, and I attempted to stammer out some words. As I did this, Jon Bon Jovi kept coming at me and said, "I heard what you said on *my stage*, motherfucker," or something like that. He then took a swing at me. I ducked. He missed. As Terry started screaming at the ensuing throng in self-defense, Fred and the Bon Jovi security guys grabbed me by the back of my stagewear, and held me by both arms, as I was most unceremoniously escorted back to my dressing

room. When we got there, they slammed me up against the concrete wall. Fred Saunders, surprisingly, then whispered into my ear the immortal phrase: "Motherfucker. I don't know whether to kiss you . . . *or kill you*."

Good times!

Jon Bon Jovi's dad, whom I had met at Mark Weiss's wedding on that fateful night so many years before, came into the room first. Followed by Jon, and then his brother Tony, who was screaming at me, "You called my brother Bon Blow Me??? On our own stage?" Bon Jovi Senior then pointed in my face as I was held against the wall. He said, "I'll fucking *kill you*," or something like that. My insolent retort was, "Oh, yeah? And who in the FUCK are you?? *Colonel Saunders???*"

Doc McGhee came into the room as well. They all screamed threats at me. Jon shouted menacingly in my face, "I oughtta kick your fucking ass." Jon and Tony and even his dad walked around in front of me and shouted threats at me. I screamed back at them, as I strained at my captors' arms, "You want to *kick my fucking ass*? Get rid of your fucking security guards. Take me into the bathroom. And kick my fucking ass. Come on, let's do it. Jon, you and me. Let's fucking go."

It was explained to Doc, by Terry, to everybody, what had happened before the show regarding the vat of freezing ice milk being poured into my hair. Doc was not aware of this. Neither was he amused. He managed us, too, after all.

After much repeated shouting, over and again, "I'll kick your ass," nobody actually kicked any ass, and nobody got their ass kicked. After more such meaningless epithets, the craziness was over. Or so we thought.

[[—WAS THIS THE SAME SHOW WHERE WE GOT TIED TO THE CHAIRS?]]

The next morning, at the hotel, we were informed that we were off the tour. We were very sad. We didn't mean for this to happen. We all thought of those guys as our friends, more or less. But we did not want to be off the tour. We were having too much fun.

By the end of the night, after a couple of phone calls with Doc and Jon, before we had missed a single show, we were *back* on the tour. I think T-shirt sales might've had something to do with it. The Bon Jovi/Skid Row tour was an immense success, even though we were basically green, little kids out to play for the first time. We were with the big boys now.

Our touring days had just begun. More insanity was just around the corner.

Next up? We were off to Europe. For another tour.

With Mötley. Fucking. Crüe.

6

ROCK IT TO RUSSIA

Bach in the USSR

June 1989
Mockba, Russkie

Before we embarked on the Mötley Crüe European tour, we had a massive one-off stadium show in Moscow, Russia. The Moscow Music Peace Festival will go down in history as the first ever heavy metal festival in the USSR. We were the opening act on a show that consisted of Gorky Park (a local Russian band) after us, Ozzy Osbourne, Cinderella, Scorpions, Mötley Crüe, and Bon Jovi. There was supposed to be no real headliner. But at the end of the day, one band clearly gave only mouth service to that idea. One band had more production than the others, and proceeded in making one of the other bands on the bill extremely unhappy. To say the least.

The plane trip over there was epic enough. We all boarded a chartered 747 at JFK and of course, we were all drunk by the time we got there. I think we did a press conference that I barely remember.

Along with every single top heavy metal band in the world on the plane, there were MTV camera crews, *Rolling Stone*, VH1, and a veritable plethora of journalists and photographers who took the trip over to the Union of Soviet Socialist Republics with us. If the plane went down into the Atlantic, it would've taken the biggest names in the music industry along with it.

Someone, I believe it was Zakk Wylde, or perhaps even myself, had smuggled a bottle or two of Jack Daniel's onto the plane. We sat in the back and Tommy Lee came back for a couple of swigs of whiskey with us. I was so excited to party with my heroes. I had been dreaming of that for years. And here it was. Even though Mötley Crüe was supposedly sober at the time, together we just ignored the fact that it was an anti–drinking and drug festival, and had another pull of the Jack. Life was good.

In 1989, going to Russia was like going into outer space. It was still communist at the time. Playing Lenin Stadium in the USSR back then was groundbreaking in every way. For the Republic of Russia, for rock 'n' roll, for the broadcast TV industry, for all of us going there. We were very excited when we landed in Moscow to get our passports stamped with a Soviet Union seal of "welcome, comrade." But they wouldn't stamp any of our passports. Maybe the Russian government didn't really want anybody to know this concert actually happened.

The whole concert was the brainchild of our manager, Doc McGhee, who was busted in the mid-'80s for smuggling 40,000 pounds of marijuana into North Carolina along with the alleged knowledge of Manuel Noriega. (See *Esquire* magazine article for details on this incident.) The *Esquire* article details how Doc came from Florida and may or may not have used drug money to launch the careers of Mötley Crüe and later Bon Jovi. He was ordered by the court to either go to jail or do something else to "pay back," as a sentence for his involvement in this incident. Doc started the Make

A Difference anti–drink and drug foundation, which gave money to organizations such as T.J. Martel. We renamed it the "Make A Different Drink Foundation." Which is what it ended up turning into for some of us.

None of us had ever been to a place like the USSR. Before the fall of the Iron Curtain, before cell phones, pagers, fax machines, or the Internet, this was truly somewhere different than North America, in every conceivable way. As we rode from the Moscow airport to our hotel, I looked out the window of the van and saw that the sidewalks were dirt. There were shacks along the dirt sidewalks that had lineups to them. I asked what they were, and through the translator, it was explained to me that these were vodka shacks. Where men would line up just for a shot of vodka. Maybe this would be my kind of place after all.

When we got to the hotel it was yet another culture shock. We had been used to the Holiday Inns, the Ramadas and Marriotts of the world. Upon check-in to our hotel in Russia, I went to my bathroom and noticed the toilet paper. You could see that there was, at one time, print on the toilet paper. After examining it, I realized that it was recycled newspaper that I was going to wipe my ass with. Only this time not because of a bad review. Hey, it made for handy reading material.

The concerts were massive: 75,000 people, each day, for two days. Broadcast by TV satellite around the world. The undisputable star of the show was not Bon Jovi, or Mötley Crüe. The biggest star on the bill, to the Russian people, was without a doubt, the Prince of Darkness Himself. Mr. Ozzy Osbourne.

I was awoken from my sleep because of the sound of sheer pandemonium outside the hotel. I walked down the stairs. Looked into the lobby and saw this huge commotion. There was Ozzy, greeting the Hells Angels of the Soviet Union, who had gathered en masse upon the hotel, in the wee hours of the morning. Every Hells An-

gel contingent from the USSR had ridden their Harley-Davidsons from the farthest reaches of the Republic to this hotel, hoping only to meet their hero, Ozzy Osbourne. So many of them had gathered outside the hotel that it became a safety concern. Ozzy had no choice but to come down and greet them. Which made most of these badass Russian bikers cry like little girls seeing The Beatles. There is footage of the gnarliest human bikers from Serbia or wherever, greeting Ozzy that night and bursting into tears like infant children.

One can only imagine the early 1970s, in a place like Russia, what hearing music like Black Sabbath must have been like. The ominous tones, the dissident chord progression, the dark power of the music must have spoken to the desolate souls inhabiting places as downtrodden and seemingly depressing as a communist republic would have been to live in, back then. Of course records were hardly available, even when we played there, most being cheap knockoffs printed locally, found only on the black market. It must've been unfathomable to live in an environment such as this and hear a song like "Black Sabbath." Everywhere we went, the whole trip, we heard the familiar refrain, "Ozzy, Ozzy, Ozzy." It was clear who most people were there to see.

We spent the day before the first show sound checking at the venue. Myself and Skid Row guitar player Scotti Hill tooled around in a golf cart on the running track surrounding the lawn of the stadium. I scored some black hash from a local member of the crew, puffing away and having a fun time. Until I was walking around near catering, and I saw Mötley Crüe coming towards me.

"Hey guys!! How's it going!"

"How are *you* doing, man?!?!" Tommy growled. He looked at me like he was pissed off.

The rest of the Crüe kept walking. Tommy stopped and came towards me.

He grabbed me by the shoulder and lit into me.

"Did you fucking TELL SOMEONE that I was drinking Jack on the plane?!?!?!?"

"Yes. I mean no. No. No, I didn't. Did I? Yes, I did. No, I didn't. No, I don't think so!! Maybe I did."

Of course I did. Tommy Lee was one of my heroes. Who the hell didn't want to do a shot of Jack at 30,000 feet with Tommy Lee in 1989? It was a complete and utter dream come true in every single way. Drinking Jack, in the sky, above the ocean, with Tommy Lee was as much a sign of *making it* as my first Gold Record. I was proud and happy to be there. Even though now, Tommy Lee was holding me up by my black leathür [*sic*] jacket, ready to punch me out for ratting *him* out. But he didn't. We have always been great friends. I would learn this later after my dad passed.

Make A Different Drink Foundation

It came time for the first show. Lenin Stadium. Not John Lennon. The other one.

We kicked off the show at 1:00 p.m. The very first words that our comrades heard, that the international audience of millions heard, broadcast live around the globe, was me uttering the eloquent phrase:

"Check *this* out, motherfuckers!"

A true ambassador of American culture, I was.

We finished our short set. It was still quite early in the afternoon. All we had to do for the rest of the day was stand by the side of the stage and watch our favorite bands play, in succession. One after the other. And since we had already finished working, it was time to party as well. Of course. Standard operating procedure.

The only thing was, we had never done a concert at one in the afternoon before. The other factor involved was that vodka in Moscow was around a dollar a bottle. So there was tons of pure vodka around. It's like water over there. Or at least it was here at the Make A Different Drink Foundation.

We started inhaling pure Russian vodka, no mixer, about 1:35 p.m. Standing on the side of the stage. Watching the bands I had loved, all my life, having a blast, in the midday sun. By 3:00 or 4:00 I was shit-hammered drunk. I have never been able to handle hard liquor. Vodka, Jack Daniel's, tequila, Jägermeister, it all Fucks Me Up Beyond All Recognition. I suppose that is the point. Nine times out of ten I react to hard booze like the T-shirt says: Instant asshole, just add alcohol.

It was around then that Scott McGhee ordered Terry Sasser to come to the side of the stage and take my bottle of vodka away from me. I was officially *cut off*. I did not understand why, since I was doing nothing but standing there watching the show. Maybe I was doing some other shit that I don't remember now, almost thirty years later. But I was finished work, so now it was Miller time. Absolut-ly. I had polished a whole bottle off by now, pretty much. There was maybe a finger left below the label. When Terry took my vodka away, I became belligerent. Big surprise.

"What the fuck are you doing?"

"Give me the fucking bottle of vodka."

"What are you talking about? You work for me. We are done with work. It's my bottle of vodka. Go fuck yourself! Get the fuck away from me."

"No, *you* go fuck *yourself*. You're drunk. You are cut off. You're an embarrassment to the whole Make A Difference Foundation."

And with that, Terry walked away with my bottle of vodka.

Let the Games Begin

I walked around the hallways of Lenin Stadium, livid and drunk. I went to the dressing room to try and find Terry, or another bottle of vodka. But he wasn't there. I couldn't find anyone. Or any more booze. So, I kept walking around the cavernous halls of the venue, looking.

I opened a door near the production office and walked in. Doc McGhee was doing a press conference in front of the world's music media. Cameras were rolling. Tape recorders were tape recording.

"Where in the FUCK is my bottle of vodka!?!?!?!!!" I shouted at the top of my heavy metal lungs, to all journalists assembled from around the world at the anti-alcohol conference.

A look of sheer terror spread across Doc's face.

Scott McGhee jumped up out of his chair. Terry Sasser was also there in the room. Scott motioned to Terry to get me the fuck out of there.

Terry, like Scott, is an ex–football player. Terry came at me like a rhinoceros with his nose snorting. Ears twitching in rage. He walked towards me while in the conference room. But once he entered the hallway, and the press could no longer see, he started running at me. I turned around and ran, in a somewhat bemused state of terror, down the hall. Scared, but also giggling. Like it was funny.

Scott McGhee came out of the room and followed Terry, chasing me at top speed around the basement corridors of the Russian stadium. Great! Now I had a pissed-off ex–NFL player, along with a running back for the Chicago Bears, after me, trying to kick my ass. In a communist country.

I *paid* these guys, no less!

I finally got to my dressing room. Slammed the door behind my back. Grabbed whatever furniture I could find in the room and put it in front of the door. Recounting this, it sounds like an action movie. This is my life, for God's sakes.

Throughout all of this, I was drunk as a skunk. Totally ripped. Kind of chuckling to myself at the action and how ridiculous the situation was. But it was about to get even crazier.

Just like in the movies, Scott and Terry barreled through the door, making a mockery of my makeshift barricade. I greeted them with the salutation, "What's up, dudes?"

As I heard the words escape my mouth, Scott grabbed me by the chest. He proceeded to slam me into each wall of the concrete room. Banging into one wall, turn around, bang! Into the other. Around in a circle. Smash!!! Into the other side of the room. Turn one more time. Straight back into the fourth wall. I ain't talkin' about Broadway, folks.

Scott flipped me over onto my back and knocked the wind out of me, as he slammed my drunken ass into the floor. He jumped on top of me and held my arms down as he jammed his kneecap into my throat. Cutting off my windpipe. Not to mention doing who knows what to my vocal cords, I remember wondering at that instant. I wasn't giggling anymore.

Scott McGhee was crying.

"I love you, motherfucker. *But you drive me fucking insane,*" he whispered an inch from my face, as his tears dripped into my eyes.

I couldn't breathe. I was going to lose consciousness if he didn't get off my throat.

As big as I am, I am not an NFL football player. I could not over-power Scott. Especially since I was blacking out drunk at the same time. I turned and saw that Terry was also crying his eyes out. Scott would not get off my neck.

"I love you. But you are nuts. You burst in on a press conference, drunk and screaming, at an anti-alcohol benefit. What in the fuck is wrong with you?!?!"

"Give me my fucking bottle of vodka. I was done working. He took my bottle of vodka." I choked out the words.

He got off me so I could breathe again, and not die. He sat down on a broken table as Terry continued to weep in the corner. None of us said anything for a couple of minutes, as our breath and heart rates returned to normal. We were all crying.

My memory is hazy of what happened after that, due to the entire contents of a quart of Absolut vodka coursing through my veins. I do know that my throat hurt.

The next day, we were onstage again at 1:00 in the afternoon in front of 75,000 people. I warmed up my voice in that exact same room where the brawl had occurred the day before. Or should I say, tried to warm up. To an Ozzy Osbourne song. I was so hung over I could barely stand up. My throat hurt from my manager almost squashing my windpipe the day before. I was also extra hung over, from the vodka. That shit really does not agree with me.

We did our show and I remember Ozzy Osbourne himself watching from the side of the stage. After, I was coming offstage and Ozzy made a point to tell me, "Hey man, great voice. You're a really good singer." I'll never forget that. Ozzy has always been one of my heroes. I have always loved his voice so much.

At the end of the show, I got to sing onstage live in front of the world on TV with my influences. Vince Neil. Klaus Meine of Scorpions. We all shared the stage at the end of the night for an all-star jam. After the concert, yet more pandemonium ensued.

Somehow, back at the hotel, I had managed to get more vodka. Not wanting to repeat the previous day's activity of almost getting my throat crushed by NFL players, I was a very good boy and enjoyed my libations accordingly. No drama. I was just really happy to be there, after all.

After Mötley Crüe's second-to-last set, Bon Jovi took the stage. All was well until the end of their set. The concert had been sold to every band as there being no specific headliner. No band would have more production than the other. Mötley Crüe was known for its stage show, fire, smoke, and production values much more than Bon Jovi was at that time. But sure enough, at the end of Bon Jovi's set, a wall of pyrotechnics exploded at the front of the stage into the skies above. No other band at the festival had gotten any pyro whatsoever. Mötley Crüe went, well, Mötley Crüe on Bon Jovi. More specifically, the man who managed both bands . . . Doc McGhee.

It was clear that Tommy Lee viewed the situation as a rock 'n' roll conflict of pyrotechnic interests. So Tommy came down the hall with some pyrotechnics of his own.

I was standing backstage, swilling from a quart of vodka. Tommy came up to me and screamed in my face.

"Your manager's a fucking asshole!!!!! *Gimme that!!!!!!!*"

He grabbed the bottle out of my hand. Immediately raised it to his lips. Bottoms up! Guzzling the entire contents, his Adam's apple protruded with each swallow. Tommy was fucking fired up and crazy. He stomped on down the hall screaming, "Where in the *fuck* is Doc McGhee??????"

I watched him lurch menacingly, disappear into a room, and heard some commotion. Tommy had found Doc, and knocked him on his ass.

Doc came out of the room and up to me. I think he'd been crying. He looked at me and said, "I didn't have anything to do with the fucking bombs or anything." He was walking around by himself, obviously upset. It was fucked up. I searched for another bottle of booze since Tommy had inhaled mine. I had one left in the dressing room. Unopened. Let's continue.

I don't know whether it was the jet lag or the vodka. Probably the vodka. But the mood after that second show back at the hotel was surly. I walked into the lobby, straight into sheer craziness. It was packed with band members and their families and crew, and everybody was drunk as hell.

Suddenly I heard someone shrieking, "Sebastian—give me the bottle of vodka! Give me that bottle of vodka!" "*It's the last one in the whole hotel!*"

I clenched the bottle for dear life. To my chest. Fuck that, it was my bottle of vodka, and after yesterday's insanity there was no way I was getting cut off *again*. They took mine away, after all, yesterday. Tommy Lee took a bottle away from me at the gig today. I was sick of people drinking my booze! Nobody was going to get this bottle out of my hands. Not even Bon Jovi's mother if she asked for it, for God's sake.

Assessing the situation, I knew I did not want to get into any arguments about anyone taking my bottle of vodka, or me keeping it. So I turned around, got in the elevator, and went up to my room. I could hear the angry mob yelling at me, pissed off as the elevator doors shut. I took a healthy swig and laughed.

On the way to my room, I got sidetracked. To some sort of party, where I got in an argument with Julie Foley, who worked for Doc at the time. We argued about who was a bigger fan of Mötley Crüe. Her or me. She worked for them and obviously had a lot to do with their success. I argued, in my drunken mind, to her that I was the biggest Mötley Crüe fan ever, and I loved them more than her and everybody else put together. It was silly. We were drunk and tired. Looking back, I would like to think we loved Mötley Crüe equally.

Last thing I can remember is being on a bus driving around Moscow at five in the morning, loaded. With Curt Marvis and Wayne Isham. We were on some sort of tour of the city. I commandeered the microphone at the front of the bus, much to the translator's and driver's chagrin. I proceed to sing every heavy metal song I know over the speakers. To the delight of some, and no doubt horror of others, who are also on the bus tour.

Flying back to America, Mötley Crüe are nowhere to be found. Mötley Crüe, along with Doc's soon-to-be ex-partner Doug Thaler, charter their own plane back to the States because they will not fly with Bon Jovi or Doc McGhee. It was shortly after this that Mötley Crüe would end their relationship with Doc. No doubt Bon Jovi getting pyro, when the Crüe did not, cemented this decision. As I suppose Tommy Lee punching Doc in the face may have had something to do with it.

Getting paid in rubles in the year 1989 was completely worthless in the rest of the world, let alone Russia itself. As the story goes, Bon Jovi got paid for their performance in blocks of wood, from Russia, from a cargo ship sent across the ocean. The wood was then sold at an American port, for American money. Or so I heard. Maybe they got paid in vodka.

Playing Russia was an amazing booze-fueled experience. Now it was time to go to Europe for the first time. Supporting our heroes Mötley Crüe on the *Dr. Feelgood* tour. They were supposed to be sober.

We were supposed to be not.

7

FEELGOOD,
AND THEN FEEL BETTER

1989
Essen, Germany
Mötley Crüe *Dr. Feelgood* Tour

I lie on the bed. On my back. Motionless. It is quiet.

This is without a doubt the smallest bed I've ever been on. I am sandwiched up against the wall. On the other side of the wall is a small commode. To my right is about an eight-inch space, where another bed lies. Exactly like mine. This is for my roommate on the whole tour, Skid Row guitar tech Chris "Lumpy'" Hofschneider, who is now at the gig. Doing sound check.

I wake up alone in the room. Can't remember going to sleep. Must've been drunk. Waking up for the first time in a European hotel room is something I'm not used to. I turn to my right. In absolute silence, I look out the window. All I see are gigantic pine trees, giants, reaching up into the German sky above. Everything in this room is so foreign to me. How do I turn on the lights? Why does that shower door only go halfway across? Why *can't* I get a burger from

room service at 4:00 p.m.? These are the problems of the late '80s rock star on the road.

This was our first time ever on European soil. European proper, that is, depending on whether or not you count Russia. Since Russia wouldn't stamp our passports, I guess they didn't count us, so I don't know whether to count them or not.

Although we were becoming huge in North America at this time, we were still pretty much unknown in many parts of Europe. Germany was one of them. I shared a room with Skid Row's guitar tech for the majority of the first Skid Row tour. None of the actual band members ever once roomed with me.

The bed I had in Germany was right next to his, as was the case in all of the European hotel rooms on this tour. As my long legs draped off the frame of the bed, the quiet of the room was remarkable to me after the mayhem and craziness of the North American touring we had done up to that point. I thought about how far my life had come. Tonight I was opening for my heroes. Mötley Crüe. In Germany. Their new album *Dr. Feelgood* had just come out, and it was a mind-blowing record. The video for that song remains one of my favorites to watch, and to listen to, to this day. The production of the title track, by Bob Rock, has often been imitated, but never duplicated. I speak from personal experience.

The Crüe were one of my biggest influences. As a kid, I remember getting their first record, in the import section, at Moondance Records and Tapes in Peterborough, Ontario. I had heard the song "Live Wire" on the Friday night Rock Show on Q107 FM, along with Accept's "Fast as a Shark," Metallica's "Seek & Destroy," etcetera. The day that I got *Too Fast for Love*, I turned over the album cover and looked at the back. I loved the pictures of the band. I loved the sound of the band. The album credits read:

Managed by Doc McGhee
Produced by Michael Wagener

I was twelve or thirteen years old. I laughed to myself right then and there, and promised to myself, and to the world, exactly this:

"*Michael Wagener is going to produce my first record. Doc McGhee is going to manage me.*"

I felt that I *knew* that would happen. I chuckled to myself. I didn't just feel it. I *knew* it. With all of my heart. It wasn't a matter of *if* it would happen. It was a matter of *when*. And I had done both of those things. The back of my first record?

Managed by Doc McGhee
Produced by Michael Wagener

Not only that, but here we were, now opening the full European Mötley Crüe tour. Dreams can come true.

It can happen to you.

I had always fantasized of touring with Mötley Crüe. But this was the Crüe's first-ever sober tour. I had been looking forward to touring with the *fucked-up* Mötley Crüe. Like we were. But this would never happen.

This time out, they were setting a brand-new precedent for me and the rest of the Crüe-tons around the world. Their new trip on 1989 was, you *don't* have to be fucked up all the time. That was a fresh concept to fans of the band. One that I wouldn't realize myself for maybe twenty-five more years or so.

No Milk and Cookie Jokes

We were touring in the winter. In Europe. It's freezing cold. We are on the bus. At an ice-cold backstage catering room, in Oslo, Norway.

Talking to a journalist at one of the lunch tables, across the room, Vince Neil is also doing an interview. I am very new to talking to European journalists. I look over at Vince, to check out how to handle all of this. Like a pro.

"Mr. Vince Neil, what do you think of the brand-new group Guns N' Roses? What do you think of that?"

"I don't *fucking know*, why don't you go interview Guns and *fucking Roses*? Why don't you go and fucking *ask them*?"

I was twenty-one or twenty-two at the time. I laughed so hard at the responses he was giving the journalist. It reminded me of when I was twelve, the very first interview/article I ever read, on Mötley

TOP ROCK
DEVELOPMENT
CORPORATION

October 4, 1989

Scott McGhee
McGhee Entertainment
240 Central Park South
New York, NY 10019

Dear Scott,

Per our telephone conversation of October 2, I am writing to
you to confirm our policy with respect to dressing room access/
decorum on our forthcoming European Tour.

We all like and respect the members of Skid Row and wish to
extend to them all of the courtesies we have always extended
to our special guest stars including the provision of the
refreshments of their choice in their dressing room.

We must, however, insist that certain guidelines be adhered to
on the MOTLEY CRUE dates which will support our band members'
own efforts to remain clean and sober on the road.

To this end, I am making MOTLEY CRUE's dressing room off-limits
to everyone except the band's immediate techs and key production
people from twenty minutes before their on-stage time until
they leave the building after their performance.

I suggest that it might be wise for all concerned if you made
it a practice to have Skid Row out of the venues before MOTLEY
CRUE's set is concluded in as many instances as practical.

Once again, I want to stress to you that we don't want to be
perceived as rude, aloof, or arrogant to our friends in
Skid Row. We are merely concerned about keeping our own house
in order as we hit the road for what we hope will be a long
and successful world tour.

I am certain there will be ample opportunities for our respective
band members to socialize without infringing upon our policy
as expressed here.

We look forward to seeing you all in Essen next week.

Warm regards,

Doug Thaler
Manager of MOTLEY CRUE

9229 SUNSET BOULEVARD, LOS ANGELES, CALIFORNIA 90069

(213) 858-7800 • FAX (213) 858-1648

Crüe. *CREEM* magazine, circa 1981. I had never read a music article like this. In this very first piece of press I had ever read on
the band, Vince Neil described, in specific detail, how to make a
pipe out of a Bic pen, so you could smoke Angel Dust at the back
of the school classroom. I was fascinated that this would be part
of the interview. Vince has never given a fuck. It's always been
hilarious.

In 1989 we did not know any other way to live, other than being
drunk and/or high pretty much all of the time. The only thing we
lived to do was rock 'n' roll, and fuck. That's all we did. In every
city around the globe. We went to Amsterdam, Holland. Before we
went there, Doug Thaler, Mötley Crüe's manager, sent a detailed
letter to our manager, Scott McGhee, about what a rotten influence
Skid Row were on Mötley Crüe. The irony is palpable. Mötley Crüe
were the baddest of the bad, and here was their manager sending
our manager a letter telling us to stay away from the Crüe. It was
understandable, because they were sober for the first time. However, I did not understand it at all.

We wanted to party with them so bad. One night we were driving through the Swiss Alps. Austria. Mountains on either side of the
bus, reaching straight into the sky. We were following Mötley Crüe's
bus. At a truck stop, outside Vienna, Nikki and Tommy ran onto
our bus.

"Hey motherfuckers!!! What are you doing?"

We were completely destroyed, as usual. Rob Affuso, our drummer, made a lame attempt at humor.

"Hey *Mötley Crüe*! Can we get you guys something? Do you guys
want some milk?? How's about some cookies?"

He was trying to be funny, but Nikki and Tommy were completely pissed. Their reputations were built on partying, as much
as music, after all. They turned around and walked off the bus as

quick as they walked on. The next day we were told to not make any more "milk and cookie" jokes at the expense of Mötley Crüe.

One day, Tommy came into our dressing room. I think it was in Finland. He had been to Amsterdam the day before and brought back the most outlandish porn we had ever seen. He showed us bestiality magazines, fat porn, pee, stuff that I did not know existed. I made a mental note to go check that shit out myself as soon as I could.

Even in Rock Circles, Considered Crude and Disgusting

Christina Applegate met up with the tour in Paris. She had the trip all planned and organized. Her mother, as well as her aunt, also made the trip with her to Paris to meet me on the Mötley Crüe tour. Even though we had not yet been intimate, she was serious about our relationship. I really liked her too.

The press had caught wind of our relationship. Driving down the interstate in the tour bus, in America, my bus driver Kenny Barnes said to me, "Sebastian, have you seen this?" He pulled out the *National Enquirer*. Inside was the headline "Christina Applegate Falls for Wild Rocker," or something along those lines.

"*Pretty Hollywood actress, innocent little Christina Applegate, has fallen for wild man Skid Row rocker Sebastian Bach.*" The article went on. I will never forget the words underneath my picture.

"*Sebastian Bach: Even in rock 'n' roll circles, he is considered to be crude and disgusting,*" read the caption.

Crude? Disgusting?

Even in *rock 'n' roll* circles? How dastardly!

Wow, I must be doing something right.

We stood on the side of the stage at Le Zénith, together in Paris.

Watched Mötley Crüe do their show, after Christina had watched us rock the sold-out arena before the Crüe did. I wore a new vest, and new blue felt pants, made by my friend Michael Schmidt. I asked her how they looked, and she said they were awesome. I really felt like she was my girlfriend that night.

We were having a great time rocking out to the Crüe. It came time for Tommy Lee to do his drum solo in his "360 degrees in the air" revolving drum kit. Outlandish to witness. Christina and I stood a couple of feet behind T-bone's kit. It started whirling around in the black light of the arena.

All of a sudden it stopped.

Tommy was hung upside down, dangling like he was on a roller coaster at Six Flags during a power outage.

I freaked out and held Christina tight to me.

"Oh my God, let's *get the fuck out of here!*"

I thought that somehow, *we* had unplugged Tommy's drum kit. That we were not watching where we were going, and in the midst of making out behind the stage, had kicked loose the power plug that kept Tommy and his drum kit spinning around like a heavy metal whirlybird on the stage. We froze, and then scrammed. They got Tommy down, and I eventually found out it wasn't our fault.

We split and went back to the hotel, not wanting to be with anybody except each other.

The next day Christina and I spent sightseeing in Paris. We went to the Eiffel Tower and took the elevator to the top. It was here where we talked about our fledgling relationship. Christina explained to me that she wanted to get married, and get a place in Middle America, Wisconsin, or Iowa, or thereabouts. She wanted us to have a farm, raise animals and stuff. I did not want this. I was busy on the road. I had Maria and Paris back in Toronto. The more I hung out with Christina, the more guilty I started to feel.

That night, Christina's mom and aunt organized a huge dinner in France for us at a beautiful restaurant. We had such a fun time. I sat there and had dinner and drinks with the three Applegate women and felt very much a part of them that night. I could have easily settled down with Christina. But that would have required me to actually *settle down*.

We went back to our Parisian suite. I remember it was raining. We flipped on the TV. It was time to get it on.

Only there was one problem. I couldn't do it.

Sex, to me, has most often been a largely subconscious act. If I *know* you are mine, and I am yours, I am the most sexual person you can ever imagine to be around. I want it all the time. Every day. Many times a day. That is how I naturally feel. But, if I get an inkling that you are *not* mine? Or that I am *not yours*? I shut down. My subconscious dictates how I feel sexually.

No matter how hard I tried, I could not get Maria and Paris out of my head on this night. It made for an extremely awkward night. I lay on the bed, listening to the rain on the rooftop above. I tried to talk myself into the situation. *For the good of the band*, I told myself. Plus, I really did like her.

But the heart wants . . . what the heart wants.

Christina went back home. I went back on the road. We drifted apart after that. The last contact I can remember with her is being extremely drunk in the lobby of the Riot House on Sunset Boulevard. It had been months since we had seen each other. I was drunk and vulgar on the phone to her. She was extremely disgusted by me, and let me know on the phone.

"How could you do this?"

"What? Huh? Whaddya mean? Hey, let's get together! Let's just *parrrrtyyyyy*," I slurred on the other end of the phone.

"Wow, thanks. *I really don't think so.*"

That was that. I feel guilty to this day about how I treated her, at our very young age. I think about her and how my life might have possibly been if I would have been more serious about her. She has gone on to a great career, and I wish her all the best life has to offer. She certainly deserves that.

We didn't hang out quite as much with Mötley Crüe as we did Bon Jovi, due to the Crüe being more or less sober. But there was one night with Nikki Sixx. In his hotel room.

He invited me and Snake up to the room. I was completely obliterated. Nikki and I were good friends at this time. He would call me at home occasionally, and we would talk. I had always looked up to him at this point and was blown away that I was now on tour with him, getting drunk in his hotel suite.

I can't imagine what kind of torture it must've been for Nikki to sit with me, as hammered as I was, and as sober as he was. As he talked to us, without any thought, I balled up my fist and smashed a wall-sized painting that was behind the couch we were sitting on, shattering the frame and sending shards of broken glass everywhere in sight.

I thought that's what we *should* do. Be wild rock stars, drunk and stupid. Nikki went, "Wow, that was wild." Nonplussed. Not impressed.

We called up the maids and got them to pick up the busted shards of glass, which covered the room. The sun was coming up.

Me and Snake kept drinking. In another foolish example of behavior on my part, I crawled out of Nikki's hotel room window onto the ledge surrounding the hotel. I was drunk and could have easily fallen to my death below.

I crept around the outer circumference of the hotel, until I was on the other side of Nikki's room, looking in the opposite window. He was on the phone to our management.

"Hey, your boy's out on the ledge. He smashed the painting on the wall behind my couch. He's gotta pay for that. You better come get him."

Todd Mackler came to the room and somehow got me down. I can't remember exactly how.

What I definitely do remember is the next morning. Being awoken with the bill. For about $15,000. For smashing the painting on Nikki's wall. What had seemed like a really good idea at the time turned out to be an idiotic move that cost me easily what I would have made personally on the whole European Mötley Crüe tour. But it also taught me a lesson.

Smashing up hotel rooms is a lot better in theory than in practice. Or:

I'd rather buy a motorbike than pay to clean up a hotel room.

On the last night of the tour, we played in Edinburgh, Scotland. I spent the day off before the gig at Edinburgh Castle, at the top of the city, with Clyde "The Spide" Duncan, Tommy Lee's drum tech. Smoking black hash and drinking beer, we studied the medieval armor and weaponry. Soaked up the sights. The next night, we were onstage at the Edinburgh Playhouse and some guy in the front row wasn't getting into our set, so I kicked him in the chest. He tried to sue us the next week. Scott McGhee was completely furious at me. Well, hey, at least I got him out of his seat.

I remember jamming with the Crüe at the end of their set. As I held Vince's hand to the air, in the obligatory bow at the end of the set, Vince started shouting, "Hey, *fuck you*, Scotland! We're going home!!! We're getting the *fuck out of here*! *Fuck you*! Later!!! We are *out*!" Of course he wasn't saying this into the mic. Just to us, holding our hands in the air. We were laughing. It was hilarious.

Next up for us? Our first headline UK tour. Then, back to the States to open up the full Aerosmith *Pump* tour.

We were getting a lot of practice.

Weird Dreams

I have a lot of weird dreams. One recurring dream I have is of heights. I dream that I am hoisted onto some impossibly high precipice. A skinny, rocky mountain type thing. There is room for only one person on top of the precipice. I climb up there. Why? I do not know. It's always windy and sunny for some reason. I am high up in the clouds.

When I get to the top, I have to freeze. I lie on my back, clutching the sides of this rock, breath escaping my lungs in short gasps, as I stare into the sky above. Feeling the height of where I am at, in the

pit of my stomach. If I move at all, I will fall off the edge. If I even turn my head, my weight will shift and I shall surely plummet to a certain death below. I spend the majority of my dream summoning up the courage to climb back down. Barely flinching, I keep my body low to the rock. So the wind doesn't blow me off. I get to the ladder, or path, down. I look at how steep and far down it is. I am too frightened to move. I freeze at the top of the precipice.

I have this dream all the time.

8

BACH THIS WAY

1989–1990
The Bazmanian Devil
Aerosmith *Pump* Tour
USA

None of us could believe it. But it was true.

We were going to go on tour with our heroes.

The original bad boys from Boston.

The Toxic Twins.

Aerosmith!

Snake called me. We were both excited after talking to Scott McGhee. We were going to be paid $15,000, every single night, on the road with Aerosmith. This was a considerable nightly sum for a band in 1989, and a new level financially for us at the time. Over the course of the whole tour, combined with headline shows on nights off, the money would add up.

Our value had increased, due to our constant touring, and chart success. Especially now, with the new top-ten single "I Remember

You" following hot on the heels of the top-five single "18 and Life."
We put asses in the seats. Especially the female kind, and that's what
Aerosmith liked about us.

As Joe Perry himself mentions in his biography *Rocks*, I was indeed enjoying our new-
found success, much like the proverbial kid in a candy store. Nose
candy, that is. Since we had money now, we did better drugs. We
started to fly girls in and out of town that we barely knew. Bringing
chicks on the bus from one city to the next, partying with them,
and then leaving them at a truck stop. Shit like that.

I perfected the art of being able to tie up a girl anywhere our
travels would take us. I would steal a towel from the hotel room.
Take my lighter, and light the edge of the towel on fire, at six or
seven equidistant points. Then rip the towel into six or seven make-

shift "ties" to immobilize the most über-hot woman in each town who would come to see us play that night.

One such ravishing beauty was from Florida. I hauled a chair out onto the balcony of my hotel suite in South Beach. Overlooking the ocean, and in full view of the hotel balconies adjacent to us, I tied this achingly hot blonde girl, clad only in fishnets and high heels, to a chair on the balcony as the evening sun set. Naked, but for her black high heels, her ankles tied to the front legs of the chair. Her wrists tied to the back. I put a blindfold on her and left her out on the balcony. Shut the door and went inside to make myself a Jack and Coke. After a while, she started to get nervous. I heard her plead my name. Crying out into the ocean air, *"Where am I? Where did you go?"* She couldn't see a thing. I was watching TV in my suite, getting drunk and high. After a while I went back out there

and . . . we got it on, in full view of the apartment buildings across the street.

A couple of weeks later, in another state, I was stumbling around, wasted, on the tour bus after a gig. The sun was coming up as I looked down into the bottom bunk near the back of the bus. That same girl from Florida was now here, in another part of the country, completely naked, in the bottom bunk of the bus, only with a different band member. I had no idea she was even on tour with us. *"Hey, I thought you were with me,"* I thought to myself, butt-hurt for a second. They were both completely asleep in the bunk, in the nude, rolling down the highway. Maybe she was with me . . . but evidently, I guess she was with him too.

Rock it up!

Touring with Aerosmith was any musician's dream come true. Listening to Steven Tyler sing every single night was a new level of appreciation for me, education-wise, as a vocalist and a performer. And, an inspiration as a person above all else. Aerosmith took us all to school. Steven's voice soared to the heavens, with the dirty street grit that set the standard for guys like me. The way he moved onstage, so effortlessly, so uniquely cool. His costuming, stage banter, but above all else, his voice, always will be second to none other. For us to spend every night opening for the incomparable Aerosmith did wonders for my own performance, and Skid Row's performance as a whole.

Although Aerosmith in 1989 were as sober as, or more than, Mötley Crüe were, they still loved sex. They loved chicks. They loved girls. They didn't sing those lyrics just for fun. That was the way they felt in their hearts, and in their pants.

I was becoming known, in tomes of backstage lore, for my prowess in procuring the most succulent lesbians in each city to hang out with us whenever we could spare the time. The quality of women on the Aerosmith/Skid Row *Pump* Tour was phenomenal. All of the coolest of the cool, hot women, who had loved Aerosmith forever, were jammed up next to Skid Row Youth Gone Wild Teen Queens in lingerie, hip-hugger jeans, and high heels. Steven Tyler? There is a method to your madness.

I flew out a girl from Atlanta to hang out with the girl I had tied to the chair on the balcony in Miami. I had asked each of them if they "liked" other girls, and they each chirped back with an enthusiastic "*Yes!*" We were in Salt Lake City, Utah, a fascinating town to play. Inhabited heavily by Mormons. Ever since the Bon Jovi tour I have noticed that Salt Lake City can be markedly more crazy, and have a different sexual energy, than other cities. The *pent-up* feeling was almost palpable from the stage. The Mormons looked at rock shows as a chance to show up in pretty much next to nothing. Lingerie, heels, and not much more than that seemed to be the dress code for the nubile rock 'n' roll chicks coming to our concerts in Salt Lake City.

The afternoon of the show, the two girls arrived at the Salt Lake airport and took the limo straight to my hotel room. The girl from Florida brought an eight ball of blow with her. This was pre-9/11, when we would bring cocaine or weed or whatever on the plane without thinking about it. Many was the plane flight I spent plopping down the dinner tray on the plane, only instead of peanuts and pretzels, we would chop out generous lines of fine *Peruvian Flake*. Freeze our faces off, at 30,000 feet.

"Excuse me, stewardess? Do you by any chance have a straw?"

It was a different time.

I was chilling on the couch, watching TV, when I had an idea.

"Hey! Let's take a *shower!*"

Before I knew it, I had one of the girls on her knees in the bathtub. She had the *other* girl up against the other wall. I was

behind the one girl as she gave lip service to the one in front of her, against the shower wall. I apologize to the hotel guests who stayed next to us that day. You should probably have gotten your money back.

After we banged each other in the shower, we collapsed in a heap back in the suite. The girl from Florida chopped out a bunch of lines and they both started getting super high. I of course didn't do any of this, as I was going to be singing in an hour or two, in front of 20,000 people.

Or more. Band members would run off the side of the stage, check out what was happening behind the scrim. A little private show, maybe a little *motorboat* action. I was really good at setting up this kind of scenario. Chicks dig singers.

One time I had two girls on the stage behind Joey Kramer, the drummer for Aerosmith. They were making out. I was spanking their asses, as they fondled each other's tits. Joey turned around and couldn't believe what he was seeing.

He was laughing and completely lost his concentration on the show. Steven Tyler ran up to him and slammed his mic stand down on the stage in front of Joey's drum kit.

"Hey motherfucker!! *Yo, Joey!* What are you doing?" As much as Steven Tyler loved beautiful women, the show came first. Joey turned around and didn't take his eyes off his lead singer for the rest of the night.

Sorry, Steven! You're welcome, Joey.

I had bragged to one of the band members about my previous exploits that afternoon with the two girls. As the three of us went backstage to his room at the end of the show, there was a selection of sex toys laid out on a table. One of the dudes in the band was supremely stoked for me to bring back the two ladies for a little Avon-style merchandise demonstration. But the two girls were so high on coke, they could no longer speak. They had been doing it since the afternoon, and they were both now chewing their lips off. The band member was not impressed.

"Get them the fuck out of here."

I guess we weren't getting paid fifteen grand a night for a case of blue balls.

I got along really well with Tom Hamilton. I asked him for some tips on our show. What would he say to make our show better? He told me that I swore too much. Which was for sure true at the time.

"You guys like to spit a lot up there, don't you?"

"I guess so."

"You guys are like *llamas* up there."

I didn't spit anymore on the stage after that.

As I said, going on tour with Aerosmith was an education. In all sorts of ways.

Watch Out for the AeroCops

Aerosmith traveled on tour with two dudes that were given the title of *AeroCops*. The Toxic Twins sure had their hands full touring with us, wandering the backstage halls drunk as they were getting ready to go onstage sober. I was a whirling dervish. The Baz-Manian devil. Snorting, drinking, smoking, screaming, swearing, fucking anything I felt like. The AeroCops were extremely nice to us during the day, but once we got a couple in us, we were *persona non grata* around the 'Smiths. I smoked pot in our dressing room after the show, and the AeroCops burst into the room. The pot smoke was wafting through the air vents of the backstage area, blowing straight into Joe Perry and Steven Tyler's room. We were ordered to stop smoking. So, I walked a couple hundred feet out to the tour bus and lit the joint back up. In bed.

Joe Perry also remarks in his excellent book *Rocks* that I personally wanted to get high with them. This is so completely true. Steve and Joe were the Toxic Twins. It seems crazy now, in this politically correct world of green smoothies and no smoking in bars. But in the 1970s, when I was a kid, and in the 1980s, rock bands partied, dude. People partied! Dentists partied. EVERYBODY PARTIED.

Aerosmith were the *kings* of partying. I had a reoccurring, vivid dream that seems like reality when I remember it today. While on tour with Aerosmith, I would dream that I was climbing under the rafters at one of the shows. In my dream, we were not playing an arena, but something along the lines of a high school gymnasium for some reason.

I crawl under the seats, over the hard metal load-bearing supports of the bleachers. Joe Perry is in the corner, under the bleachers. As I make my way over to him, I pull out a bag of weed and a brick of black hash and roll up a big joint. I smoke with Joe. In my dreams would be the only place we would smoke together.

I was only twenty-two at the time. Still extremely juvenile in my thought process. What I failed to realize was that Aerosmith had done the impossible. They had turned their lives, and careers, around. Put down the heroin, the substances, and made the most successful album of their career. *Permanent Vacation* was a landmark album, and the first one they had ever done sober. The album we were on tour supporting, *Pump*, had the hit single "Janie's Got a Gun," which was released not long after we had put out "18 and Life." Those two videos dominated television sets in 1989. "Janie's Got a Gun" was a whole new sound for Aerosmith. They had achieved a level of success and critical acclaim they had never achieved while shooting heroin.

The tour had reached epic, legendary party status by the time we got to Los Angeles. We played four nights at the fabulous LA Forum. Tonight, on this run with Aerosmith, was remarkable for two reasons.

This was the night I met Axl Rose. The man who would become my friend, tour companion, and partner in debauchery for decades to come.

Another gentleman who joined us in the festivities that evening, in Southern California, was none other than Mr. Diamond David Lee Roth himself.

Axl came into our dressing room for a specific purpose. He had been asked to jam on the song "Train Kept A-Rollin' " with Aerosmith, but he did not know the words. I knew the words, and agreed to write them out for Axl in my dressing room.

Axl came in our dressing room before Aerosmith went on. He was very nice, and we got along great. He told me later that everybody told him, Del James included, that he and I should be enemies, not the buddies, which we fast became. I don't know what that says about me. But we have been friends for decades. Axl was cool to me from the very start. Tonight was the first night we met, and it would turn out to be an evening that would set standards for the many, many parties to come.

We wrote out the words. Lonn Friend, Wayne Isham, and Snake were in the room. After exchanging pleasantries, we smoked a joint or six and had some drinks. We went to the side of the stage and watched Aerosmith together from the monitor board. Axl danced around and we had a fun time watching our heroes only feet away from us. It came time for Axl to jam, and he went up there with his lyrics that we wrote out in hand. He rocked the LA Forum crowd hard.

Pretenders to Mah Throne

I had met David Lee Roth twice before. First in Phoenix, when I was in Madam X. Somehow we had got backstage on the *Eat 'Em and Smile* tour. I was quite impressed that Dave had a blowup swimming pool backstage, filled with suntan oil, for girls to wrestle in after the show. The room was all set up with stage lighting and a mammoth stereo, to create the proper hot-oil wrestle vibe.

Talk about backstage hospitality!

The second time I met David Lee was on the Bon Jovi tour. I remember the backstage area of the Forum being so crowded, it was next to impossible to walk around. To get from our opening band dressing room, to the end of the hallway, was a production in and of itself. Someone came back and asked me if I wanted to meet David Lee Roth. I was like, of course I want to meet David Lee Roth! As security ushered me into the packed hallways of the Bon Jovi/ Skid Row LA Forum throng, up the stairs, to the legendary, ultra- exclusive VIP Forum Club, I couldn't believe that David Lee Roth would be hanging out in such a packed environment. It took twenty minutes to get from our dressing room to the Forum Club, which was only up one flight of stairs. We got to the door of the club.

Where was David Lee Roth?

My security guard opened the door. There, at the bar, was one person. Mr. Diamond David Lee Roth. In this giant, ornate, *Old Hollywood*–style room. The rest of the backstage was a complete madhouse. You couldn't walk or breathe. Yet, inside of this giant room, which was completely empty except for the legendary David Lee Roth, was an oasis of peace and tranquility. Somehow, Dave had the *entire* LA Forum Club all to himself.

He summoned me in to say hi. I was blown away.

"Heyyyyy Baz!!! A toast to you!" As he raised up his glass. Bottoms up!

I used to go running! But the ice cubes kept popping out of my drink!
—David Lee Roth, *Creem* magazine, 1982

While all the peasants milled about the backstage halls, not unlike cattle, we were the two Rock 'n' Roll Kings of LA, in our private castle.

Back to tonight. Aerosmith tour.

A knock on the dressing room door.

"Excuuuuuuse me!!! Is BAZ in here?? Where is BAZ???"

I turn around, and his head sticks into our quarters.

Oh my God!!! It's Diamond David Lee Roth!! LOOK AT ALL THE PEOPLE HERE TONIGHT!!!

"Hey Dave!!!!!!! *Come on in!!!!* Sit down, man!" David Lee Roth sits down right next to me.

"Hey Dave!! You want to roll a joint?" I offer the salutory gesture.

"You know what, BAZ?? Why don't *you* do the honors??!!!!"

And so commanded David Lee.

I did exactly that. As we sat backstage and smoked, Axl Rose came back to the dressing room. All of a sudden, Rick Rubin showed up. In our tiny dressing room, we had Rick Rubin, Axl Rose, and David Lee Roth. As the pot smoke billowed out into the hallway outside our dressing room, the outgunned AeroCops peeked in and just held their hands up, flailing their arms in surrender.

I had been drinking Jack Daniel's steadily throughout the evening. Rick Rubin had an idea. To take Axl and me to the Rainbow. David Lee Roth said, "Hey!!!! I'll meet you guys there." This was going to be an interesting night for sure.

Axl and I got in the backseat of Rick Rubin's insect-like automobile. I don't remember exactly what kind of sports car it was, but it was some sort of small, extremely fast contraption that I was in the back of, with Axl.

We sped away from the Forum, the car as well as the Jack Daniel's starting to kick into overdrive. As we weaved our way to the Rainbow, at high speed, through the streets of Hollywood, I opened up the door of Rick's car. Axl holds me, by the collar, on the back of my jacket, as I vomit all over the pavement zooming by. We were all laughing, as I was retching, with my face mere inches from the street below.

Speeding down Sunset Boulevard, Axl pulled me back into the car. Now, I was definitely ready to party. We were off to a good start!

We pulled into the parking lot between the Roxy and the Rainbow, and out of the car. Rick Rubin and I discussed how he would like to make a record with me. This was around twenty-five years ago. I'm still waiting, Rick. For God sakes, let's get on with it now. Call me! I promise I won't puke in your car.

We sat down at the center, main large table in the middle of the revered rock 'n' roll establishment. Myself in the middle, Axl to my left, and David Lee to my right. It was absolute bedlam. It was so packed in there, that the only way I could walk to another table in the room was to stand up on our table, and walk *onto the other table*, like a giant, fucked-up alien spider. As I continued to pound the Jack with Dave and Axl, someone would shout to me from across the room. I would place myself up on our table, extend my pointy-tip heeled boot to the table opposite ours, plant my foot on top of some stranger's table, and walk around the Rainbow.

Instant alcohol. What an asshole!

Tony, an amazing guy and the manager of the Rainbow, flipped the fuck out. I was banned from the Rainbow for a long time after that night. Tony called Doc the day after and informed him that I was not allowed back in, due to me walking around the establishment on top of everybody's dinner rolls.

I sat down again between Dave and Axl and we let the shots fly. Bret Michaels walked over to our table. He asked if he could sit down with us. We all looked at each other, laughed, and turned to him and said, "No." What a bunch of dicks! It was nothing personal against Bret. It was what Poison represented at that time. Somehow, it felt appropriate to deny Poison from the table where Van Halen, Guns N' Roses, and Skid Row sat. This was 1989. The whole music industry was about to change. A move away from pop, and more into the dark side of rock. I have toured with Poison since then. Bret is an extremely nice guy. Maybe a little *too* nice to sit with the three of us that night, so many years ago.

Diamond Dave downed shot after shot of the Jack. I cannot handle Jack Daniel's. It always makes me violent in some way. Either towards others, or in my stomach, violently retching, as it had earlier in the evening. The Jack seemed to be taking the same sort of effect on our hero, David Lee Roth.

Axl, to my left, sat mostly quiet. Brooding. Intense. It was somewhat poignant to sit between the two. Axl talked in a quiet, understated tone, whereas David Lee was the over-the-top ultimate front man, as we all love him to be. But as we knocked back the Jack, Dave's mood began to sour.

"*Well.*" He slammed down the shot glass. "It looks like I got a couple *pretenders to mah throne* sittin' right here, I said, I said, ahhh . . ."

Axl turned his head and stared straight at me in disbelief. "*What the fuck did he just say?*"

"I said, it looks like I got a couple *pretenders to mah* THRONE sittin' right here!!" Dave was talking to us.

This came as a shock, yet not really surprising. After all, David Lee Roth had set the standard for what Axl and I did. Not specifically, but nobody was cooler than David Lee Roth onstage, in interviews, on television, on record. David was the coolest. He certainly sat at the "throne" of rock 'n' roll. I myself was completely stoked to be sitting at whatever table it was that David Lee Roth was sitting at. Maybe it was just the booze talking. But Axl cut him no quarter.

"I'm not a fucking pretender to *anybody's* fucking *throne*. What the fuck are you talking about?" Axl leaned across my chest and let David know exactly how he felt. I leaned back into the red leather couch and braced myself for two of the most intense personalities in music history to go at it. On my lap.

The storied establishment known as The Rainbow was writing itself yet another story.

"Well, you know the way I see it???" Dave shot back. "You two are the *pretenders* and I'm on mah *throne* and that's the way I see it! I said, I said ahhhh . . ." Dave slammed the shot glass down and turn to the waitress, and implored with thirst, *"Medic???"*

Axl was cool, yet quite clear.

"I ain't no *pretender* to nobody's fucking *throne*. I'm not influenced by *you* or anybody else. I don't give a shit about your fucking throne. I don't know what the fuck you're talking about, but this night is fucking over."

It felt as if Axl was about to fight Dave. Dave was a kung fu master. Axl was a street urchin. Living under the street. So the song says. I did not want to know who would win this battle. I loved both these guys.

The old guard facing down the new, this night was indicative of both their personalities. Dave was always the flamboyant, ego-charged, ultimate front man of all time. Whereas Axl was coming from a much darker place, lyrically and musically.

Axl got up and split, leaving me and Dave there to get more and more soused.

A couple days later, I was back in Florida recording the *Slave to the Grind* record. David Lee Roth had faxed me a letter explaining his behavior that evening at The Rainbow. It said, "Sebastian. When I hear your voice on the radio, it reminds me of everything I like about music. I love your voice. The way you sing. You remind me of the reasons why I got into music in the first place. What you guys saw the other night was my *love of rock 'n' roll*, my pride talking. My bravado. *My fighting spirit*. None of that was meant personally against you guys." I kept the letter for years but after Hurricane Irene, I don't know where it is now. I hope to find it again someday.

I talked to Axl on the phone from New River Studios in Fort Lauderdale, Florida.

"Oh my God, dude. David Lee Roth sent me a letter."

"He sent me a letter too."

As I described the contents of my letter, Axl related that he got pretty much the same letter. We were both blown away that David Lee Roth would send us each a handwritten note like this. He was an inspiration to both of us. Probably to myself more than Axl. Dave obviously had one of those *"Oh my God, what happened last night"* morning moments that made me quit drinking whiskey myself. Jack Daniel's will do that.

I was banned from the Rainbow for a long time after that. After I quit drinking whiskey, and switched to wine, I was let back in.

"Hey Baz. Will you be ready to go on tour in two months?" Axl asked me on the phone. We were still in the studio, recording *Slave to the Grind*. We would not be done with our second record in time. But I said "Yes" anyway.

We accepted the offer. For us to tour the United States, and Europe, with Guns N' Roses.

Let the Mayhem Begin

By the time the first album's touring cycle was over, our lives had changed immeasurably. We had come to the stark realization that we had been ripped off royally. Fucked up the ass. Taken down the Hershey highway. Screwed, blued, and tattooed. As far as the business went? It sucked to be us.

The same goes for the name of the band. It happened at rehearsal in Toms River, New Jersey. In Rachel's garage. Dave "The Snake" Sabo burst through the door.

"Oh my God, you're not gonna believe this. Gary Moore, from the band Skid Row *in Ireland*, won't let us use the name unless we give them some money."

There was in fact a band from Ireland called Skid Row that featured members of Thin Lizzy, before Thin Lizzy. They had released albums in the early 1970s. They still release CDs (Greatest Hits compilations and the like) today.

We all looked around the room.

"Oh my God that sucks," we all said.

Skid Row was a band from Ireland in the early '70s, with the legendary guitar player Gary Moore, and Brush Shiels on drums, who started the band. Snake explained to us that Gary Moore's lawyers

had contacted ours and we needed to pay Gary money for use of the name Skid Row. The exact figure was US $35,000.

Rob Affuso, the drummer from Skid Row, remembers this exactly the same way as I remember it.

All five of us looked around at each other and said, "Oh fuck, we got to pay him." So $35,000 was taken out of the band account.

9

BUNCH OF BOOZE, MOUNTAIN OF BLOW, QUAALUDES, AND TENNIS: MY TIME WITH METALLICA

Moondance
Ontario, Canada

The record store. My happy place.

I can spend hours in a record store. More than happily. It's always been that way. I purchased my first album at Sam The Record Man on George Street in Peterborough. A compilation record containing the song "Convoy," which I thought was the coolest song of all time. *Breaker Breaker 1-9 . . . We got ourselves a convoy.*

Something about a record store has always felt like the womb to me. Flipping through the racks, the feel of cellophane wrap opened with your fingernail. The smell of the inner sleeve packaging and fresh wax. When I go to a record store, I literally look at every single record in the store. It makes me feel good. Even now, thank the Lord I live blocks away from the formidable *Amoeba Music* on Sunset

Boulevard in Los Angeles. There are many great record stores in Los Angeles. I frequent them all.

My first favorite record store in the world was Moondance Records and Tapes. Run by my friend Mike Moon, who was close to my mom and dad. When we first moved to Peterborough, this was the store that made sense to us. They even had long hair in there. They sold hippie-esque fashion. Smoking supplies on one side of the store. Records on the other. I love the store. Incredibly, it's still in operation here in 2016. Thankfully, some things never change.

I would ride my bike down to Moondance, having saved up five or six bucks over the course of the week with my paper route or whatever odd jobs my dad could cobble together for me. I would sweep up the art gallery, paste ads for art shows all over telephone poles and foyers of local businesses in Peterborough. My dad would give me a stack of flyers with a couple rolls of tape. I go into a store and implore, "Can I please put this poster up in your window, ma'am?" Some would say yeah, some would say no.

I learned to sell art at an extremely young age.

One day at Moondance I was looking for anything Cheap Trick, Van Halen, Rush, whatever I didn't have in my collection yet. As I got to the back of the *M* section, past Moxy, Boney M., Motörhead, and Melissa Manchester, came an album by a band I had never seen nor heard of before. The band was called Metallica. The album, *Kill 'Em All*.

Turned over the album jacket. Looked at the back. Shocked at what I saw.

In the age of super glam, KISS, Rush in silk kimonos, in the era of Van Halen with bandanas tied from the knee down to the ankle, tight spandex pants, light shows, laser shows, everything *looked cool*.

Not this band.

Quite simply put, they were the ugliest rock band I had ever seen in my whole life.

The picture puzzled me. How the fuck did they put this picture on the back of the record? Lars had a wart on his face. True, Lemmy did too, but at least Lemmy wore black flared pants with conchos down the side, with tassels, and white pointy-heeled boots. Lemmy dressed like a rock star. Metallica dressed like bums.

Collecting music was my hobby. Anything interesting, anything that caught my eye, I collected. Here was an album by the worst-looking musicians on the planet. I had to have it!

When I put it on at home, I freaked. This was the *heaviest shit in the world*.

"Seek and Destroy," "Hit the Lights," "Metal Militia," "Jump in the Fire." I totally loved these songs. We would smoke pot and crank "Phantom Lord." Metallica were heavy and sleazy and cool. I went to see them live at the Masonic Temple in Toronto with W.A.S.P. and Armored Saint in the front row. I was a Metallica fan from the first second they came on the scene.

The first time I met Alcoholica, as they were fondly referred to in those days, was when we opened for Aerosmith at the Cow Palace in San Francisco 1990. After our set, there was a knock at the door. "Hey guys! Metallica want to meet you." Wow, this is crazy. I loved the band and I couldn't wait to party with these wild motherfuckers.

The door opens. James Hetfield walks right up to me. He grabs me by both sides of the head and stares into my face. He is an inch away from my nose, staring deep into my eyes. I am scared shitless. "Holy fucking goddamn shit!!" he says. *"You really do look like that."* It was then he let me go, and started laughing. I was already digging these guys.

We started the night partying with Alcoholica. They lived up to their name.

Kirk Hammett I had known about since I was a little kid. He had worked at the Record Exchange in Walnut Creek, California. The exact store that was blocks away from my grandma's house on Creekside Drive. I would just hang out in there for hours on a summer day. This is where I got my first Mötley Crüe record, first *Kerrang!* magazine. W.A.S.P.'s "Animal (Fuck Like a Beast)" single. Twisted Sister's "I Am (I'm Me)," with the iconic Dee Snider stage raps on the B-side. I heard Twisted's live "It's Only Rock 'n' Roll" playing as I was going through the racks. *What the fuck is this?* I never laughed so hard in my life.

I also got my first marijuana joint there.

One night playing in the Bay Area, possibly in Sacramento, Kirk came to the show with a bag full of mushrooms. I split it with him after the gig and we ended up laughing, uncontrollably. Unable to find his car in the parking lot after the show, we stumbled around, incapable of speech due to our laughter-induced paralysis. I don't know how, but it was just me and Kirk, looking for his car in the dark, after some huge show, walking around with the audience. Through tears of hilarity, we asked the fans if they might know where Kirk's car was. Not knowing where the fuck we were, I don't even remember what concert this was.

1990
Canadian National Exhibition Stadium, Toronto

Ring! It's Tommy Lee on the phone.

"Hey doooooood!!!! Are you going to see Aerosmith tonight????"

We are in town hanging out with family. Aerosmith is in town tonight with the Black Crowes and Metallica on the bill. Yes we are going to the show.

We agreed to meet Tommy down at the CNE Grandstand. Aerosmith had been so generous, giving me as many guest passes I want, backstage, including my mom, brothers, sisters, my whole family. It was great being friends with the Bad Boys of Boston after our tour together. At this time, I could indeed say we were friends.

We drove down the Don Valley Parkway in my Camaro IROC-Z. Upon arriving backstage, we had agreed that we were going to jam that night. I realized that Steven and Joe wanted me to warm up with them vocally. I couldn't believe it. I went into a tiny closet-sized room. Joe Perry was in there with his guitar and Steven Tyler was next to the piano. We started doing scales together in preparation for the show. We had agreed to do the song "Last Child" together, in my hometown. What an honor!

Stood on the side of the stage next to Tommy. Ian Astbury and his girlfriend Renée were there. I asked Ian, why did they still live in Toronto?

"Because it's civilized," came his reply.

And then it came time. It was kinda cold that night, so Tommy Lee gave me his *Dr. Feelgood* tour jacket to keep warm. He was freaking out, dancing and jumping up and down on the side of the stage.

Steven Tyler uttered the immortal phrase, "Hey TORONTO!!!! Put your hands together for your *hometown boy!*" He welcomed me onto the stage. One of the highlights of my whole life.

After the gig, we all went up to the Four Seasons hotel, where Aerosmith and Tommy Lee were staying. I had a big bag of weed and we ended up in Tom Hamilton's room. It was great to see him again. He sat on the bed, and me and Tommy were having a great time, laughing. I'm freaking out because we are hanging with Aerosmith. I pulled out the bag of weed. Tom Hamilton said, "Hey, Sebastian." And I look at this dude. I was being a complete jerk, and insensitive to his sobriety.

"Come on, man, it's not big deal, it's just weed!"

"But Sebastian, you don't understand. If you pull that out, I'll have to leave the room." And it was his room.

So I put it away.

The next day we decided to go to hang out with our good buddy Lars Ulrich. The first thing he did was tell me that he *filmed* my jam with Aerosmith the night before. He promised me a copy. This was in 1990. Hey Lars! It's twenty-six years after the gig. Can I please have my copy now? I cannot think of anything I'd rather see, to be honest. Seriously.

We started our day going down to the CN Tower and getting drunk. Lars was in tourist mode that day, and being European, probably felt the Canadian vibe. Up to the top restaurant we went, to the bar of course, for brunch. Drank a bunch of booze, and then decided to leave. The restaurant was the "spinning" kind, revolving 360 views around the city of Toronto. I don't think we realized it was motorized. Any room would've been spinning in the state we were achieving.

We made it down to the bottom of the CN Tower and drunkenly bought trinkets at the gift shop. Into the cab, up Yonge Street, to the Gasworks. My old haunt. It felt great to strut in there with the drummer of Metallica on a hot summer day. We proceeded in the Canadian national pastime. Sit on the patio and drink beers.

In my experience, partying with Lars, decades ago, he was never content with only drinking beers. There was the time at the top of Le Mondrian in West Hollywood, after doing mountains of cocaine, Lars and I challenged each other to an early morning tennis match. We went up on the roof of the hotel, after partying all night, and had our own little mini-Wimbledon up there. A bunch of booze, mountain of blow, and tennis. That's how we rolled back in 1990.

This day was similarly debauched. Rolling onto the Gasworks patio, I had somehow let my friends know we were going to be there. Rick and my buddies from Peterborough showed up. We all started drinking. Lars, at about three in the afternoon, whips out a bag of cocaine. Dumped it down right on the table, while businessmen and families were walking past. We started snorting lines in the middle of the beautiful sunny day, on a quaint, Canadian terrace, breathing the fresh, crisp air through the pure cocaine we shoved up our faces. The owner of the establishment came up and said, "Sebastian!" He looked horrified. "I can't let you just do that here right in the middle of the table!" Lars and all of us, fueled by booze, just turned and looked at him and laughed. Like this guy was going to throw out me and Lars Ulrich? Out of his rock 'n' roll bar? In 1990? Of course he wasn't. So, we kept inhalin', like Van Halen.

Metallica had a photo sesssion set up the next day with the world-renowned rock photographer Ross Halfin. They asked me to come along and hang out. We ended up at a studio somewhere on Queen Street, I believe. When I walked in the studio, as a joke, all of Metallica had their hair done just like Skid Row. We were the originators of the side part, giant hairdo, which wasn't exactly original, but we had perfected it down to hair spectacularness. People dug our hair, man. For sure! They still do. It's wild.

So I walk in, and they all are making their Sebastian faces at the camera.

I had brought a case of beer, probably Labatt's Blue. We cracked it open and started drinking. Jason Newsted was brand-new to the band. Started copping a pretty good buzz. Someone had the idea to take the photo shoot up onto the roof.

By this time, we had killed half a case and were feeling pretty good. Since I wasn't working, I probably imbibed more than the guys in Metallica, but I remember James in particular was feeling no pain for sure. We are on top of the roof with a great view of Toronto. For some reason, there was a bicycle up there, next to some air ducting. I got on the bike and started riding it around the roof. We laughed.

As I put the bike back, I discovered that the front wheel was detachable. After a couple more Labatts, I started rolling the wheel of the bike around the roof of the building. Just for fun. Got a little carried away. Gave it a little more torque than I should've.

The front wheel of the bike went flying across the roof of the building. It hit the lip of the eavestrough, and soared into the air above. James and the rest of Metallica ran to the edge of the building and looked with shock into the sky above, at this lone bike wheel, spinning madly in space.

Collectively, we gasped in horror at what might happen. On the streets below, this was a busy day, in the middle of the city. There were people going to work. Coming home from school. Going to the grocery store. This was ridiculous.

The bike wheel shot up through the air, and then began its descent to the ground far below. We were next to some sort of alley. Underneath us was a brand-new Mercedes-Benz SUV sports-truck-type vehicle. Black. Shiny. Obviously, this year's model. Somebody had worked super hard for this vehicle, and had gone to the necessary precaution of parking in this alleyway, where surely no harm could come to it.

That was before Metallica decided to do a photo shoot on the roof.

With a sickening *crrrrasshhh*, the wheel sailed through the air straight through the windshield of the SUV. Neat and precise, the whole windshield was destroyed. Nobody was hurt. But at the sight of this brand-new SUV, with a bicycle wheel now lodged in between the driver and passenger seats, smashed glass all around, and the alarm sounding, James Hetfield let out a roaring laugh, turned around, and said, "Oh my fucking God." We got the fuck outta there.

The rooftop photo shoot was over.

Time to go party!

Went to a club somewhere that night that was full of, how shall I say, *colorful* characters from the Queen Street/Yorkville community in Toronto. Not exactly Metallica's crowd. I just remembered at the end of the night James Hetfield screaming in some guy's face, as we pulled him away before he destroyed the man. Then, in the cab ride home, one of the band members trying to eat my girlfriend's sister's arm.

I had to tell him to stop biting her.

Rock 'n' roll.

San Francisco. Metallica stomping grounds. Live. Playing in Oakland, headlining, with Pantera opening the show. Grandma is there. Even though this was a very wild show, Grandma was always there. After *Slave to the Grind* came out, she said, "Sebastian. Does the music have to be *so* heavy?" I told her, "Oh, well, yes at that point, it does." She respected my work ethic, and believed in me since I was a little boy. Gave me Frank Sinatra cassettes when I was in Madam X. Always told me that Frank was the example of as fine as a singer could be. She was right. She taught me about good singing at an early age, but Pantera was a little different than Ole Blue Eyes.

The day after the show, me and Lars decide to hook up with Steven Tyler. At San Francisco's infamous Mitchell Brothers O'Farrell Theatre. The place they made that movie about. This is one of the original vaudeville strip clubs in San Francisco, with a crazy story and reputation to match the craziness that went on inside. Upon entry, we were handed laser pointers, to highlight any *naughty bits*, as they say. We had some fun with that. But after the strip club, me and Lars wanted to step up the fun meter a little more.

We decided to go score some blow. Lars knew the place, but it was in a shady part of town. We went driving his car and ended up at some dudes' house in the middle of a residential street. Got out of the car. Went up the sidewalk. Excited to score, we were drunk, and we were loud.

Went up the stairs, onto the porch. Lars knocked on the door. Nobody came.

"Dude, are you sure this is the right place?" I helpfully inquired.

"Yes, Sebastian, I been here before, I know this guy. He's got the bad shit. This is the fucking place."

Knock knock knock knock.

"Dude, where is this guy? This is bullshit. What the fuck is going on?"

Knock knock knock.

"I swear, it's cool. Just chill out, this guy's got the blow. Some fucking good shit, too, man. Chill out. Trust me."

Knock knock knock knock.

BANG! The blind behind the window on the front door on the porch shoots open. And there, standing in the doorway, right in front of us, is a long-haired man in a bathrobe.

With a shotgun.

Pointed right at Lars's head.

"Holy fuck, dude!!!!! What the fuck!!!!!! Come on!!!!!! It's me!!!!"

"Who is it and what the fuck's going on????" the guy says, greeting us with his hand on the trigger.

"Oh, LARS!! Right on, man!! What's happening??" He puts the gun down, and lets us into the house. Actually he just lets Lars in. I go wait in the car.

Lars returns excitedly with a bunch of coke. It was party time. Time to go back to Lars's house, talk, a lot, and solve the world's problems. Before the sun came up. Then, watch the sun come up. This night was getting weirder and we were determined to see it through.

We made it back into the winding hills of the East Bay, where

Lars lived. Cranking tunes on his stereo and having fun. When we got to his house we noticed something weird. Two guys running around in the street, in front of his garage. Lars said, "Who the fuck is that? That's weird." Having never been there before, I had just had a gun pulled on me. So I didn't think it was that weird.

We pulled in the garage, next to his other car. He noticed that the windows were down in the other vehicle. "That's weird," he said. What I thought was really weird was that he had an elevator. In his house. The hill was so steep getting from the garage up to the dwelling that we got in Lars's little elevator and were promptly elevated to the top of the hill. To Lars's house. We jumped into the living room, cracked open some brews, snorted some lines. Let's get this fucking party started.

Dad having been an artist his whole life, having been surrounded by art myself, I marveled at the artwork on the walls. Lars was the first rock 'n' roller I had ever met that appreciated artwork like my family did. Big, large pieces. Huge, surreal paintings. Abstract, realism, both. I was blown away by the art.

And the blow.

We did what rockers back then did. We sat up all night, doing coke, drinking, listening to music, and talking. That's what blow used to do. Before it started to freeze my brain, make me unable to speak, breathe, or sleep, the blow made me talk. A lot. Lars too. Sebastian Bach and Lars Ulrich, together, high on cocaine, ended up doing A LOT of talking. Not a lot of sleeping.

Sometime before the sun came up, Lars was bragging to me about the stereo he had in his car. Not the one we came home in, but the other one in the garage. He told me that this was the most insane car stereo ever invented by human beings. "The amplifiers and speakers are the most powerful known to man," he declared, the small Danish sound enthusiast that he is. Suggesting we get some beers, take the elevator down to the garage and check out some Mercyful Fate in the car, I was totally into the scene.

We got off the elevator and stepped back into the garage. Laughing, drinking, and having fun. Got into the car. Shut the door. Lars puts in a CD, and says, "Wait till you fucking hear this." He turns the stereo on, and I look at the dashboard. It was all lit up. I braced myself for the heavy metal onslaught that was about to shatter my brain.

"Your're naaaaauught gonnaaa belieeeeeve this," Lars says to me in his Arnold Schwarzenegger high-on-crack accent. "This is the most unbelievable newwwww speaker in the world for heavy met-al music." He turns it louder, and louder, and louder.

But nothing.

No sound.

He looks at me.

"What the fuck?" he says. Then, turning around, Lars looks into the backseat of the car and notices that the two backseat windows are not rolled down. They are actually *smashed in*. And, where once lived the most valuable, loudest, most important heavy metal speaker of all time, now was just a hole, in the wall, of his car, with wires hanging down out of it.

We clued in.

Holy fuck! Those guys that were running around the street in front of the garage when we pulled up? They had actually been in Lars's garage, smashed the windows out of his car, and stolen his speakers.

We just looked at each other and laughed. Most people would be freaked out. Pissed off. Lars looked at the smashed windows, the wires hanging out of the speaker, and erupted into laughter. This dude was so rich he could have anything the fuck he wanted. We just kept on laughing, drinking beers, and saying, "Jesus fucking Christ, can you believe this shit?" Not even concerned that they could still be in the area or anything. We were invincible. We were true rock stars. We stumbled out of the car, into the elevator and back up the hill. To do more blow, drink more, and play some more rock 'n' roll.

The night went on and on. And on. Into early morning. Then, it was 10:00 a.m. And then 11:00 a.m. Yes, dear reader. We were still up into the afternoon, playing *Don't Break the Oath*, snorting, drinking, and talking.

Knock knock knock comes from the door. Surprise! Me and Lars turn and look at each other. I gasped in fright. There's not supposed to be anybody here. *Shit, it isn't those dudes coming back? Who stole the speakers? Is it the guy with the blow with the shotgun pointed at our heads? Only hours before? Is it the cops? Come to bust us for all the drugs?? And all the fun we were having?* We were so fucked up, we couldn't believe somebody was knocking at the door. It was past noon. We were so high on blow, I'm surprised we had any lips left.

Knock knock knock knock knock.

"Hide the blow!!!!" Lars went over to his elevator, told me to hide out in the living room and chill out. I sat on the couch keeping as low a profile as I could, after doing mountains of cocaine and having been up all night drinking.

"Oh my God!!! Sebastian!!! You're not going to believe this!!!!!"

I turned to my right expecting the worst. Not ready for who I was about to see in front of me.

And there, stepping off the elevator, into our world of debauchery, was . . . my grandma.

Yes, that's right, dear reader. My grandma was there! At Lars's house. In his living room. I had forgotten that I had made a date to see her that day, and hang out with my family that night, at our family reunion. Completely had escaped what was left of my mind.

She walked in the room. We hid the blow.

"Hi, Bass!!! It's so wonderful to see you!!!" God bless her soul. She had no concept of what we had been doing for the last twelve hours or so. None of which had involved sleeping.

Lars Ulrich could not contain his glee at the situation. As he was about to have his last beer, and attempt to form some semblance of sleep, my grandmother was elated at the prospect of spending a quiet afternoon with her grandson and family members. We would have a lovely dinner, take pictures, and have a quality family time together as I was coming down off a blow and booze bender with the best of 'em.

We say goodbye to Lars, and take the elevator back down to the street below. Past the smashed windows of his car in the garage, and into my grandma's new Honda Accord. The same car that I had bought her in 1990 for her birthday. It was the very first brand-new car she had ever had in her whole life. Now, she wanted me to drive it home from San Francisco to Walnut Creek. I was so high I could barely keep my hands on the steering wheel.

My grandma's positivity, and attitude, got me through this day. Never once did she comment on my appearance, which was no doubt disheveled. All she did was smile and tell me how great I looked, and how happy she was to see me. I concentrated on driving the car as best I could, after not having slept for two days. We left and I felt the same as I did when I used to come stay with her every summer as a child. She lived in the same place on Creekside Drive and miraculously I pulled the car into her driveway. Made some coffee and had some chocolate chip cookies. The same kind she used to make back in the '70s. I chilled out and then made it to Auntie Margaret's for dinner, where my cousins, brother Zac, and my dad had flown in from Canada. Along with my aunt and uncle, we had a giant family dinner together. At dinner I overheard my uncle Bill said, "Well, I don't know, it looks like he hasn't slept that much in a couple days. He looks kind of *burnt out*." If you only knew, Uncle Bill. If you only knew.

1991
Toledo, Ohio
Raceway Park

Maybe you can tell by this book, back in the 1980s and early 1990s drugs were definitely a part of rock 'n' roll. Part of the scene. This is nothing new. Any other rock book on the shelf next to this one will contain similar tales. On the Guns N' Roses tour, they had the MGM Grand plane as a mode of transportation. I had asked Axl many times, "Hey dude, can I come on the plane? Can I come on the plane? Seriously, can I come on the plane?!?!"

"No, no, no, no, and no," I would always get told.

"I *really* want to get on the fucking plane with you guys!"

"No."

One day, after a gig, I went out to the fence where all the fans are standing. Looking for some weed. I asked a hundred or so people, "Any of you guys got any weed?" This was in Toledo, Ohio. I remember distinctly. A couple days after the St. Louis riot. Nobody had any weed that day in Toledo. Then, some guy said, "Hey, I don't have any weed, but I got this." I go, "What's that?"

"It's opium." I had never seen opium in my life, and I have not seen it since that day. I said, "What the fuck is *opium*?" I didn't know what it looked like, or what you even did with it. Smoke it? Shoot it? Snort it? I didn't know. But since there was no weed, I was willing to find out.

Dude came to the front of the fence. Big Val let him through. He then reached into his pocket, and pulled out a cellophane wrapper. Unwrapped it. Inside was a round ball of dark goo-like substance that he told me was *pure opium*. I said, "Sure, I'll take that, dude," and gave him a couple backstage passes. I now had a large ball of opium, whatever that was, but I still had no idea what to do with it.

Saw Axl that night backstage. "Hey dude, can I come on the plane, man?? Seriously! I think we would have fun."

"No, Baz, you still can't come on the plane."

"Come on, Axl, please let me come on the plane, dude, for reals."

"No, I really don't think it's a good idea, Baz. Sorry, maybe tomorrow."

"You know what?"

"What?"

"I just got this big fucking huge ball of opium."

"Hey Baz."

"What?"

"Get on the fuckin' plane."

That's kind of how it was then. Fast-forward to Castle Donington, 1995. The bill is Metallica, Skid Row, and Slayer. Yes, you read that correctly. Here today it might sound incredible that Skid Row would be on the bill between Slayer and Metallica. But that's the way it was.

I remember this day for many different reasons. Backstage, walking around the Donington race track concert site, everybody drunk, in the mud, drinking beer, pissing everywhere. Hot dudes in denim jackets. Not many bathrooms.

Hanging out with Tom Araya of Slayer that day. I have been a Slayer fan since *Show No Mercy/Haunting the Chapel* EPs back in the early eighties. I went to their first ever Toronto show, at Larry's Hideaway, and ended up smoking hash with them that night at Larry's. It was amazing to play Castle Donington with them a decade later.

Tom Araya and I were walking around the backstage area, when a drunken British musician came up to us. "Hey Sebastian!" the lout shouted in my general direction.

"Hey dude, how are you?" I said, annoyed.

"Oh yes, *Sebastian*!!!!" he said, with a hint of "mock" in his tone.

"Guess what the name of my band is?!?!?"

"What is that?" Like I gave a fuck.

"The name of my band is . . . KID WIKKID! Ha ha ha ha haaaaaa, yes! That's right, Sebastian!!! Kid Wikkid! What do you think of that, Sebastian?? Do you *like* the name of *my* band???"

I was like, "*What?*"

Obviously, he knew this was my band before Skid Row. He thought it was hilarious that he could run up to me and report to me this piece of information. "Yes, that's right! We saw your name, Kid Wikkid, in a *magazine interview* you did, and we thought, bloody hell! What a good name for our band! So we *knicked* it!! Ha ha ha ha haaaa!"

I swallowed my pride and tried to brush it off my shoulder. This, certainly, did now have me feeling *well-chuffed*. I was much more interested in talking to Tom Araya of Slayer, someone I had immense respect for, than this drunken fool, who was only trying to piss me off anyway.

"You know what, dude?" I told him. "That's cool, man. You took my name, that I invented, when I was fifteen years old, that I saw in the subway when I was a kid. Okay, fine. All I ask is that you maybe mention that? Where you got the name? If you ever do an interview in a magazine? Is that fair?" I queried.

"Bloody hell, Sebastian!! We could actually *use some press*!!!" By this time he had his arm around my shoulder, pulling my neck in close to his face. In my face, spitting as he talked. I was starting to fucking lose it. "I have a better idea!" he blathered. "Why don't you *punch me*? Ha ha ha ha ha ha haaaaa," this guy said.

I looked at Tom Araya. I looked back at the guy. I couldn't believe what he was telling me. He was actually *asking me to punch him*. I had tried the nice approach. So, fuck it. Give the people what they want, I always say.

I remembered distinctly, from Shao Lin Kung Fu, Sifu Damien

would tell me in training that the flat, front part of your forearm is the hardest area of the human body to strike somebody else with. With no nerve endings, the forearm is also one of the hardest bones in your body. If you wind up, and really want to fuck someone up, the forearm smash is the way to inflict serious damage without feeling any pain whatsoever yourself. Also very useful in *close proximity*, which this drunken Brit was definitely in. Perfect for this situation.

I was just giving this dude what he wanted. You want me to punch you? Alright. Want to mock me in front of my friends and steal the name of my band? That's your choice. But then I get to make my choice. And, with that, I folded my arm and planted my right elbow into the side of this dude's cheek, knocking him completely unconscious. He crumpled into the ground, at Tom Araya's feet. We stepped over the unconscious man and went to find some beers.

I never read any interview with this dude about how he got the name Kid Wikkid. I never read any interview with this dude ever at all.

We kept the party rolling. Lars showed up. The first thing I told him was, "Hey, listen. I don't do blow anymore." Which was true. I realized long ago that cocaine did not agree with me anymore. I saw a TV show once on cocaine and what it does to the body. When you first start doing it, it *stimulates* your serotonin levels. Makes you talk, babble, and engages you with others who are feeling the same way. But the more you do it, cocaine in fact *depletes* your serotonin level. That is the worst fucking feeling I can think of in the world. When you are trying to sleep, coming off blow, there is no worse way to feel. When it's noon, you are staring at the ceiling, pleading with the Lord, "Please God, I promise to you I'll never do this shit again if you just let me go to sleep. Please *just let me go to sleep.* Just this once, please, I promise I'll stop."

Then you do it again.

Well, I was tired of that feeling. I genuinely did not like the way cocaine made me feel anymore.

I explained to Lars that I had stopped.

"Hey, you know what, Sebastian? That's a real nice story. But you wanna know what I think???"

"What's that, Lars?"

"Maybe TONIGHT is a good night . . . *to start it back up again!!!!!*"

And with that, he reached in his pocket and pulled out a gigantic bag of blow. It was on.

Let's get frozen.

We kept partying backstage at Donington, drinking beers and doing blow. When it was time to go back to the hotel, Slayer invited me onto their bus with them. We were staying at the same hotel. Their manager was the guy who actually invited me on the bus. A man by the name of Rick Sales. A man who would be extremely important in my life and career in the years to come.

We got on the bus, my teeth rattling from all the blow shooting through my veins. The soundman pulled out the oh-so-familiar silver Halliburton briefcase. Filled with either cash or drugs, or both, this was the ubiquitous fixture on many rock 'n' roll tours throughout the 1970s and '80s. Rolling down the highway, "Hey man, what you got in the briefcase???"

"Oh, you don't want to know, Baz." Fuckin' bullshit I don't wanna know. "Crack that fucker open!" I was pretty sure I knew what was in there.

He opened up the briefcase. Rick Sales shook his head no, no, no. I nodded my head and said yes, yes, yes. Inside the briefcase were sacks of blow. It was time to get into the scene.

By the time we got to the hotel I couldn't form a sentence. My last memory of this bus ride with Slayer was them all checking into the hotel, as I sat out in the front valet area under a tree, talking to myself. This was back in 1994. I don't do that shit anymore. I count myself lucky at how I have abused my body, over the years, and am still here to tell the tale. Sitting under a tree talking to myself is not my optimum idea of a *good time*. Cocaine sucks.

Don't ever find yourself alone, talking to yourself, under a tree.

The next time I saw Lars was at the Rainbow in Hollywood. Duff McKagan was there, back when he still had an intact liver. This was one of the nights we were out to do some damage.

I had heard about, but had never actually seen, the legendary drug known as Quaaludes. Always in stories regaling the '70s, there would be mention of this mysterious drug that I had never encountered or come in contact with in my time. I heard about it and wondered about it. This night at the Rainbow would be the one and only time I have ever seen, and tried, Quaaludes.

After who knows how many hours drinking with Duff, we found ourselves somehow underneath the back corner table of the Rainbow, which has always been the best place in the world. Always open to serious rock 'n' roll animals such as myself. The recent passing of Lemmy is just yet another marker of the end of an era. It is incredible how the Rainbow is still there today, surrounded by development, major hotels coming up all over the Sunset Strip. The Rainbow remains. This is where Joe DiMaggio got engaged to Marilyn Monroe, back when it was called the Grove. And this is the only place where Sebastian, Duff, and Lars did Quaaludes. Talk about Hollywood history.

You would be surprised to see the underbelly of the Rainbow. I had never been, nor have I since been, *underneath* the tables in this fine establishment. But on this night, I found myself looking up from the floor to the underside of the table. All kinds of graffiti, autographs, and of course, chewing gum, stuck all over the place. Me and Duff did a couple of bumps under there, and then came back up top. Somehow we had Quaaludes. *Fuck it, let's do Quaaludes now! Finally!*

Who knows how or where we got them, but we put them into our mouths. They were big, hockey-puck-shaped pills. As the night went on the drug began to hit me. I became very, very, very, very, very *relaxed*. Very, very *slow*. As I was talking to Duff, I noticed the oddest thing. The shape of Duff's mouth was changing. He was talking, but I couldn't really understand what he was saying. He was mumbling. I looked down at my jacket. For some reason it was wet. I looked back up at Duff. He was drooling. And then I realized the same thing was happening to my face. I had lost control over the muscles in my mouth. My lips were slack-jawed. I was drooling all over myself.

This is fucked up.

As I look up, I see the laughing little heavy metal gnome known as Lars Ulrich dancing merrily around our table. He's like a little leprechaun, doing a pixie dance.

"Ha ha ha ha haAAAAAAAA!!!!! Hey, everybody! Line up! Come and MEET YOUR HEROES!!! It's your dream come true!!"

What the fuck was he talking about?

Zzzzzzzzzzzzzzzzzzzzzzzzz.

By this point, me and Duff are falling asleep on each other's shoulders. Drooling on each other. Unable to speak. Drifting in and out of consciousness. Partying like rock stars at the Starwood in '77, we think.

Then we realize what Lars was up to. This little demon was talking to the fans. He had them lined up in front of our table.

"Hey everybody! Come get your picture taken!!! With a real rock star!!! Come meet Skid Row!!! Guns N' Roses!"

"Heyyyyyyyy, mmmmmaaaaaannnnnn, that'ssssss nnnnot cooooooooollll, mmmaaaaannnnn . . ." *Click, click, click* go the flashbulbs.

Lars is *charging* fans *five dollars each* to come sit next to me and Duff.

To get their pictures taken with us. We are too 'Luded out to protest. Attempting to stop this madness, we tell LLLLAAAAArrsssss to stop iitttttttt, through drool, in excruciating slow motion.

Welcome to the Rainbow! I never did Quaaludes again.

Never Had Nothing to Do

1990–1991
New Jersey

I had never had money to do just whatever I wanted with. Nobody in my family, or nobody I knew for that matter, could live the way we were living now.

One of the things I loved to do, when I was twenty-one years old, was drink beer. I drank a lot of beer in those days. When we were first off the road, I literally had nothing to do. Or, to be more specific, I didn't *know* really what to do. I had never had *nothing* to do before. Everything I had done since I was eight years old in the church choir had led me up to this moment. I specifically asked myself, *"What in the fuck am I supposed to do every day now?"* When you are on the road, working and playing every night, your days are structured. Every moment is spoken for. Your time is maximized to the fullest. Coming *off* the road, however, was the exact opposite of that. I looked at the calendar, having nothing on the schedule at all, for the first time in my life. And, also for the first time, tons of money in the bank. What a neat combo. But totally foreign to me.

I began to collect rock 'n' roll memorabilia, movies, and bootleg VHS tapes, etcetera, with a vengeance. I amassed a large collection of unreleased concerts on VHS, mostly from Japan. It was legal to buy bootlegs in Tokyo that you could not find anywhere else in the world. We would go into the store called Airs Rock, and since they were bootlegging us as well, they would let us walk out with as many VHS tapes as we could carry. I would walk out of the store with five or six garbage bags full of unreleased concerts, promos, and television appearances by KISS, Van Halen, Mötley Crüe, Judas Priest et al., on VHS tape. Before the days of the Internet, this was an *extreme* novelty to my friends back in New Jersey. We would regularly have my friends over at night to drink and watch old Van Halen or KISS concerts on the big screen, cranked through the speakers like a PA. This was a great way to have fun with my friends and not have to deal with the public. Not such a great way to ingratiate myself to the neighbors. I ended up with the cops coming over numerous times. My landlord of the condo in Freehold sued me. In chambers, she testified that I acted like "an animal." I told her lawyer, "It wasn't an act."

Regardless of these messy details, the band was so big now that we each were able to buy our own gigantic houses in the New Jersey countryside. After looking for a couple of months, we found a beautiful secluded place in Lincroft, New Jersey, a sprawling property on Swimming River Road. Little did I realize in 1990 how the name of the street would be so prophetic, decades later.

My house is situated on three and a half acres of pristine New Jersey real estate, in the woods. At the time of this writing, I still own the property. The house was destroyed in Hurricane Irene in 2011. My property abuts twenty-five acres or so of government land, so it's literally as much woods as anyone could handle. It was always so great coming off the road and wandering the paths in the woods. Paths that I would cut myself, through running, or hiking on the trails with my children. I knew every single leaf. Every rock. Every tree. Nothing was a more soothing escape from the insanity of heavy metal rock 'n' roll than walking around in the woods on my New Jersey property. I miss that greatly. When the house was destroyed, it was so overwhelming that it was hard to process. I thought it was interesting that the time I actually broke down was walking around on the trails in the woods in the back. That is where I felt the most sadness. Having the house destroyed was so painful I could barely process it. But walking around in my woods was where I dropped to my knees. And cried.

My house also had a large basement, which Skid Row used to rehearse in, since the day I moved there. The material for the record *Slave to the Grind* was mostly written and worked on in my basement, and Rob Affuso's garage. I wrote the music for the title track "Slave to the Grind" on my mini-cassette Dictaphone handheld recorder in Freehold, New Jersey. I had felt that, on our first album tour, we really didn't have a great opening song for our set. Our opener, "Makin' a Mess," was a song I wrote on the first Skid Row album with Snake and Rachel. But I thought it was just not quite fast, or badass, enough to open the show with. I thought we needed a real mean, up-tempo rocker to grab people by the throat the minute we walked out onto that stage. "Slave to the Grind" became that song. Originally inspired as a sped-up version of Van Halen's "Dead or Alive," I hummed that riff into my microcassette recorder, walked into rehearsal the next day, and said, "Rachel. Snake. Scotti. Play this riff as a whole. In unison. Rob. Play this drumbeat." *Rat-a-tat-tat* . . . I air-drummed Rob the drumbeat. Then, Rachel said, "It sounds like a grind."

"*Slave to the Grind.*"

YEAH!!!

Rachel and Snake worked more on the music that very night, and the classic Skid Row opening song was born. Written between the three of us. As the best songs on the record were.

"In a Darkened Room," to me, is the "best" Skid Row ballad. I don't like to use the word *best* or *better* when describing music. It's not sports. But this song hits me quite hard when I listen to it. It's a song that I wrote with Snake in Tokyo, Japan, at the Roppongi Prince hotel. Snake had the music for the verse, but no melody. He had no music to go to after the verse. We wrote the bridge together. "*Forgive me please, for I know not what I do*"—that led to the chorus. After the record came out, Slash pulled me aside at his house and was perturbed at this particular song. I didn't understand why. He explained to me that the guitar pattern in the chorus was his signature guitar pattern from the Guns N' Roses classic "Sweet Child o' Mine." I did not realize this whatsoever. But when I listen back, I do indeed hear the similarities. Sorry, Slash. I had nothing to do with that part!

The sound of our second record was very important to us. We wanted people to know us not just for our hit ballads, but for rock 'n' roll. Michael Wagener and I drove around the back streets of New Jersey looking for the ultimate Marshall amplifier.

We listened to bunches of different local bands and found one particular amplifier head, owned by a guy by the name of Dave Linsk. We went to his house one snowy afternoon and heard the amp that we eventually used on "Slave to the Grind." There was also a new amp company out of Florida called Riviera, and we used some of their amps as well. It was Michael Wagener and myself who were most concerned with the production of this album. On all of these excursions to find and listen to different guitar amplifiers, it was always just us two. The metal heads inside the two of us wanted to beat "Live Wire" and "Balls to the Wall." How ironic is it that as I am writing this I started my day today by putting on the TV and the "Slave to the Grind" video is the first thing I see. I still hear it all the time. The album still stands up.

The opening track on the album is called "Monkey Business." The song turned out to be incredible in the final result. But when I first heard it, I thought the main riff of the track sounded too much like the Guns N' Roses song "Paradise City." I got an idea for how "Monkey Business" could sound more unique and hummed Snake the new chords. We then hammered out together what eventually became the main riff of the song. Of course I didn't get songwriting credit on this. Which makes me bristle. Again. The song would've been completely different without my melodic input on that riff. It also would've been completely the same. As "Paradise City."

We worked on the songs in my basement. One day, Steven Adler came over to visit. We had planned for him to stay at my house for a couple of days. Until I came down the next morning, and opened the door of my main-floor bedroom bathroom. Steven was sitting on my toilet with a syringe in his arm. Blood was splattered all over the white walls. I told him that he had to get out of my house immediately, if not sooner. Some girl came and picked him up as I wiped his blood off of my bathroom walls.

Much has been said about the sophomore slump, and how easy it is for an artist to come out with the big debut, only to not be able to come up with a sufficient follow-up. This precedent, combined with the financial pressure due to the horrific *Underground* contract, added an extra level of pressure to the recording sessions. Not to mention the fact that the first album was now well over 4x platinum, which for any artist would be tough to beat.

We decided to once again work with Michael Wagener in the producer's chair. We would record the album down in Florida, and live in Fort Lauderdale for a couple of months. First, we had to come up with the material. This created a unique challenge. Although we were a hard-rocking band, our two big radio hits were both ballads. This pissed us off. In our young, piss-and-vinegar style, we made a conscious effort to make the album as hard as it could be. While playing in Daytona Beach, Florida, in 1990, I was walking in the ocean. Two silly dudes were walking on the sand a couple yards away for me. They yelled out to me, "*Iiiiiiiiiii Reeeeeeeemember Yoooooooooo*" in a mock sarcastic voice, and laughed. I understood where they were coming from. At that moment, in the "I Remember You" summer of 1990, Skid Row were an overexposed band. Our videos were over-saturating the public's mind, and even my own. You could not get away from us. I could not get away from myself. I was as sick of me as the dudes mocking me on the beach were.

Our answer to being perceived as balladeers was to come out as hard-ass screaming metal as we possibly could. And we definitely accomplished that goal.

Living in Fort Lauderdale for a month or two was really a lot of fun. We recorded at New River Studios. Frequented the local strip bars, of which there were plenty. Pure Platinum and the other gentlemen's establishments became our stomping grounds while recording the album. We had a drunken blast, as any hot-blooded young men would. I, as had become my pattern by now,

of course took my fun to extremes. Which was starting to become the norm.

One night in particular stands out. I went out to one of the local Fort Lauderdale strip clubs, drunk on Jack Daniel's and ready to kick some fucking ass. After drinking, smoking, and snorting who knows what, I managed to wind up in one of the cages on the strip club floor.

Naked.

Where the dancers dance. I pulled my pants down, in public, onstage, in a cage, and then had another stroke of brilliance.

I proceeded to light my pubic hair on fire.

To the dismay, and considerable hilarity of the shocked establishment. In actual fact, as fucked up as I was, no one was that shocked.

It was a different time.

I had forgotten about this incident until decades later, when some dude came up to me backstage.

"Man, I was with you that night. When you set your pubes on fire."

"Excuse me?" That's not exactly something you hear every day.

Dude reiterated the story back to me.

"In Fort Lauderdale. We were sitting there having some cocktails. All of a sudden you jumped out of your seat, into a cage, on the stage, and lit your jungle bush on fire, dude." It all came flooding back to me.

This was so long ago that people actually had pubic hair. We're talking medieval times here, folks.

After I lit my pubic hair on fire, onstage, I continued drinking Jack Daniel's until I got so drunk I got kicked out of the club, and wound up passed out in the parking lot in the back of someone's pickup truck. I slept off the booze, walked back in the club, and gave the guy who owned the truck my black leather Skid Row tour jacket. He drove me back to my place with Lumpy, who was so high on speed he asked if he could get out on the side of the road and *walk* the rest of the way home. On the highway. The sun was coming up. It was beautiful. We let him off, in his bare feet, as he walked towards the next town. He never made it. Lumpy was picked up by Florida State Troopers. They took him to the Dade County jail for a week or so before they let us bail him out. He had no shoes.

When we got back to the hotel, I fell asleep for twenty hours. When I woke up, I came to the realization that I had given some guy my leather fucking jacket. My one-of-a-kind, personalized, First Album Tour, Skid Row Leather Jacket!! *Oh my God.* We went back the next night, found the dude, and he gave my jacket back. As crazy as shit got, us rockers usually looked out for ourselves. We were like a gang. A gang of drunk people who liked to set their pubic hair on fire.

Recording of the record went well. We came up with some kick-ass heavy metal music, and performed the songs as if our lives depended on them. Because they did. In my case, the incident with the bottle throwing in Massachusetts on the Aerosmith tour had cost me pretty much every penny that I had. I paid over $300,000 in settlements and lawyers' fees, after all was said and done. That also added to the fuel and fire of the *Slave to the Grind* album. Looking at all the platinum records on my wall, in my brand-new house on my own sprawling property, I had the distinct feeling of "*Oh my God, we did it. Now we got to do it again* if we want to keep all these houses and shit." So we came out with all guns blazing.

I sang so hard, I actually blew my voice out for the first time in my life. For the *Slave to the Grind* record, I was warming up my voice in the usual Bel Canto singing scale style, and then I began to end my warm-up with Whitney Houston singing the "Star-Spangled Banner" in the 1991 Super Bowl Halftime Show. It was the most amazing vocal performance I had ever heard, and I wanted to see if I could do it. I practiced singing it until I could nail it. I would sing The National Anthem in the foyer of New River Studios, at the top of my lungs, with fans outside the building, listening. Then the song would end, and they would all would clap and cheer for me. I laughed. When you listen to it today, it seems amazing that a male voice could do the same thing. But I could do it, full voice. Then I would walk in the studio and sing the vocal tracks for the album *Slave to the Grind*.

The moment I knew I had pushed my voice too hard was when we were in Florida, cutting the song "Wasted Time." I had screamed so much on that song that I couldn't sing it anymore without shouting. My *ballad voice* in "I Remember You" and "18 and Life" is never shouting in any way. That vocal sound is a very controlled technique known as *speech-level singing*. I save all my power for all those high-scream vocal histrionics. I had overused my pipes to the point where I just couldn't get that *floating sound* that is one of the trademarks of my voice. I had simply sung too much, too hard. I had pushed my throat muscles and vocal cords to the point where they couldn't be subtle anymore. Just full out.

I went down to the beach, alone on a rainy day, to the Fort Lauderdale Howard Johnson. Got a coffee. Went up and down the sand, torturing myself as to what to do. The band was depending on me. The record company and management were depending on me. Most importantly, the fans and my family were depending on me. I decided to take a couple of weeks off from singing. I would rest my voice, and pick it back up in California a couple weeks later.

We moved the whole operation back to California. The guys in Metallica were in town making The Black Album. When I sang the beginning of "Monkey Business," Lars Ulrich came to the studio. He was actually sitting behind the board the night I recorded the vocal to "Monkey Business." He dug that opening scream and told me, when we both thought it sounded right, that I was "roaring," which was certainly my intention.

James Hetfield came by a couple of days later. He took me for a ride in his truck as we listened to some of the new tunes we had cut. James turned the music down as we got back to the studio. As we entered the parking lot, he said in a hushed tone, almost under his breath, "Sebastian. I want to tell you something. My favorite singers are . . . John Bush. Of Armored Saint. And . . ." he cleared his thought, and forced himself to utter the words. "And . . . well, and you." For a moment there, I was very flattered. For a second. "But don't tell anybody that," said James Hetfield. *Gee thanks. I'll promise I won't let anybody know.*

We had demoed the whole record in a very small studio in nearby Colts Neck, New Jersey, prior to going to Florida. We had cut most of the record, and in particular, a really vicious version of the song "Slave to the Grind" that was so potent on that original demo. But it was not recorded with the same sonics as New River, or any of the places in LA we were at. So we decided to re-record that song along with the rest of the demos.

For some reason, we just could not capture the original fire of the demo for the song "Slave to the Grind." The demo blew away the album version in every respect. No matter how many times we tried, we couldn't capture the same magic as that original take. I was adamant that the demo was the version of the song that should go on the record. Michael Wagener battled me on every front in this respect. He tried his hardest to beat the demo. We just couldn't do it. The album was completely done and mastered. He brought me, alone, to the studio, to listen to the "final" version of "Slave to the Grind." After all, this was our baby. I listened to it, turned to him, and said, "Nice job dude. But the demo is better."

"*I know.*"

And that's what ended up on the record. The first time we ever cut the title track. To the first #1 heavy metal album in the history of *Billboard* magazine charts.

The first cut is the deepest.

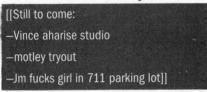

[[Still to come:

—Vince aharise studio

—motley tryout

—Jm fucks girl in 711 parking lot]]

10

LOSE YOUR ILLUSION!

1990–1991

I had developed quite a good relationship with Guns N' Roses' mercurial front man, Mr. Axl Rose. We spent time at his apartment in West Hollywood, at Shoreham Towers, where he came up with the idea for the GNR song "Right Next Door to Hell." Dedicated lovingly to his neighbor.

Bang! Bang! Bang!!! went the door.

"Open up! It's the West Hollywood Police!"

We looked at each other in shock. Well, me more than him.

"BAZ! Hurry! Go lock yourself in the closet!!"

I was like, "What?"

And so, being that it was Axl's apartment, I followed Axl's directions. I went into his living room closet, leaving the door opened slightly. I peeked out and witnessed a scene I have not seen before. Or since.

There were about seven police officers, male and female, assembled at the door. Axl opened it up, and spoke to them in a quiet, understated, yet undeniably aggressive manner. I could not hear exactly what was said. We had been drinking and smoking and doing who knows what else. Cranking Dread Zeppelin, a bizarre musical cross between Led Zeppelin and Reggae music that Axl thought was hilarious. He liked to crank it. Very loudly.

From my view in the living room closet, I could see the cops arguing with Axl. But they never entered the apartment. Whatever they had to say, Axl responded to, out-reasoning the authorities in his *Clint Eastwood/Dirty Harry* baritone voice. It wasn't too long before I watched him literally talk seven police officers into leaving his premises. I came out of the living room closet as he shut the front door. We continued to rage all night long.

Surprise! We had some great parties. Someone at Axl's house showed me how to smoke dope. Something I had never done before. We broke off sheets of aluminum foil, put the dope on it, heated it up with a lighter, and then rolled up a piece of Reynolds Wrap to use as a pipe. This was all new to me. The sensation was indeed pleasant, but I didn't really enjoy it all that much. It was like going to sleep while still being awake. I remember it felt really good to scratch my face. I would smoke some, and then talk to Axl about all sorts of crazy shit.

We called Howard Stern one morning, as the sun came up, with Erin Everly and Maria partying along there with us on the balcony. It took Howard and his radio staff ten minutes to believe that it was really us. But once we did do the interview, it became one of the most replayed interviews on Howard Stern to this day.

We were smoking dope.

It was a different time.

Axl and I were like partners in rock 'n' roll crime. We kinda sorta ruled the world from 1987 to 1991.

He would call me at home in New Jersey and we would talk and laugh. We became friends quite quickly. Erin Everly became friends with Maria for a time. It was on their hips, the first time I ever saw *hip-hugger* jeans. Sitting on Axl's couch, Erin and Maria walked in with jeans so tight they looked painted on. They had shimmied their pants down to be barely above the ITG. This was the first time I'd seen that look. It was a good look.

I have never, and will never, use needles to do drugs. I snorted dope for the very first time with Steven Adler, at his house, the night before Skid Row's first ever photo shoot with renowned rock 'n' roll photographer William Hames. Steven invited me over, as we had made plans to go out on the Sunset Strip later that night. But we never made it that far.

When I got to his house, Steven was lying in bed watching *The Love Boat*. I snorted dope for the first time, in Steven's bed, as the familiar theme song played on the TV.

> *Love,*
> *exciting and new*
> *Come aboard,*
> *we're expecting you*

I looked over to my right to the most amazing scene. As Steven was rolling up a joint in his hands, with his head against the backboard. He had nodded out. Yet his hands remained vertical, above his chest, with the unrolled joint perched precariously in his fingers. For about eight hours. As Steven settled into his nod, no marijuana leaf whatsoever dropped out of the unrolled Zig-Zag paper. For the whole time that he was asleep. I was completely amazed. When he came out of the nod, around 2:00 a.m., he yawned like the Cowardly Lion in *The Wizard of Oz*, looked around the room, at me, and finally at the unrolled joint in his hands. He then nonchalantly resumed rolling up the joint that he had started on about eight hours previously.

By the time we woke up, all the bars were closed. So we stayed in bed and watched TV. How wild can you get!?!

The next day, at the William Hames photo session, I had the distinct feeling that I had been *changed* somehow. A *je n'est c'est quoi*. A feeling of *innocence lost*. I only touched heroin two or three more times in my life. It did not hold the romanticized allure for me that it did for some other poets, writers, and musicians of the past. I thank God for that. Wine and weed is more than enough for me. Being at that photo shoot, I felt *different*. Like I had crossed a line somehow. Which I had.

Steven Adler would walk around his house explaining to me how everybody was mean to him, and how he would never let the band down. As he would tell me this, he would walk into his bathroom, look me straight in the face, and tell me he didn't even *do* dope. Then, he would remove a loose brick from the wall behind his toilet. Reaching into his bathroom wall, he would pull out a stash of dope. Which he would then do in front of me. The whole time, explaining to me how he didn't do it.

It was bewildering to witness. I was with him the day that he was told he couldn't play the drums to the song "Civil War," and that Guns N' Roses were going to have to bring in Matt Sorum to finish the track. Steven was absolutely heartbroken. He stammered on to me for hours.

"I can play it! I know I can do it! How can they do this to me???" But none of this slowed down the pursuit of "good times."

Duff "The King of Beers" McKagan was also super fun to hang out with. I would go to Duff's place, on Mulholland Drive, where he was always hanging out with his friend "Nasty," who was lead singer with a band called Creature. They looked like early KISS, wore full face paint and costumes, and had neon green glow-in-the-dark Creature T-shirts that I used to love to wear.

Duff would send me and Nasty out on booze runs in Duff's black Corvette. Nasty would drive at 100 miles an hour, catching air off every bump in the street, screeching the tires on every turn. Drunk and high on coke, we would speed through Beverly Hills. The whole time Nasty would be laughing and cackling, like the evil rock 'n' roll coke-fiend clown on *Metalocalypse*.

"Dude! Slow down! We're going to crash! We shouldn't be doing this to Duff's car!"

"*Ha ha ha ha ha.*" Cackle cackle cackle. Nasty thinks this is all funny.

It was a different time.

The album *Slave to the Grind* wasn't exactly a rush job, but we were under pressure to finish the album as quickly as possible. Axl called me and asked if I could be ready to tour, in only two months' time. We were not done with the record yet, but we made the decision anyway to go on tour with no new record out at all. Guns N' Roses had also not yet finished the *Use Your Illusion* double album set, so they were going out with no new record either. That illustrates just how big both of the bands were at the time. It was unheard of in 1991 to go out on tour with no new record in the stores.

The album situation did not make a difference in ticket sales. We sold out multiple nights, in the biggest venues, in every single city around the globe.

Alpine Valley has been home to some of my greatest concerts. The venue is so electric. Outside, summertime, rock 'n' roll at its finest. But Alpine Valley is also known for its tragedy.

Due to its remote location, Alpine Valley was only accessible at the time by one single, solitary road. For all the fans and the bands. This makes it impossible to get there on time for the show if you have to wait in line with 25,000 other people, also headed to the same destination. The answer to this was to fly the bands, in helicopters, from the nearby hotel where we were staying to the backstage area of Alpine Valley. All of the bands did this. On the Bon Jovi tour, the day that I was picked up to fly, I couldn't believe that the pilot took it upon himself to give us a joyride in the air. Reckless and crazy, he was laughing and quite obviously star-struck from us being in the helicopter. Doing all he could to impress, zigzagging around, dipping in altitude, accelerating, decelerating, etcetera. At one point he came dangerously close to a set of power lines running up the side of the mountain. I was glad to get to the gig in one piece.

When I returned to New Jersey, about a month after that experience, I was driving around in my 1989 Camaro IROC listening to the radio. I pulled over the car, not believing the news I was hearing.

"Stevie Ray Vaughan has been killed in a helicopter crash, going to his concert at Alpine Valley in Wisconsin" said the DJ, choking on his words. I stopped the car and wept. Only three weeks before, I had been in the same helicopter, staying at the same hotel, playing the same stage that Stevie Ray Vaughan played that fateful night. It was only a simple twist of fate that it was Stevie Ray Vaughan who was tragically killed and not any of the other musicians who played the legendary venue.

The very first night of the Guns N' Roses/Skid Row tour held at Alpine Valley was a harbinger of things to come: magical, loud, crazy, violent, weird.

We went onstage just before the sun set. I was so skinny at the time due to my kung fu regimen that I had worked on prior to the tour, with Sifu Damian Cordisco back in New Jersey. How ironic that my kung fu instructor, who got me in shape throughout the Skid Row years, died recently of a heroin overdose. Makes no sense at all. But very few things do.

It was a glorious night for rock 'n' roll. The sun was shining down on me, in my brown leather pants, no shirt, the omnipresent Peter Pan boots kicking ass all over the stage. We were veritable hellions of heavy metal rock 'n' roll, at its apex, in our early twenties, in one of the biggest rock bands in the world. Opening for what was undoubtedly, at that moment in time, *the* biggest band in the world: Guns N' Roses.

I had an eight ball of potent, high-powered cocaine that night. When we were done with our set, I dug in and the party was on. Duff McKagan invited me to sit under the stage next to his bass rig and watch the show from there. I crouched under the awning, and was actually sitting cross-legged, so the crowd wouldn't see me. I chopped up lines of coke, on a handheld mirror, as Duff would run over between songs to take snorts of blow off the mirror.

The crowd went wild.

I was guzzling Jack Daniel's. Duff was hammering Vodka and Cranberrys the whole show, while snorting blow at the same time. It was already becoming a crazy evening and we hadn't even got backstage yet.

All of a sudden some guy I don't know staggers up to me. He's obviously drunk, like everyone else. He crouches down, to my level, and leans into my face.

"Hey! Sebastian Bach!! Is that you?" the man slurs.

I go, "Yeah. What's happening??"

"Because you're a fucking *faggot*. You're a pretty-boy *faggot*!!!! You know that, right? Fag boy?"

And with that, as he uttered the words, spitting into my face at the same time, I stood up, cocked back my arm, and punched this motherfucker right in the face. As hard as I could.

I always chuckle when people think that they can come up to me and talk to me in this way. Maybe because I was sitting down, he didn't realize that I am in fact six foot four, as well as way drunker and higher than he was anyway. I had no idea who he was. He went flying, from the backstage area, straight onto the side of the stage. He was lying on his back as the security guard John Reese picked him up and took him out of harm's way. Out of *my* way.

I sat back down and chopped out some more lines.

Near the end of the show, the same security guards that hauled off this drunken dude picked me up, by the scruff of my neck. From the side of the stage, they took me off to a remote backstage room. One guard on each of my arms. I was saying, "What the fuck??" the whole time.

"What's going on?"

I could not understand why I was in trouble. After all, if some guy called me a pretty-boy faggot, it was my sworn rock 'n' roll duty to punch him in the nose. I should be receiving a round of applause, not being reprimanded. For this?

There was just one problem.

This guy wasn't just some dude.

The guy that I had punched, in the face, turned out to be Izzy Stradlin's *brother*.

Izzy Stradlin.

I had punched out *the guitar player for Guns N' Roses' brother,* on the *first night of our tour opening for Guns N' Roses.*

Not a good way to start the tour. Not exactly a wonderful way for an opening act to ingratiate themselves to the headliner.

I was in some seriously deep shit. Here I was, again, being held up to the wall by security guards. Much as I was on the Bon Jovi tour. Only that was at the end of the tour. This was the *first night.*

Izzy Stradlin entered the room. He was not happy. Followed by GNR manager Doug Goldstein, he addressed me as my arms were pinned to the wall. He had dark black shades on. It was about 1:00 in the morning.

"Sebastian. Why did you do that?"

"I didn't know it was your brother, dude. He called me a pretty-boy faggot. He was drunk off his ass." Then, unexpectedly, he shrugged and said, "I know."

Izzy didn't really say much more after that. Doug Goldstein did the talking.

"Well, we really know don't know what to do with you, Sebastian. You're a loose cannon. We can't have any more incidents like this, obviously."

Izzy kind of shuffled around the room. He looked like he had been through stuff like this before. He left.

"No more of this kind of shit, okay?" And then everybody split. I went back to my dressing room and chopped out some more lines.

The tour had just begun.

When the album *Slave to the Grind* was released, in June 1991, none of us could have been ready for the reception it received.

We were on the road with Guns N' Roses the day it happened. Since both bands had been out together for a month now, neither with a new record to promote, the demand for *any* new music from this tour was unprecedented. Guns N' Roses were so big they didn't need a new album to tour. We sold out Wembley Stadium, two nights. Nine Inch Nails opened the shows. We did multiple dates in the biggest arenas all over the planet. This was rock 'n' roll on a bigger scale than we had ever seen.

Billboard magazine had recently announced plans to change their system of ranking album sales. Before 1991, I was incredulous when I would hear my manager say things like, "Oh, we talked to Whitney Houston's manager this week. We're going to take number 20 on the Top 200, and they're going to take number 18." I am paraphrasing. But I did hear discussions, on Skid Row's first album, of

managers speaking with other managers, bartering chart positions. This is the way the record industry worked back then.

The new system was to be called *SoundScan*. We were putting out our second record the second week the system would be implemented. This was all brand new. *SoundScan* required a device to be installed, on every record store counter in the country, which would register each individual sale in America. For the first time in the music industry, this would be a *true* tally of what album sold the most that week in America. We were the guinea pigs. Nobody knew what was going to happen.

What happened was we sold over 100,000 copies of *Slave to the Grind* in the first week of release. Skid Row became the first hard rock band ever to debut at number one on the *Billboard* chart. Ours was the first record to debut at number one since Michael Jackson's *Bad*, four years previously, in 1987.

On the bus, going to play the Capital Centre, in Landover, Maryland. Masa Ito, the celebrated Japanese heavy metal journalist, was on the bus with us, covering the tour. I come into the front lounge. Masa goes, "Baz-U!" As they call me in Japan. "Guess what-are your album comes out to????" He can't contain his excitement, even through his broken English. "Number-o ONE!!! HAHAHA-HAHAHA!!!!" I go, "What? Number One *what*?" "You are-eh Number ONE!!! Yeah!!" Masa repeated, many times. I could not believe what he was saying.

To say this was a feat, to say this was unexpected, would be severely understating the case. Quite simply, no one on the planet Earth ever expected Skid Row to ever have a number-one album. Except, possibly, Ahmet Ertegun. I was at Atlantic Records' office a week or so before the record came out. Ahmet said, "Well, Sebastian. It sure looks like we're going to sell a lot of records. At the beginning, anyway." A backhanded compliment, but he was right. We were at number one for all of one week. Like N.W.A. was, for one week before us. But, we had defeated the sophomore jinx. No one could mess with us now.

For the album cover, we asked my father to do the art. This was very kind of Rachel and Snake. For them to realize Dad's talent, and to have him do art for the band, was very cool and something that meant a lot to my whole family.

He modeled an image after a Caravaggio painting, and the result was a three-panel foldout CD package designed by Bob Defrin. Especially with the now defunct long-box format, it looked quite unique next to other CD artwork on the shelf. On the day it came out, I was in a record store somewhere in Middle America.

The people in front of me all had copies of *Slave*. I was standing right behind them in line. I smiled, and looked over their shoulders. "Hey, that's a good one!" It felt amazing to be there and see people holding my dad's art, with a CD of our band. This is something I will never forget.

After Masa Ito told me that we had the number-one album in America, the bus pulled into the parking lot. I ran into the Cap Center for sound check. Excited beyond belief. There was my buddy Duff McKagan on the stage. I ran up to him.

"Guess where our album came out!!!!!"

"Where is that, Baz?"

"Number ONE!!" Duff was visibly shaken. He stopped playing the bass, and put his hand up to his chin, looked at me, and raised his eyebrow.

"You debuted at number one?? On the *Billboard* chart?" He spoke for the whole world. It was the surprise of the year.

When my father passed away, in 2002, on his deathbed, I held him.

"Dad. We had a *Number One Album*!!!!" In his opiate-induced haze, he burst into tears and held me close. These words made a dying man laugh with joy. We smiled through the tears. It was one of the pinnacles of my life, and my father's life. He knew that his art would live on, forever, on the cover of that record. What a feeling. To die with. Perhaps, even a sense of immortality.

What beauty art and music can bring to this world.

I thank the Skid Row fans, and rock 'n' roll in general, for making this happen in our lives.

Wine, Women, Song, and Duct Tape

Your basic stadium backstage. Always real consistent. Shower stalls. Where the football teams live. Where the hockey players change their gear. Gray, concrete, sterile environment with shower rooms designed for full football teams. Not a plush, extravagant rock-star entourage. This is why most bands lug around drapes, and lighting, and other *creature comforts* to transform the drab walls into something more appropriate for a backstage party.

Backstage at one show, our guitar player Dave Sabo and myself decided it would be a good idea to drop some acid. Now, in the late '80s and early '90s, this was not a usual occurrence. I never ever saw Dave, Rachel, or Scotti even touch coke. So when Dave and I decided to do some acid, it was a very unique circumstance. And a very unique situation in which we soon found ourselves.

The party continued into the other band's dressing room. I remember being very, very high and laughing a lot. All of a sudden a girl came into the room in high stiletto heels. I don't remember who, but somebody said the immortal line: "Let's wrap her in duct tape!"

It sounded like a good idea at the time.

One of the road crew members proceeded to procure a roll of silver duct tape and a roll of black duct tape. Two substances that are never far from reach in the midst of any rock 'n' roll concert tour. Duct tape has many uses. We were just about to discover how versatile duct tape can really be.

We proceeded to apply the duct tape.

We kept on partying, laughing, drinking, smoking, snorting, doing whatever the fuck we wanted to. We were rock stars playing stadiums with a girl wrapped in duct tape teetering around in stiletto-heeled boots with her naked ass and tits in our face. As we enjoyed exchanging regalia of the tour, and the night's show.

Somehow, we moved the party from the backstage greeting area into the shower stalls themselves. Well, some of us did. Actually, it was me and the leader of the other band, the girl wrapped in duct tape, and some other guys standing around watching what was about to unfold.

Suddenly we tumbled down into the middle of the shower stall. I was on the bottom, on my back, with the girl on her front lying on top of me. Grinding and writhing around in the shower stall. All of a sudden the leader of the other band got on top of her. She was in the middle of us. The guy from the other band's face turned flush.

High on acid, seeing the walls of the shower appear to move in on the scene that was happening on the ground, with the girl wrapped in duct tape writhing on top of me with a guy from another band on top of her. It was fucking crazy.

The girl was perched back up onto her heels. Identity unknown. Not able to speak, or move. Stiletto heels remained on, throughout.

The next thing I remember is leading her back into the backstage room. Us going back to our drinking, smoking, and carousing. All of a sudden, management burst into the room and exclaimed, "What the fuck is going on in here??"

The leader of the other band exclaimed, "I know what to do!!!! *Let's shave her head!!*"

The room erupted into laughter.

Management said, "Absolutely *not*!! The party's over, boys!!" And with that, the girl was teeter-tottered out of the room. Never to be seen again. At least she left with the hair on her own head intact.

Just barely.

[[—st Louis
—eating pussy w matt
—chicks in Scandinavia
—too high to fuck in Germany
—stage diving in Germany, asked to sing Nuremberg

—too tired to be in November rain

—slash's house nude boxing

—smoking coke believe in me Wembley curses under door

—Ecstacy first time too much carried out of party too high

—Iceland getting in fight coming down from ecstasy fighting on Jack

—PANTERA TOUR

—SOUNDGARDEN]]

11

EVERYBODY IS MAD AT ME.
ALL OF THE TIME.

Seriously. Did you ever feel like that? That no matter how hard you try, no matter how good you try to be, somehow, sometimes . . . it just comes out . . . well, . . . bad.

So many instances of this.

One that comes to mind quickly is that nobody really understands what it truly takes for a singer to do what a singer does. To live up to people's expectations. To live up to my expectations of myself.

A typical day for me is this: I usually wake up and have interviews to do. I am lucky to do them. But those close to me sometimes can't believe that I sometimes spend four or five hours a day on the phone talking about myself. Answering the same questions over and over again, ad infinitum. The first day or so of this is like a novelty. But those closest to me often tire of listening to me waffle on and on about me me me, for hours on end. I want to hang out with those I love, and they want to spend time with me. Usually halfway through the interviews of the day, I get a look that says, "Are you done yet? Can we do something?" No, I am not. No, we can't.

After interviews, I like to go for a run. I have found through the course of trial and error that my body responds best to a seven-mile run. Five miles doesn't hurt enough. Eight miles is way too much. So seven it is. This usually takes me about an hour and twenty minutes. It takes me thirty minutes or so to get psyched to actually start the run. And about thirty to forty minutes after the run to recuperate. The more I run, literally, the better I look. People expect rock stars to be "ageless." We are not. I am supposed to look like the dude in the "18 and Life" video . . . for the rest of my life. The more I run, the more I look like that dude.

After the run, I get on the floor and do push-ups and sit-ups. I am no bodybuilder by any means. But I have a routine of 50 push-ups and about 200 sit-ups a day. If I have shows coming up in the schedule, I have to sing. For hours. Every day. Singing on my own in preparation for tour is a very methodical, somewhat boring exercise. I do a vocal scale called "Bel Canto" which is about thirty minutes long. After that, to get my counter tenor range working, I vocalize to Steve Perry of Journey. Lastly, to work the absolute top register of my voice, I sing to Rob Halford of Judas Priest. In order to get my voice really cranking, I have to sing properly for about an hour a day. To my neighbors in hotel rooms around the world, I must say . . . *this is my job. This is what I do.*

Many times I have held up reservations at the nicest restaurant in Madrid, Barcelona, Quito . . . because I have to hit the high note at the end of the live version of "Genocide" for the millionth time in my hotel room. Oftentimes we play in cities that are very exotic. Usually restaurants in Belgium, or Germany, or Sweden close no later than 9:00 p.m. I am always racing to finish my routine before there is no dinner left to be had in whatever city we are in. To my band and crew, I say . . .

Sorry, dudes!

People get mad at my sleep schedule. When your job is to be *firing on all cylinders* at 8:00 p.m. every night, after decades and decades, your body and circadian rhythm becomes acclimated to this. I am built and conditioned to kick ass every night at 8:00 p.m. When the show is done around 10:00 p.m., I am conditioned to party after the show and drive all night to the next town. Where we do it all over again. It's great work if you can get it. But what happens is when the tour is over, you go home. And then you are expected to wake up in the morning and go to sleep at night. Like a normal person. But the human body is not designed to work like that. I don't know about you, but I cannot just will myself to sleep. When I get home, my body doesn't know the difference between being at home or on the road. So I end up staying up all night, crashing about 4:00 a.m. in the morning, and sleeping till 11:00 a.m. or noon. This pisses people off.

My humblest of apologies.

I can remember one Christmas when my family came from Canada to New Jersey to celebrate the holidays with us. I had just gotten home from a European tour only days before. My mom and sister and brother were so excited to see me.

I was completely exhausted from the road. Wiped out. Destroyed. People have always told me I have "a lot of energy" on stage.

I leave it there.

Coming home from a European tour to Christmas with the family was pretty much fucked for me. Not only was I on show time, I was on European time. Which meant that I was all but useless when I got home to my family expecting me to play Santa. I can remember being completely comatose in my bed. Physically and mentally spent. Unable to move. Not capable of joining any "reindeer games" at this point in time. My sister Heather came into the room and said to me, very sweetly, "We just want you to know that we are really missing you." It was very nice. But I had no more energy to give. I wanted to. So very badly. But I just couldn't.

I am sorry.

I remember being asleep, with the water pipe next to my bed. My brother came into the room, trying not to wake me. I blew up at him.

"Get the fuck out of here! I'm tired! I'm sleeping! I can't believe you would wake me up!" What a dick. My brother, flustered, tries to back out of my room and be nice to me, apologizing and being totally cool. I, however, am a complete prick. To him, I say . . .

I'm sorry.

All of my life, I have done pretty much one thing. I am a singer. I do what I do well, because that is all I know. But the flip side of this is that I don't really know how to do normal, everyday things. That other people have to accomplish every day. Because I have never done many *normal* things. Put quite simply, I am good at doing hard things. Like making dreams come true. Envisioning concepts, and turning thoughts into reality. It's the easy things in life that are difficult for me.

Relationships. Family. Home. Sleep.

These are things that elude me.

When I went through divorce at the age of ten, I flipped a switch in my head. I swore on my life that I would never have a son or a daughter and leave them. I would not be capable of inflicting this pain and confusion on a child of my own. All through my teenage years, into my twenties and thirties, I held on to the pain I felt when I was ten watching my dad walk out the door. They say that there is no lead singer of a heavy metal band that does not come from a broken home. I think there must be some truth to this. When I sing with emotion, be it aggression, sadness, pain, or loss, it is not a contrived emotion you are hearing come from me. When I sing "I Remember You," and you feel it in your heart, that is because I am feeling it in my heart. I can cry very easily when I am singing a song. With a song like "18 and Life," "By Your Side," or "Wishin'," I record the song literally on the verge of tears. Then I take one step back from that emotionally naked place. Those are usually the takes that end up on the record.

I Like to Run

I am a tall guy. My friend John Rich described watching me run one time. He said it was like watching Bigfoot come out of the woods at you. Chewbacca is also someone I get mistaken for. Frequently.

The other day, I went on my normal run. I enjoy running because not only is it a great physical workout, but mentally it clears my head, and no doubt one of my addictions is the *runner's high*. The endorphins make it quite exhilarating and keep me coming back for more.

What a way to see the city. There is no better way to immerse yourself in the culture of wherever exotic locale you are in than hitting the pavement and getting right in the faces of the locals. Who have never seen anything up close quite like me.

I remember the first time I played in Beijing, China. 2005 I think. Played there with my solo band. Some people have the misconception that somehow all my greatest shows were done with my old band. This is simply not the case. As you get older, it becomes all the more precious and valuable to you. What, you ask? Pretty much everything. Time becomes more critical. Your days mean more to you. Your legacy becomes something you think about. Experiences you have when you are in your teens and early twenties tend to be taken for granted.

We headlined Beijing and to my shock and amazement, we sold out a 10,000-seat outdoor arena. The Chinese Military Police were in full force throughout the gig. As I looked from the stage into the seething crowd, I saw the Chinese Army troops in their jackboots marching in step through the crowd. None of the audience seemed to notice them. They were all standing on their feet, rocking out, having a great time. But the soldiers' presence implied that if the people had too good of a time, they would be brought back into line. Posthaste.

I will never take for granted the incredible places I get to go. Not just go to, but be treated like royalty from the people who brought us there, and gods by the fans who have been listening to us for years. To play in Beijing, to drink beer on the Great Wall of China, is something I could never do if I wasn't a rock singer. I was so completely stoked to put my kicks on and see what Beijing was really like. From the ground level.

I hit the sidewalks of China. Hot. Buildings are huge. Square. Not really tall and skinny, but short and fat. Like a little sumo wrestler.

I run as fast as I can through the streets of Beijing. No shirt. Headphones on. Cranking Phoebe Snow. Listening to "San Francisco Bay Blues," thinking back to being a little boy at my aunt Leslie's house in suburban Toronto. Hearing the same song on the streets of China all these years later is truly surreal.

As I stop on the sidewalk, at red lights, I am surrounded by the locals, who stare at me like I am from another planet. Which, in some ways, I guess I am.

I run further and further into the city, not knowing or caring where I am going. Just taking it all in. Feeling literally lucky to be alive. I reach an area of Beijing known as the Catacombs. The houses are all connected. The structures are all very, very short. I am very,

very tall. I notice that the people who dwell in The Catacombs are quite small in stature as well. When they see me, shirtless, long blond hair flowing down my back, covered in tattoos and sweat, wearing gigantic headphones running through the alleyways they call home, it truly becomes a freak show. Very old men and ladies come out to stare at me. The look on their faces is a mixture of wonder and apprehension. Mixed with fear. "Who or what is this crazy man running through our home?" I laugh. The elderly members of these communities are no taller than my waist. Some of them look to be in their eighties or nineties. I doubt they had ever seen a rocker dude running through the streets of their catacombs.

There is no better way to see the city. Runs like this one are something that I will never forget. I have run along the beaches of Lima, Peru, suburban streets of Zaragoza, Spain, Bondi Beach, Sydney, got lost in Hyde Park, Perth, Australia. The backwoods of rural Sweden and the sunny hot climes of Southern California are my personal outdoor treadmills. It makes you really feel like a part of the community where you are at. I can't think of a better way to see a place than be all over it.

Alas, as with anything, sometimes things do not go as planned.

Recently I was on my current run in Beverly Hills, California. In the back trails off Coldwater Canyon. Ho hum. Out doing my usual route, listening to Hatebreed or Alan O'Day or my new demos or whatever. I turn a corner on the trail. There, standing before me, is a woman and her little dachshund dog. Off leash. A little wiener. Here comes me. The big weiner.

The dog is startled. I run down the trail, towards the tiny pooch. He cranes his little doggy neck as far up as it will go. He gets one good look at me, turns, and bolts down the trail as fast as his little body will take him. The lady, surprised, looks at me with a quizzical expression. I keep on running, not sure what to do.

As I make my way down the trail, I turn and look back once

again. The dog is nowhere to be found. The lady is standing there. Alone. She is as unsure as to what to do as am I.

About an hour later, I make my way back down the trail. Feeling incredibly guilty. Looking for the little pup. That I scared away. Hoping he's okay. Wondering why, when I try to do my best, try to do the right thing, it can sometimes all go askew.

The lady is now in her car. By herself. I see her driving around the parking lot, looking earnestly for her dog. Eyes darting back and forth. Searching.

I keep on running. Head hung low. I look for the dog.

I am so very sorry.

I remember when my parents divorced, when I was ten years old. I used to go to California every summer to see my grandma. She was a big part of my life when I was a little boy. My dad had done a painting of my mom, about six feet long and four feet high. Grandma hung this painting, with pride, in her living room. I loved the painting. When I visited my grandma it felt like Mom and Dad were there with me. Looking at that painting seemed like a very real expression of love between my parents. The texture and strokes of his brush. I could see and feel my father pouring his heart and soul into the canvas. I imagined the look on my mom's face when it was done. What an awesome thing to do for the woman you love!

When I went to Grandma's after my parents broke up, to my shock and dismay, the painting was gone. I did not understand why. Yes, my parents had broken up; our family did not exist anymore; but it was still a cool painting. I didn't quite yet grasp the life changes that we were all going through. How could a ten-year-old?

I asked Grandma about this the very second I walked into the room. "How come you took down the painting of Mom? That Dad did?"

She looked uncomfortable. Her eyes shifted around the room. She appeared as if she did not know what to say.

I continued. "I know when parents get divorced, they're no longer together. But does that mean you divorce your whole family?" I remember this moment quite clearly. Not being quite sure of her response. I wanted Grandma to give me a hug. Tell me everything was okay. She was going to tell me, "*Of course not, Sebastian. Families are forever. We will never be apart. I will always be your grandma and I will always love your mom.*" I knew for sure this was what she was going to say to me.

I was not prepared for her answer.

"Well, Sebastian, that's *just what happens* sometimes."

I couldn't believe this was true. Not only was Dad leaving mom. Grandma was leaving Mom too.

I never saw the painting again in my life. I don't know if Grandma threw it in the garbage, gave it away, or sold it. If anyone reading this book knows where it is, I would certainly love to see it again someday. I'll bet Mom would, too.

My great grandparents on Mom's side were "rum runners." From Windsor to Detroit. They owned their own family bar. On my dad's side, our ancestors came from a town in Norway, called Elverum. When I play shows in Norway and ask the locals about Elverum (which was actually our family's last name centuries ago),

the Norwegians just look at each other with a knowing smile and tell me, "People from Elverum are *crazy!*"

My aunt Margaret, of Norwegian descent, was a piano player in World War II. She toured the world during the war and played music for our troops. Auntie Margaret lived to be ninety-seven years old. She drank alcohol every night at dinner, as I recall. She had a fun life.

I cannot exactly say the same about myself. Do I get into trouble every time I drink? No. But every time I get into trouble, am I drinking? Probably. Drinking was always fun when I was growing up. But, I guess I am one of those guys. There was a reason I got such good reviews on Broadway playing the dual role of Jekyll and Hyde.

We used to love our Jack Daniel's whiskey. Before Skid Row, I was always a Labatt's Blue beer kinda guy. That was my drink of choice. Like a good Canadian, I loved my beer. I used to joke around, "In Canada there are three pastimes: Hockey. Beer. And Rush." Funny, yes. Truthful, more so. When we made it big, Skid Row were marketed on the front page of *Billboard* magazine as "The New Bad Boys of Rock." I remember thinking, "*Wow, what a lame ad.*" But another part of me said, "*Well, it might be fun living up to this job description.*" We certainly gave it our best shot.

AA, or perhaps a doctor, will tell you, "All alcohol is the same. Alcohol is alcohol. It all does the same thing to you." But in my case, I have found this to not be quite so cut and dry. Beer does not do to me what wine does to me. Jägermeister, vodka, champagne . . . all of them give me a different, distinct buzz.

But no alcohol does to me what whiskey does.

If you met me when I was drinking whiskey . . . I'm sorry. You wouldn't like me if you met me drinking whiskey. I didn't like myself. My wife did not like me. My kids did not like me. My coworkers did not like me. Complete strangers really didn't like me.

I thought getting fucked up was part of the gig. All my heroes got fucked up. David Lee Roth, Mötley Crüe, Ozzy, The Stones . . . a bottle of Jack Daniel's was as prevalent on the posters adorning my teenage bedroom walls as was an electric guitar. Jack Daniel's and rock 'n' roll just seemed to go together. Like chocolate and peanut butter. Only different.

There are so many stories of me getting hammered on Jack Daniel's and making an ass of myself, I don't even know where to begin.

But I know where it ended.

Saturday Night Live 1991: Heavy Metal ABCs

Growing up in the 1970s, appearing on the show *Saturday Night Live* was a big deal. No, a huge deal. Next to Johnny Carson's *Tonight Show*, *Saturday Night Live* was the biggest variety television show of the decade. Perhaps of all time. Along with being on the cover of *Rolling Stone*, the childhood boy inside the man could never fathom me being on *SNL*. Even now, it is still a huge deal for any performer. But in the '70s, '80s, early '90s, playing with your band on *Saturday Night Live* was pretty much being on top of the world.

I have never sold a ticket to a show of mine and then drank alcohol before I sing. To me, this is a disgrace. The stage is sacrosanct. If you are charging money for people to hear you play music, in my mind the right thing to do, the only thing to do, is to give 100 percent of yourself. Leave it all up there. Blood, sweat, tears . . . give it all you got.

If you want to see a real disgrace? You should have hung out with me *after* the show, the night we played *Saturday Night Live*.

I wanted to perform better than I ever had before. I wanted to sing my best. I wanted to look my best. So, that meant no drinking beer all week before Saturday night. I wanted to be a lean, mean Bach 'n' Roll Machine.

Well, I certainly was lean. And thanks to the Jack, no one was meaner.

Jack Daniel's turns me violent. Beer made me silly, pass out early, and pee a lot. I always used to say, you don't drink beer, you rent it. Because you have to return it as soon as you get it. Wine makes me amorous. Like they say, drinking wine is like drinking love. It also makes my lips purple. And my teeth black. But I digress.

I was the mean drunk at the bar when I drank whiskey. The guy doing shots at the bar, looking at you from across the room. Who said, "Are you lookin' at me? What the fuck are you lookin' at? *You're looking at me!?!?* Fuck you!!"

"But I'm not looking at you, dude!"

"Fuck *yes* you are lookin' at me! What the fuck are you lookin' at?"

Oh yes, I was so tough. With my ex–NFL linebacker security guard standing next to me. Paid to punch whomever I deemed was "looking at me." Yes, I was *that* guy.

I can remember the exact instance described above happening after a show in Reykjavik, Iceland. Just drinking whiskey and looking for a fight. Good times.

I would wake up the next morning saying to myself, "*What is wrong with me?* That guy wasn't even looking at me. Why do I always want to get into a fight when I drink the Jack?"

Which brings me to the night of *SNL*. I set up the after-show party as a reward for not drinking beer all week. All week I told myself, over and over, "*When this is over I am going to get SO much more FUCKED UP than I EVER got. In my whole life.*" Which, at that point, was saying something.

When I set a goal, I usually achieve it. Tonight was no different.

The pressure of doing the show was enormous. It really was LIVE. From coast to coast, all across the USA, rocking out in everyone's living rooms. They would hear our big heavy metal sound at a quiet volume, coming through one single, solitary, tiny speaker on their TV set. Every note, every inflection, had to be note-perfect. This was before Pro Tools. This was before in-ear monitors. This was old school.

This was nerve-racking.

Flew Mom in from Canada to be part of the show. She was so proud. Kiefer Sutherland was the host that night. During rehearsals, Chris Rock was so hilarious. He was brand new to the show. In 1991, I didn't know who he was. We rehearsed on the set every day that week, leading up to the live broadcast on Saturday night. One day, Chris Rock is in front of the stage, rocking out, with his hilarious moves. I started laughing and came off the stage. "Skiiiiiiidddd Rooooowwwww!!!" Chris exclaimed, jumping up and down in front of my face. "Yeah dude!" I replied. "I loooooove me some SKID ROW!" Chris shouted. We laughed again.

I saw Chris years after that, on the street in Manhattan. He told me how he ran to the store and bought *Angel Down* the day it was released and how much he dug it. Whenever I have seen him, he always seems to know what is up with me and my career. He is a great guy and a true rocker.

Anyways, we kicked total ass on the show. Which wasn't without its fair share of drama.

We did a skit together with Adam Sandler and Kiefer Sutherland called Heavy Metal ABCs. It was written to be Adam playing Axl Rose, and Kiefer playing Slash. They have a duel of heavy metal ABCs in a kids' dream, and Rachel and I come into the dream and join the proceedings.

We certainly did have some fun after the show. *Reward time!*

We went to a local bar after the show. With Kiefer Sutherland, the whole cast of *SNL* (including an extremely inebriated Chris Farley—you can see us head-banging together in the closing credits of the show), my manager Scott McGhee, my wife, and my security guard Big Val. I would definitely need him later.

I started rewarding myself. Heavily. I was real good at rewarding myself. After a week of no drinkin', I started to hammer down the Jack. I remember sitting at a table with Kiefer, my wife, and Scott our manager, and doing shot after shot of whiskey with anyone and everyone. Weeks later, Scott told me that Kiefer contacted him and said, "Wow, your boy was really fucked up that night." Ummmm, yes. That would be correct.

I don't remember much after that.

I have not touched a drop of Jack Daniel's since that night.

My Voice Has a Life All Its Own

My voice has always had a life of its own. In fact, my voice has given me a life of my own. Without my singing voice, I cannot imagine what I would've become.

I was always the class clown in school, until people heard me sing. Then they treated me seriously. With a modicum of respect, even. It was so wondrous and joyous to me as a kid (and to this day, when I think about it) when all of a sudden I would have more friends than I ever would have had before I sang.

Sometimes my voice gets me noticed in the most random ways. Like going to Home Depot with my next-door neighbor Kevin McCallion, and standing in line at checkout. Hair tied back, base-ball hat on, the standard celebrity attempt at incognito. We have our items in hand, are ready to pay, chatting about something or another. An elderly lady, in line ahead of us, turned around and said to us, "Excuse me." I said, "Yes?" She says, "What do you do for living?" She was at least eighty years old. Not your typical Skid Row fan. I didn't know what to say. She said, "You're a singer, aren't you?" I replied, "Well, actually, I am!" She responded, "I knew it. I could tell by your speaking voice. I could tell by the way you speak that you're a singer." My neighbor and I looked at each other. How would this lady know such a thing?

Many times people have told me, "Hey, I thought it was you standing there. But when I heard you talk, then I *knew* it was you." I'll never get used to it.

I'll tell you another time that my voice definitely had a life of its own.

I am sitting here writing this at Le Montrose Suite Hotel in West Hollywood, California. I have some very vivid memories of staying at this place.

One time, I was staying on the ground floor of the building. In the corner room. Right on Hammond Street. I had the balcony suite, leading right out onto the sidewalk. Encased with bamboo and other lovely floral fauna, it was but a mere jump down a step or two to get onto my balcony from the street above. This was one of these nights.

My driver that day came into Le Montrose to have a great time. We were standing out on my balcony when we heard two girls walk down the street in front of us. They could not see us through the bamboo, and because we were down a couple of feet from the actual street itself. It was more like we were at ankle level. Or crotch level, to be more exact.

My driver and myself kept on smoking and drinking. Watching the girls walk down the street. All of a sudden, one of the girls exclaimed to the other, "I will never find true love!" We looked at each other and thought, this was funny. She kind of shouted it. Without missing a beat, I said something along the lines of, "Say it isn't so! Don't despair, fair maiden! True love SHALL prevail!"

As soon as I said that, the girls, who were halfway down the street by now, stopped. They looked at each other. Slowly, they turned around, and started walking back up the street. From where they came. Towards us, standing on our balcony. We looked at each other and said, "What the fuck?" I turned and looked at the girls again. When they got closer, they said, "Sebastian . . . is that you?" I had never met these girls in my life. They kept saying it again and again. "Sebastian, is that you? It sounds like you, Sebastian." I didn't understand. So I said, "Yeah, it's me." They came up to the balcony, where they could see me standing there. "We knew it was you by the sound of your speaking voice!" This was different than being at Home Depot. I said, "Right on! Cool!" In my drunken state, I motioned for the girls to jump down a couple steps. Into my room. Into my lair.

We talked about how crazy it was that they knew who I was by the sound of a couple of words spoken half a block away. We laughed and got into some drinks. As the night went on, we laughed a little more and had a couple more drinks. My driver had had enough and bid us good night. Which left me alone in a hotel room with these two girls, who I had met only an hour or so before.

One of the girls went back out onto the balcony.

She comes into the bedroom and . . . you know the rest.

When we are done, she stands up, rearranges her clothes, and goes out onto the balcony to rejoin her friend. I say good night and goodbye, as they hop back up onto the street above. And walk back down the street, strangers in the night. Where they were going in the first place. Before she uttered the words, "I'll never find true love." Well, maybe not true love. But she certainly found something resembling love on the way home that night. Just chalk it up to another thing that never would have happened, if I didn't have this voice!

Pantera

1985

The first time I ever heard of the band Pantera was in Madam X. We were playing Cardi's in Fort Worth, Texas. Or was it Savvy's? This was a club in which, yes, there was a chain-link fence separating the band from the crowd.

Godzilla came backstage. Excited as could be. "Oh my God! You're not gonna believe this!! Pantera is here!!"

Who the fuck is Pantera?

He then went on to explain to me how Pantera was one of the tightest, most hardworking, successful, and well-liked bands on the circuit we were on currently. Southern United States. Texas, Louisiana, etcetera. We were booked by the same agency, American Artists. We played the same clubs. I was seventeen years old, headlining shows in Texas. Tonight, Pantera is in front of the chain-link fence, watching the band.

1991

Coming off our first record, recording *Slave to the Grind*, we were out to rock 'n' roll as hard as we knew how. After the touring we had done in the last three years, most recently around the world with Guns N' Roses, we were now ready to headline arenas ourselves. This meant we wanted to take a real heavy band out with us as openers on the tour. Pantera would be that band.

I was over at Scotti's, the guitar player's house, writing songs one day.

"Hey Baz. You gotta check out this band. They're unbelievable." I was curious.

He dropped the needle on *Cowboys from Hell*. Immediately, I was stunned.

This was a completely new sound. Much as the world was not expecting *Appetite for Destruction* years earlier, none of us could foresee a ZZ Top meets Slayer meets Van Halen meets Rollins Band approach that these Texas wildmen hit us all with. I picked up the cover and realized that this was the same band Pantera that I had met back in Madam X at Savvy's. *Wow, good for them*, I thought. They were the best at what they set out to do.

Right then and there, I decided that I wanted Pantera to open the *Slave to the Grind* tour. I asked the other guys, and since Pantera were on ATCO, a subsidiary of Skid Row's label, Atlantic, we worked it out to go on tour together. We met Vinnie Paul at Starplex in Dallas on the Guns N' Roses tour. We told him we would love for his band to open the tour, kicking off in New Orleans on New Year's Eve 1991–92. After discussing our business proposition with Mr. Paul, he then left our backstage area, and proceeded to fall asleep in his own vomit in the parking lot of the Dallas Starplex.

This was gonna be one *hell* of a tour.

1992

I simply had never met anybody in my life that partied as hard as Pantera. Guns N' Roses liked to have a grand old time, but in a different sort of way. GNR were more high *class*. Models. High-priced drugs. Cocaine. Caviar. Expensive cars, presidential hotel suites, the MGM Grand plane on call. Bon Jovi liked to party their asses off as well, but would aim to be sober, together, during the show. We would do shots of ginseng before we went onstage with the guys in Bon Jovi. Whereas Pantera would line up forty shots of Crown Royal and Coke before they went out to perform. Going on the road with Pantera was like being on tour with Mike Tyson. An incredibly talented fighter. Who would think nothing of biting your ear off.

Pantera redefined heavy metal in the 1990s. When grunge came around, they defiantly thrust their middle finger in the face of everything popular, while continuing to make the heaviest metal albums imaginable. We spent months together on the road, taking them on their first arena tour of the United States and Canada. These were magical times. When the tour started, Pantera were all but unknown to the mainstream of North America. Their album *Cowboys from Hell* had been out for a while, but had yet to go Gold. They were out to support the *Vulgar Display of Power* record, which would be released about a month into *Tour Grind*. In Rex Brown's book, roadie Guy Sykes is quoted as saying, "We came out on stage and blew Skid Row away every single night." Well, that's not exactly accurate. If the question is "Which is a heavier band?" obviously Pantera would win that contest against pretty much any *band in the world*. You can't compare Mötley Crüe to Slayer. It's a different style.

Guy Sykes and Rex Brown miss the point. It was the side of Pantera that *allowed* them to tour with Skid Row, that helped the band to achieve their first dose of mainstream popularity. Any Pantera fan, or even any member of Pantera, will tell you that *Vulgar Display of Power* is the commercial and creative apex of the band. This album achieved its initial success with Skid Row fans. Every night we played to packed houses across North America. Guy Sykes should *thank* Skid Row.

The night Pantera found out the first-week position for *Vulgar* on the *Billboard* chart, we were in Vancouver, British Columbia, playing the PNE Coliseum. Tommy Lee was backstage that night. Pantera was shaving his head. For the first time since the late '70s, the drummer for glam metal titans Mötley Crüe would have *short hair*. Phil Anselmo and Pantera would do the honors. It is a significant moment in metal. The passing of the bald torch. Tommy, all excited, came out of their backstage room with a mohawk. It was crazy.

Phil Anselmo was hilarious that night. When he found out they debuted at number 44 on the Top 200, he freaked out. It was a very high chart position for such a brutal album.

"Hey BIERK!" That was Pantera's name for me. They always called me by my real last name. They said calling me *Sebastian Bach* was just *too much*, for some reason. My dad absolutely loved that about the band. "Hey *Bierk*!!" Dad would hear through the concert halls. "Who is calling you *that*?!?!?!" Dad was the biggest Pantera fan of them all.

"Here's the deal. You seen the latest *Billboard* chart???? Okay then. I need roast beef every night. Bing cherry sauce. More booze. More

weed. I need a couch, curtain, and a disco ball. What have you." We both started to laugh. He was very funny. Whereas the rest of the guys in Skid Row would not ride the bus with me anymore, Phil was the one who would jump on the bus and party with me going to the next town. We are the exact same age. I think that had something to do with how good we got along.

I must admit that following Pantera some nights onstage was a gigantic bummer. When they got going into their unique, heavy groove, they were like a machine. Add this to the internal band fighting starting to happen in Skid Row, and some nights ended up being not so much fun. They were together in every way. Whether we knew it at the time or not, we were in the initial stages of falling apart.

This tour was nothing like those with Aerosmith, Bon Jovi, or Mötley Crüe. This was a more extreme environment. We continued to be serious drinkers. There was lots of cocaine around as well. I should say that I never once ever saw Snake or Rachel or Scotti do cocaine. But there was lots around, with the extreme metal fans that were coming to this particular tour.

One line in particular stands out. I had already begun to realize that, in fact, cocaine sucks. I truly hate cocaine today. The way it makes you feel is awful. Hanging out with people that are doing it, when you are not, is excruciating. They chew their lips. Eat their face. They stink. The cocaine sweats are so horrible to endure. *Coke farts* are the most lethal and deadly of their kind in the world.

Beware the Satanic Death Metal Telemarketer

We were playing Pine Knob Music Theatre in Detroit. That day, one of my old telemarketer friends from the Madam X days was wandering around backstage. This guy was a serious death metal fan. Long black hair. Sunken eyes. And a necklace of a pentagram dangling below his Satanic face. He looked evil. And that day he brought some evil with him. In his pocket.

It was a hot, sweaty summertime rock concert. Outdoors. Humid. In the thick of the Detroit summer. We did our usual high-octane set, and I ran off the stage shirtless, dripping in sweat. There was the Satanic Death Metal Telemarketer waiting for me. With a line of blow chopped out literally the size of my forearm. Well, at least it looked like blow. Could have been speed. Could have been Ajax. At that sweaty moment in time, I didn't really give a shit. It was one continuous line of what I thought was coke, from one end of the bench to the other. Sports teams would use this surface to lace up their skates, put on shin guards, etcetera. We were utilizing this service for rock 'n' roll means.

Huffing and puffing from the two-hour show, my heart was beating as quick as it could go anyhow. From adrenaline. From music. From the sheer aerobics of running around on the stage and screaming. My heart could not possibly take what it was about to.

I bent over with a rolled-up hundred-dollar bill and started vacuuming up the line with my nose. I don't think I was ever really a cocaine addict. But I did like the way it smelled.

I got to the end of the line in more ways than one. The blow hit me. Maybe it was cut with speed. I didn't even bother to ask. I couldn't, because I was now blacking out. All I knew was that my blood was rushing to my heart and everything was starting to slow down. I backed up and hit the wall. And then slumped to my knees. Before I knew it, I was on my back on the floor of the dressing room. Clutching my chest. Fearing for my life.

Time started to slow down. I started to see things in a vignette. The center of my vision was lit, but the perimeter darkened out. Surely this cannot be a good sign. Then, the Satanic Black Metal Death Telemarketer leaned into my face, and started to laugh. More like a guffaw. In slow motion.

"Ha . . . ha . . . ha ha ha haaaaaaaa!!!!!!!"

The pentagram dangling from his neck weaved back and forth in front of my eyes. The laughter coming from the evil telemarketer . . . was like a distorted . . . slow . . . monstrous sound. Laughing, at my impending death, surely.

It was at this moment Phil Anselmo came backstage to say hi. Lying on the floor, I could not speak. I could not breathe. He asked me some sort of question and I tried to tell him I needed help. I can't remember much after that.

About a week later, the whole band had to take physicals, for our upcoming tour of Japan. This was required for insurance purposes. The doctor told me.

"Hey, you realize you have a heart murmur, right?"

"What are you talking about?" He told me that my heart had an irregular pattern. This was the first time in my life any doctor had ever told me such a thing.

I knew exactly what line of cocaine caused that to occur.

It took about five years of going to the doctors, to have him tell me that my heart had returned to normal. The murmur took that long to correct itself. Thank God I am here to tell you it did. The moral of the story? Cocaine sucks!

I tell this to you, dear reader: that shit is horrible. What an awful drug to do. It doesn't even make you feel good after doing it for a while. I think if you're going to party, all you really need is weed and wine. Anything else turns you into a Satanic Death Metal Telemarketer. Let this be a cautionary tale.

I began to feel alienated from the rest of my band on my own bus. Usually it was me, Big Val Bichekas, sometimes with Phil from the opening band. One night we were on our way to the hotel in Philadelphia when our driver got a call on his cell phone, which were a brand-new thing at the time.

"Oh my God, we can't go to the hotel. Everybody's been kicked out."

"What the fuck?"

Apparently Dave the Snake and Dimebag had done acid together. Upon checking into the hotel, Dime pulled out a knife and proceeded to slice up the couch in the foyer of the building. Resulting in both bands and crew being forced to seek out new lodgings that night.

What the Fuck's a Shortfall?

At the end of the *Tour Grind*, we all had a meeting at the McGhees' office at 240 Central Park South in Manhattan. We were totally stoked to be home; now it was time to wallow in the riches of our latest world tour. Surely we were all rich beyond our wildest dreams, and would be able to live the rock-star life to the fullest, after all of this success. Instead, that day we all learned a brand-new word.

That word was *shortfall*.

It turned out that instead of each receiving a giant check, each one of us would receive a *bill* for the year-long *Slave to the Grind* tour. How could this possibly be, dear reader? We were just as confused as you are.

As Scott McGhee dunked his Nerf basketball through a hoop affixed to the back of the office door, it was explained to us that our pyro was one of the reasons for this new word we had just learned: *shortfall*.

"You guys want to be like KISS?? Well, each time you blow up one of those bombs, it's three G's." Not the Verizon Wireless kind.

This was also the day we learned the difference between *net* and *gross*. How it was possible for us to sell out a 6,000-seat arena and not make any money. Management and accountants, received commission off the *gross* of the tour. Meaning that if we blew up too many bombs, drank too much booze backstage, all of that fun stuff would be paid for after we paid the management and accountants. We would pay to play if we didn't watch the budget. We thought we had people watching the budget for us. Once again, we found out that we really had no one watching out for us. Not even ourselves.

12

JUST JOKIN':
END OF THE ROW

Mid-1990s
Westchester, New York, USA

Ace was always my favorite.

Out of all the members of KISS, I gravitated toward Ace. The Spaceman. Maybe he had a gravitational pull. From the Planet Jendell, there was something so cool about him. I think of the cover of *Love Gun*. The painting, arms folded, an orbital, all-knowing, all-seeing, alien smile upon his face. Willing and nubile young denizens sprawled amongst his silver stacked heels. His guitar solos touched me so very deeply. On his solo record there is a song called "What's On Your Mind?"

> *I can't express the words to tell you about the feelings I got*
> *locked up inside*
> *If only you would give me a reason why you're so uptight*
> *What's on your mind?*

Dear "Dreamsville",
I would just be thrilled to have a KISS color pin-up autographed by Paul, Gene, Peter, and Ace, The 1st issue of KISS magazine (by Marvel Comics), and last, but certainly not the least, any "KISS album.

Sebastian Bierk,
RR2 Cavan
Bests Pond
Ontario Canada

There is a lead guitar section that he plays along to these words, on the outro of the song, that is so beautiful to me. Ace Frehley's solo album quite literally kicks the shit out of all the other KISS solo albums. I just bought all of them on Pono and the quality of the songwriting, production, playing, and energy makes it quite evident how talented Ace is.

Imagine how honored I was to be invited by the Ace himself to write songs with him, at his house in Connecticut. When I first went there it was like another time-travel, space-continuum kind of deal. I told Jeanette, Ace's wife, that when I was a kid in Canada I would dream about going to Connecticut and sitting in the bushes, looking out at his house, to see if I could see Ace walking around the yard or something. Jeanette told me that if I would've actually done that, they would have invited me to come on in and hang out. Mind-blowing stuff. Here I was with my hero. About to write songs with him?!?! How could this be real????

I had hired Richie Scarlet, Ace's rhythm guitar player, for my solo band. Along with Richie and Anton Fig (the legendary drummer of KISS's *Dynasty*, *Unmasked*, and more importantly Ace's incredible first solo album), we all went up to Ace's to put some songs together. Describing Ace's house always gets a laugh. I knocked on the door, and it took about forty-five minutes to get an answer. After repeated calls on my cell phone, trying to make sure I was at the right house, Jeanette, Ace's wife after all these years, answered the door in stack-heeled sky-high platform boots. This was in the mid-'90s. With a laugh, she welcomed me inside.

Immaculate, nice and normal on the upper levels of the house, on one wall was the KISS Monopoly Game from the 1970s that was famously presented to Bill Aucoin and all four band members only. But then, when one went into the basement, it was like some sort of crazy fucked-up drug-crazed man-cave. Knee-high in debris. *Expensive* debris. Laptops. VCRs. Computer cables. Videotapes, records, turntables, just all kinds of musician-computer-spaceman–related ephemera that you literally could not walk through without kicking a laptop, or moving a VCR off the couch. Wading through spaghetti rolls of wires, cables, busted-up CDs, shrink-wrapped copies of *KISS Alive II*.

Ace said, "Hey *bubbe*." This was an old slang word for *buddy* that he called me, and a lot of other people. None of us had any idea what it meant. "You wanna watch a video?" he intoned in his Curly-meets-Shemp Three Stooges voice. I said, "Sure." He walked over to the other side of the room, and there was a television set with RCA cables that were no more then three inches long. Ace had a VCR plugged into these RCA cables, which meant the VCR itself was dangling in midair. I had never seen this before. I said that if he used some of the longer RCA cables that we were kicking out of the way underfoot, he could put the VCR down on a shelf, or on top of the television set itself, perhaps. He goes, "Fuck that!," grabs a porno tape, and puts it in vertically underneath the VCR. There were other things, amongst the debris, that were for the *big kids only*, if you know what I mean. I laughed as we did a couple of lines of coke and watched porn.

I couldn't believe Ace had asked me to his house to write music. Skid Row had invited Ace to jam with us the first time we ever played the Meadowlands Arena, in 1989, opening for Bon Jovi. He got onstage in front of 20,000 people, as we did "Cold Gin." It may have been the first time Ace had been on an arena stage in quite a while. He was our hero. We were tripping over ourselves to jam with him. We had become great friends in the Skid Row years, and even before, when I had first met Ace in 1987 at Rock 'N Roll Heaven in Toronto. When he was playing near me in his solo band, I would always go to his shows and hang out. Still, that was nothing compared to creating new music together with my childhood hero. To collaborate with the guy I had stared at on my wall when my family was breaking up. The guy who threw me his cup from the stage at Maple Leaf Gardens in 1979 while I was perched upon my father's back for the last time. The guy I put all my hopes and dreams into. This was going to be the pinnacle of my career, of my life, for sure.

I went around the house and got all my song ideas together. My microcassette recorder that I hummed songs into. My notebook full of ideas, lyrics, titles, verses, etcetera. I began to specifically think of Ace himself, writing an album, and I started putting more ideas together that I thought would be great for the Ace. Inner Space/Outer Self. My cousin Kevin was in town. We loaded up the car and went up the turnpike to Connecticut. I jammed on the ideas on my cassette recorder the whole way up there. We were so excited! Here we were, two card-carrying members of the KISS

Army of the '70s, going to Ace Frehley's house. This was a fairy-tale dream come true.

A *rock 'n' roll* fairy tale, that is.

We kicked the computers out of the way and began to rock. I guess in the lore of ancient *KISStory*, this should be called the *ACE-ment*. Anton Fig in one corner, me in another, Richie on bass guitar over there. Ace, although we were huddled together in a wood-paneled, suburban basement, had a full arena-sized Marshall Stack setup, at pretty much full volume. Although it could've been on one, with the proximity I had to it, it was completely deafening.

The Ace was ready to rock. "Sebastian! What do you want to do?" With this, he played a sequence of two chords, which happened to sound a lot like the first chords of the Mötley Crüe song "Shout at the Devil." Richie and I looked at each other. "What else do you got?" He played the exact same sequence, only now the very last chord was different. It went one chord higher. Which happened to be . . . ummmmm . . . the exact second two chords of "Shout at the Devil," if I wasn't mistaken. "Is that it?" Ace goes. "What would you sing over that?"

I wanted to say, *"Shout at the Devil?"*

But instead, I closed my eyes and went to the microphone. Pressed record on my microcassette and put my voice into Ace mode. More specifically, the first Ace Frehley solo record. Released in 1978, I bought it the day it came out. Went to *Artspace*, with the biggest speaker in the whole city. Dad let me play the record through the full system as I lay down on my back. From the opening crack of the snare drum into the first riff, this was the heaviest album I ever heard. Anton Fig's monstrous drum fills.

> *Rip it out*
> *Take my heart*
> *You wanted it from the start*

Some of the heaviest music of all time. I closed my eyes and imagined that.

I started singing a melody line over the three chords he had. I let the melody flow out for the vocal in the verse of the song. Ace and everybody in the room loved it. We had nowhere else to go, musically, in the song. The three chords he had lasted all of about six seconds. But he liked what I was singing, so we worked on it. "What do we do after that?" We looked around the room. Ace goes, "I got nothing, Bubbe." We all start to laugh. It was funny.

This was gonna be a pretty short song.

"What do you think?" We jammed on what we had. Again, I thought back to the album *Slave to the Grind*. When I wrote the riff for the title track of that album, I was just looking for something fast. What this song needed was something sleazy and cool for the chorus. I tried to feel what would fit.

Back in Skid Row, in Rachel's parents' garage in Toms River, we used to talk about the early KISS albums and how they would go *Pa-whooooom!!!* Ace, Gene, and Paul would run their fingers from one end of the guitar neck, low on the frets, up to the high part of the neck, as a bridge to another section in the song. We thought this was so cool, to the point where we would try and put as many *Pa-whooooooms* into Skid Row songs as possible. We were also *very* fond of what could quite possibly be the coolest instrument in the world, the Cowbell. Yes, I capitalized that.

Right after the verse, I hummed out the guitar riff I heard in my head. To everybody in the room. I sang it to Richie and Ace. "Hey Anton! Try this!!" I hummed the riff again. Anton played a beat, then I suggested he slow it down and put the almighty cowbell behind the snare beat in the chorus. This was very much like the song "Creepshow" on Skid Row's *Slave to the Grind*. We now had that kind of sleazy vibe, on that record, that I was trying to inject into this Ace song.

I hummed the whole chorus's main guitar riff to Ace, very specifically. It contains a chugging section that Ace first played with *up-and-down* strokes on the strings. I explained that the riff needed to have all *down* strokes on the chugging part, to give it the aggression it needed. Like Johnny Ramone of the Ramones.

Once Ace and Richie did the down strokes together, the song had a machine gun–sounding style. With the cowbell part behind the beat, it was really badass and sleazy. Once we had the music down, Ace pulled out this incredible book, full of lyrics and ideas, all in his inimitable handwriting style, that he had since the '60s. We sat on the couch, did blow, and went through the book. Stopped on a page of lyrics with the title at the top, "You Make It Hard for Me." We laughed. That was the best title we saw, so we called the song "You Make It Hard for Me."

> *You make it so hard*
> *To see*

Not the best lyrics. But we came up with the tune, right there and then, and it really was badass. I recorded it on my microcassette, and Kevin, my cousin, Richie, Anton, Ace, and myself were all very stoked. We wrote other songs as well. But "You Make It Hard for Me" was the one we all really dug.

I could not have been happier. To make a kick-ass song with my ultimate guitar fantasy hero, in his house??? With my friends, and my cousin even, all right there with me??? This was a night I would never forget.

There was something else there that evening. The most cocaine I ever saw in my life.

After the session, sitting on the couch amongst the debris, Ace says, "Hey. You want some of this?" Underneath the coffee table, in front of us, he pulled out a large mirror already filled with cut lines of coke. We inhaled the flake and enjoyed the new song on tape. About an hour and a half later, I find Ace in the other room, next to the VCR dangling from the TV set. He had a clear plastic bowl-like kind of thing. With a rotating crankshaft grinder on the top. I had never seen something like this before. Was it for cooking? I queried. Not really.

Ace cranked the shaft, around and around, as we both grinded our lips. Then I saw what was inside. Giant rocks of coke, the size of softballs. The lever, on top, attached to a circular blade, which ground the coke into powder. Ace, chewing his teeth, as I was, in anticipation of the outcome. The sun would be up in a bit. Here we were, in the basement, turning boulders of cocaine into pure powder.

This was my dream come true. This was what it was like to really make it.

One time, I recorded in the studio with Ace, in the city, in an extreme snowstorm. A classic winter nor'easter, the drive from New Jersey to Manhattan and back would not be easy.

"Ace, are you sure we're gonna do this?" I gulped over the phone. It was around Christmas time.

"Of COURSE we are doing this, Bubbe!! It's time to ROCK!!"

"But it says on the radio that the highways are going to be shut down. They are saying to keep off the roads!! Are you sure we can't do this tomorrow? Or another time?"

"No, we gotta do it tonight. The studio is booked. I already got a car set up. I'll see you in there!"

"Okay," I stammered.

My car at the time was a silver-blue Jaguar XJS. Which was about as heavy as a skateboard. An extremely light vehicle, the Jag was *not* made for snow or the icy conditions the nor'easter was dumping upon the whole eastern seaboard on this day. But, the studio was booked. I said *Fuck it, this is the Ace-man. This is my hero. I would do anything for this dude. Would I die for him? For rock 'n' roll? Umm, I guess!* What a great last memory. Dying for the Ace. *This was everything.*

I bit my lower lip and grit my teeth. Drove an hour or so up the parkway to Manhattan. The snow/sleet/rain on the way was ridiculous. But I was in a silver-blue Jag, going to rock 'n' roll. What else matters in life? Of course, nothing. Not even life, really.

I was glad I had made it to the studio in one piece. There was Richie, and a bunch of studio cats, along with the producer. Some tiny studio in the city. We had a bunch of beer, and weed, and almost as much snow as was on the streets outside.

This is *rock 'n' roll.*

As the nor'easter continued to dump on the city, we rocked and rolled and partied long into the night. When it time came to leave, in the wee hours of the morning, I looked out the window and was aghast at the conditions I saw. Facing my journey home. I told Ace, "Hey man. There's no way I can drive in this."

"What do you want to do, stay?"

"Yes. Just let me crash here in the studio. Till the roads clear. I want to stay here."

"You can't. The studio's going to close. We all gotta go." And that was that.

Oh my God. But, what's the worst that could happen? I was a good driver. Even though I was drunk and high, I had to make the trip home. No matter what. I had no choice.

The next hours are among the most scary I can recall in my whole life.

I steered the Jaguar, through the snow, so high on coke, I was like one of those guys on steroids who tries to bend the steering wheel. I white-knuckled it to the point (or so I thought) that my fists were going to break. I clenched my jaw, and chewed my lips to the point of injury. I was by myself. The snow was pummeling the northeast relentlessly. I drove through the city wanting to die. Maybe tonight, I would get my wish.

As I exit the Lincoln Tunnel, already in the car at least an hour, I realize the great mistake I have made. In my twenty years of liv-

ing outside of New York City, this is the only time I can remember where only one lane on the Garden State Parkway was open. The snow was piled up as high as it could go, on either side of the one open lane. The only other time in my life I have ever seen snow like this, was on tour in Fairbanks, Alaska. In the distance, all you could see was the grim flashing light of the snowplow. There were no cars to be seen hardly anywhere in any direction. Except for the idiot high on blow, and drunk in a silver Jag with no snow tires. That idiot was me.

I fixated my eyes upon the one, endless, snowy lane, and began to cry. I remembered in my coke-induced haze, that if you stay below 55 mph, your tires will not spin out of control on the black ice, and you should be okay. So, let's do that. I kept my car under 55 mph for the whole drive. This was a long drive. From Manhattan to Red Bank, New Jersey, is about forty-five minutes with no traffic . . . doing 70 mph. Or 75 mph. Driving 55 mph, in the snow, would take excruciating *hours*. Which it did. I cried the whole way, with my heart jumping out of my chest. *This is the last time I will ever do something like this,* I swore to Christ, as an exchange for me possibly getting home.

The drive was pure torture. But somehow, I made it close to home. I couldn't believe it. I had the windshield wipers cranking the snow out of the way. I have been on the road for hours. Out of my mind. Barely seeing a car. But, somehow I was approaching my exit. This is looking good. I was going to make it. I was going to rock 'n' roll with Ace Frehley, and live to tell the tale. Or so I thought.

As I saw the first sign for my exit, about two miles away, I burst into peals of rapture and joy. My tears turned into laughter. I felt like I cheated death that night. I looked at my speedometer. I was going about 50 miles an hour. The vehicle was in control. I had done it, man!!!!! I had made it home high on coke *and* drunk on booze. Way to go, rock 'n' roll!!!!!

Dude, Where's My Car?

I saw the sign for my exit and said, *fuck it*. I dared to press down on the gas. So excited that this nightmare was over. So excited to be home. The car went from 50 miles an hour, to a little under 60. I came down a hill, on the other side, in the one lane surrounded by snow. And then it happened.

What?

The back of my Jaguar started to sway. Gently, at first. From side to side.

swish

I actually didn't think it was a big deal at first. Only a couple blocks away from my house? There's no way I could've made it through hours of snow and slush only to crash within walking distance of my home. Or was there?

swish swish

I'll just slow down the car. Thinking, *that'll straighten it out. Easy peasy!*

swish swish swish

But it did not.

swish swish swish swish

Back-and-forth. Into a full 360 *loop*.

I was now doing 360s, one after the other, on the Garden State Parkway in the snow. I started going around and around, screaming, crushing the steering wheel, fearing for my life. This was it. For sure.

Luckily, there were no cars around me.

Smash!!!!

There is no sound like that of a silver-blue Jaguar, crumpling, into a heavy metal guardrail.

Crinkle

Like a chandelier dropping from a cathedral ceiling, a piece of silver tassel snapping on Christmas Day, *Pshhhhhhhhhhhhhhhttttttt* goes the ornate vehicle. I imagine the sound of a dump truck, in a collision, would be different than that of a Jaguar.

Luckily, by the grace of God, I hit a guardrail, which are not on the whole of the Garden State Parkway. This could've easily happened on another part of the road, where there was no guardrail. Where I could've gone spinning off the side, into the woods below. Instead, I smashed the front end of the Jag, somewhat like an accordion. But I was alive.

After the crash, the car was not moving. The engine was off. I looked up, and to my horror, I was now facing the *opposite* way on the Garden State Parkway. And, for the first time in the early morning, I can now see cars.

Which are headed right towards me.

I turn the key in the ignition. The car refuses to start. *Pitter-patter.* Nothing was happening. I turn the crank one more time. Then, all of a sudden, the car miraculously starts. With smoke bellowing from under the hood, I loop it around so I am pointing the right way on the parkway. I pressed the gas. I was moving. And crying. This really sucked.

I get to my driveway, somehow. The driveway, unplowed, had at least three feet of snow on it and was impossible to drive onto.

But I had had enough.

I cranked the car to the left, and went as fast as I could. Straight into the snow. Hoping I could move it, with the momentum of the destroyed Jaguar. No such luck. I hit the snowbank, and the poor car went off the side, into the woods below. Hit a tree. *Fuck this.*

What a long night. I got out of the car, and left it there, smoldering in the snowbank.

"Hey babe! I'm home!"

"Where's the car, honey?"

"Oh, it's out front, in the snow. I smashed it!"

My wife went out and looked into the front yard. There was the Jaguar. Wrecked. Smoking. Broken. In the snow. In the woods.

But, we have got a great song out of this. Me and The Ace. So, destroying my Jaguar really didn't matter to me. I got to make a song with my hero. And that's what I had always intended to do.

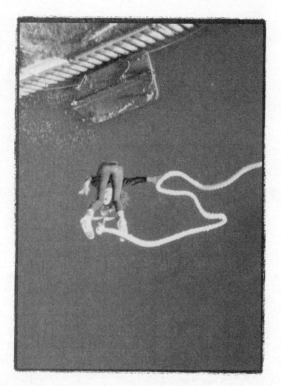

1993-1997

The time after my dismissal from Skid Row was fraught with disappointment. Sadness. Pain. An extreme sense of loss. An unbelievable amount of stress. For the future. For my family. Guilt. For letting down millions of fans. For letting down ourselves. I literally had no idea what to do when I got kicked out of the band that we had taken over the world with.

Nobody really understands why we broke up. Anyone you ask, band members included, gives a wildly different and always extremely vague account of what they think happened back in 1996. At the time of this writing, we're talking twenty years ago. Or should I say, not talking. It's all a bit hazy, talking about something that happened two decades ago. Events that happened that

long ago are all but meaningless today. I will try to explain it from my side as best as I can. It still makes no sense to me.

My whole frustration with the breakup of Skid Row really boils down to the fact of letting down all of our fans. All those who supported us. Who made our dreams come true. Who paid for our family's hospital bills, our children to go to school. Everything that the five members of Skid Row ever got was because of the fans. Nobody else. Letting them down is the ultimate dream *killer* of all. How can it be? A whole *generation* related to our music. "Hey! We were just joking!"? This will haunt me till the day I die.

Decades later, it's amazing to realize what success can do to people. In the case of Skid Row, our success tended to *isolate us* from each other. When we first started the band, I lived at Rachel's house. We were close friends for all those years. Sharing dinner together. Weddings. With our families. Dave "the Snake" is the godfather of my first child. It has to be said that, the first couple of years after the breakup, "the Snake" would continue to send his godson birthday cards. A very religious guy, Snake may or may not have been my best friend in the band. I was impressed that he would try and honor his role as godfather. After a couple years these cards stopped as well.

Any contact I have had with him since then has been merely by chance.

All of the friendship, and most of the good memories, pretty much are all based on the time before we made it. Once we all started making money, the first thing each of us did was buy a big huge house of our own. Although we were only twenty minutes or so from one another, we might as well have lived on opposite sides of the world. I hardly ever saw those guys after we all bought our own homes. *Before* we had success, we were undeniably best friends. Once we each got our own places, the walls of our homes became walls in between one another.

We came off the road. Took a couple months off. Then, missing my friends, I would want to hang out again. Calling them, wanting to write songs, get together, just to see each other. It rarely happened. I never understood why.

I guess I should've taken it as a sign, when on the *Slave to the Grind* tour with Pantera, that the band decided that I would have my own bus. With my security guard "Big Val" Bichekas, I spent much of the *Slave* tour alone, while the rest of the band hung out and whooped it up on their bus together. Phil Anselmo would ride with me sometimes, but for much of that tour, I was pretty much alone or riding with a couple crew members. Not my own band.

Although we were not getting along as good as we used to, we really did still enjoy making music together. After this latest tour ended in Australia in January 1993, it would be well over a year before we would even start to talk about making new music again.

We entered the studio in 1994 for what would be our last album, *sUBHUMAN rACE*. Recorded in Vancouver, with Bob Rock in the producer's chair and Randy Staub at the engineer's helm, there are some great songs on this record. Lauded with much frequency, and passion, by Eddie Trunk on *That Metal Show*, *sUBHUMAN rACE* remains a fan favorite. However, to my ears, although I do enjoy some of the songs on the record, it doesn't sound as "Skid Row" to me as it could have. A lot of the production and musical choices on this record sound more like decisions made by Bob Rock, not Skid Row. "My Enemy," "Beat Yourself Blind," and the ballad "Breakin' Down" I think are very good representations of the band. "Breakin' Down" ended up as the theme song to the Christopher Walken movie *The Prophecy*. I still perform this song live from time to time, to this day.

It was on the *sUBHUMAN rACE* 1995 sUBHUMAN bEINGS oN

tOUR where we noticed a decline in the popularity of the band. After an extremely successful tour of Europe and Japan, we even made it to Seoul, Korea, to play for the first time ever. By the time we got to Korea, we had spent three weeks touring just in Japan, an unusually long tour for any Western group. From Narita, we headed straight to Taipei, Taiwan, then to Bangkok, Thailand, and lastly our Headline Show in Seoul. We toured this area in the monsoon season. After all this time in the rain, I was being seriously seasonally affected by the gray skies and no sun for a month long in Asia. On the flight to Korea, I remember the airplane briefly breaking through the clouds in the sky. Like a man starving for water, I placed my face up against the window of the airplane. Felt the sun's rays hit my skin for the first time in a month. The vitamin D soaking into my skin felt like the most powerful drug I had ever taken. I longed to be sitting outside in the sun, somewhere, anywhere, instead of flying to yet another foreign country in the rain.

We landed the plane, got into the limo, and went straight to the ubiquitous *lonely hotel room in a foreign country* where none of us spoke the language.

God, I miss my family.

The morning after we get there, I am recuperating from the travel all day before, which we had spent totally drunk, flying, and then in the hotel lobby when we arrived. My sleep is so completely fucked from all the touring, by this time, that just *falling asleep*, in and of itself, is a miracle. It was on this tour where I first encountered problems sleeping. Mostly due to my father being diagnosed with leukemia and bone marrow cancer. I also could not deny another dying member of my family: Skid Row was on life support as much as anyone with a terminal diagnosis. No wonder I couldn't sleep.

Poor Sandy Rizzo at McGhee Entertainment. The Korea trip was her first on the road with us. Very few bands had played in Korea in 1995 and it was quite groundbreaking for the music industry

to make inroads into the Korean market. Doc McGhee sent Sandy over to coordinate the press and general overall proceedings.

After checking into the hotel room, I flick on the TV in an attempt to wind down. Of course there is no English television in Seoul, Korea, in 1995. The Internet was not available for the public. And no one had cell phones. Calling home, from a hotel room in Korea, to New Jersey, would cost thousands of dollars. So I sit, drink beer, and stare at the walls. Daydream of being on a beach somewhere.

Morning happens. No sleep at all.

Knock at the door. Sandy Rizzo from Management.

"Time to go to the press conference!"

There's only one problem.

I am so tired I cannot form a sentence.

I try to explain this to Sandy. From behind a closed hotel room door.

"But, Sandy! You don't understand! I haven't slept in days! I can't speak!!"

"Sebastian, you *have* to come. It will be a serious *loss of face* if you don't. They take this shit very seriously here in Korea!! We have to *save face*, go down to the lobby right now, and do the press conference."

"Okay. So should I go like this???"

I swing the door open.

Naked as the day I was born, I look at her, as if to emphasize my point.

"There is no FUCKING WAY I am going downstairs right now!! I am FUCKED UP!! I have no clothes on! I can't sleep!! I'm drunk!" Looking me up and down, in a state of shock, Sandy glances over her shoulder at the housekeeping staff and other hotel guests, who are straining to see what all the commotion was about. I back into my room. She has nothing more to say.

I slam the door. Crack open another Budweiser from the mini-bar. Suck it back. Finally, I go to sleep.

Sorry, Korea. Dennis Rodman I'm not.

Returning back to America, in 1995, it was quite evident to see. Heavy metal, or hard rock, whatever you want to call us, was no longer in fashion like it was on our previous tours. We attempted to headline the sUBHUMAN bEINGS oN tOUR in America, with disastrous results. Pulling into four-thousand-seat arenas, in the Midwest, to play for less than a thousand people. Something that no band ever wants to see happen.

We did have some great shows on this tour. The Palladium in Hollywood was a memorable show. But we all knew the truth. We were on the way down. Not on the way up. And that was hard to take.

All of this just made us more distant. When we went to play the Monsters of Rock Festival, in Brazil, in 1996, none of us knew that this was going to be our last-ever show. We had no idea. Just another show for us at the time, we were put on a bill with thrash metal bands, such as Motörhead, King Diamond, Biohazard, Anthrax, Mercyful Fate, and Iron Maiden. The extreme Brazilian metal crowd did not want to see Skid Row alongside these other, heavier bands. We went out and played to an abysmal reception in São Paulo, Brazil. Dodging rocks, spit, flying bottles of piss, this tour would be the last Skid Row would ever play.

We have never played again.

People ask me all the time, why we don't have a reunion? The press constantly writes about this. No one understands why we are not touring together, this summer, or right this very second. The real reason we are not together, in my mind, is publishing royalties. Publishing is where the real money is in music, and publishing royalties go to a song's writers. But when I was singing the first album, and rewriting the melodies to suit my vocal range, I did not realize that I should have been asking for co-writer credits on all these songs that would sell so many copies worldwide. I did not understand the monetary implications of getting my name on a song, as much as the other, older guys in the band. This is why it is always such a fight in the industry to get credit. At the time of recording my first Skid Row album, I was nineteen or twenty years old. Never in a million years could anyone foresee 10 million people buying the first Skid Row album. But, they did. My name is *not* on some of the songs where I, in fact, contributed greatly to the vocal melody of the song. On any given Skid Row song that goes up into the higher vocal register, there is one person who thinks of singing those notes. That person is Sebastian

Bach. You'll know what I mean when you listen to me sing these lines in "18 and Life":

Fingers to the bone

. . .

Child blew a child away

And these from "I Remember You":

Oh my darling, I love you

. . .

Through every endless day

I am not named as a writer on either of those songs (two of our biggest hits), but these screaming parts of the melodies are what many fans tell me they actually enjoy most. The other guys might disagree that I deserved an official writing credit because they wrote the original versions before I joined the band.

The final contact the five of us had involved the 1996 KISS Reunion. This was an incredible time for any KISS fan. The reunion of our favorite band!!!

Snake and I went to a bunch of the shows, including New York City, at Madison Square Garden. After one of those shows, Snake, myself, and our women went to a local bar. On the cab ride over, Snake and I got into quite the verbal brawl, which carried into the bar itself. I was pissed off that he wouldn't return my phone calls. We never hung out. We never rehearsed. We never wrote songs together anymore. I asked him why.

"What is taking so long?"

"Well, you don't have to write the songs!!!"

Incredulous, I reminded him that both the albums *Slave to the Grind* and *sUBHUMAN rACE* had no less than *five* songs, each album, that I had co-writes on. There was no reason to change things at this point. But it felt like these guys just would not let me into their club anymore. I still do not understand why some of them personally have a problem with me. I can't help but think there was jealousy over the attention I had received, and this is what ultimately came between us as people, and altered our friendships.

The thing that hurt was that I never asked for any more attention than the other guys. I never asked to be treated different than any of them. The individual attention I received was not of my own design. Fame is uncontrollable. You either have fame or you do not. It is impossible to control once you attain the level of fame Skid Row achieved.

Rachel had started a "side project," another band, featuring members of our road crew. Instead of recording and playing with Skid Row.

We were asked to open up the KISS Reunion show, on New Year's Eve 1996/1997, at the Meadowlands Arena in New Jersey. Our hometown jam. I couldn't believe that we had the chance to open up for my favorite band. In our hometown!! *On New Year's Eve!!*

Alas, this was not to be.

I was told that Rachel was "busy with his side project" and that this would make it *"impossible for Skid Row to play with KISS on New Year's Eve in New Jersey."*

I couldn't believe what I was hearing.

Are you fucking kidding me? Really?

Obviously, I freaked out. What the hell would you do?

I was then told that Rachel was so mad at me that this was merely "the last straw." Of what, I did not know.

Our fans loved us. I didn't see what was evidently going wrong. Everybody goes through life's ups and downs. Why should we be any different?

"Hi."

I called up Snake. As usual, got no answer. Although at this point I was completely used to nobody in the band accepting my calls, it still really pissed me off.

"I can't believe you would allow this to happen," I said to no one, talking into a machine that cannot speak back to me. My anger is building.

"This is complete BULLSHIT. How in the FUCK can we turn down opening up for KISS??? ON THE REUNION TOUR??? In New FUCKING JERSEY???"

I left a nasty message on his answering machine. What do these people expect? I voiced my extreme displeasure over the situation.

How could we as a band turn this down? Obviously we were not thinking of what was best for Skid Row, or the fans, in any way. I found this to be unacceptable.

After I left this message on Snake's phone, he called me back and left a message for me.

"Hey! Nice message you left on my phone. *You don't have a guitar player anymore.*" Since Snake and Rachel trademarked the name of the band only to the two of them, this meant I was no longer a member of Skid Row if they didn't want me to be.

This was Snake's way of kicking me out of the band.

Skid Row breaks up because KISS asks us to play a show? Be careful what you wish for.

Things were worse than ever.

What in the fuck am I gonna do now?

1997

Phone rings. It's Ace Frehley.

KISS has now reunited. It's the most incredible rock 'n' roll happening of the century. All Original Four Members. Full makeup. Costumes. Blood. The fire-spitting demons of rock, returning from decades of not rocking. For my buddy The Ace, this was so incredible. We were so happy for him. His solo career was cool, but there was *nothing* like reuniting the original KISS. It was so surreal to see. With their makeup on, putting all that on their faces, they were the definition of timeless. No band, no entertainer, could have ever been more timeless. All wrinkles, any signs of old age, were impossible to see under layers of clown paint, silver glitter, stars, and whiskers. It was crazy when they came back. Like being transported through time. For us fans, too.

It came to pass that the inevitable KISS reunion record would end up being titled *Psycho Circus*. The band headed up to Vancouver, to follow the lead of Bon Jovi, Aerosmith, Mötley Crüe, Metallica, and yes, even us goofs in Skid Row before them. They made the album with Bruce Fairbairn, the go-to producer in the go-to studio for hard rock hits. This would turn out to be one of Bruce's last-ever records.

Ring. "Sebastian!! It's The Ace!" I was excited to hear from him. It had been a while.

"Are you sitting down, man?????" I was now. "Okay, well, you know we've been working on the new KISS album."

Of course I knew that. I was as die-hard as they come.

"Well, we just got through playing all the songs for Bruce Fairbairn. And I got just one thing to tell you."

"What's that?"

"You're on the new KISS record!!!!!!!"

Excuse me?

Think I might have dropped the phone. This was incredible news, for sure. What was he talking about?

"We played all our demos for Bruce. Do you remember that song we wrote in my basement? 'You Make It Hard'? 'For Me'? Bruce loves it. It's going on the new KISS record." I couldn't believe my ears. Yes, it was a cool track. But to be on the KISS Reunion album? It was too insane to be possible. The last I had heard about the song was when I recorded with Anton Fig for his solo record. Anton said, "Hey Sebastian! Your song that you wrote with Ace? We recorded it!! And it's amazing!! Did you hear it??" No, I had never heard it. I did not even know it was being recorded.

As it turned out, the song never made the KISS record. Never happened. I got a story later on, from someone at Electric Lady Studios in New York City, that an engineer on the KISS record thought it was horrible, so it didn't make it. The title, from one of Ace's old books, was probably shown to Gene and Paul before. I guess they couldn't have liked it that much either. In any case, our song did not end up making the KISS reunion record. But Ace was right. It would, eventually, make it on to a record.

Just not now.

Under Attack:
"You Don't Have a Band Anymore"

1996–1997
New Jersey

When I was kicked out of Skid Row in December 1996, I was completely mystified as to what to do. For the first time in my life, I was not in a rock band. A Bass fish out of water.

That Christmas, we were out in the woods on the grounds of my New Jersey property. Mom and me and Aunt Leslie, in the snow collecting wood for the fire. Nobody could believe that I was no longer in the band.

To our Canadian sensibilities, it seemed unfathomable to reach such success, especially in the United States of America, only to turn around and dissolve everything we had fought so hard to achieve. Two thoughts occurred to me.

How in God's name could this have happened?

and:

What exactly in the fuck was I going to do now?

Around this time I got a call from Barbara Skydel, the talent agent who, along with Frank Barsalona at Premier Talent, signed Skid Row when we first started. I had been approached by some other agents to book me for shows. Barbara found out about this and called me, completely incensed.

"What is this shit I hear? You are working with other agents?" she admonished.

I myself was slightly confused by this. I had naïvely assumed that since I was no longer in Skid Row, then I would no longer be with Premier Talent, or William Morris Endeavor, which is what Premier eventually morphed into.

I was completely mistaken about my situation.

"You tell those other agents that you *already have a fucking agent!* I am your goddamn agent! Do you understand me?"

I was surprised by what she was telling me, at the same time being bemused, and very touched, by *how* she was telling me. In actual fact, when Skid Row kicked me out of the band, Premier Talent dropped Skid Row. While *keeping* me as a client. And they were not about to let me go.

Barbara Skydel was the best. She signed me when I was nineteen years old, and continued on as my agent up until the day she passed away. Guided me through Skid Row, Broadway, television, and now my solo career. She took me with her from Premier Talent to William Morris Endeavor, as well as working with my current manager, Rick Sales, in 2006. She never let me go. A true friend, as well as being hard as nails, Barbara was the sweetest lady you could ever want to know. We would talk all the time. She was almost like a family member. Her funeral was attended by the biggest luminaries in the music industry and I wouldn't have missed it for the world. A true rarity in the music business, Barbara Skydel stuck by my side her whole life. More than anyone else from when I first started to rock. She is sorely missed.

It was Barbara and her assistant, the amazing agent and friend Lachlan Buchanan, who approached me with a couple of offers for some solo gigs in the Northeast of America. I had no clue that it was possible for me to be in a solo band. But, at the same time, I also had no choice. I wasn't in the position to turn down work after getting booted out of Skid Row.

The money I was being offered for these initial solo shows was not great. It would have been impossible to do them if I would have had to give management commissions to the McGhees. I called Scott McGhee and asked him if he still wanted to manage me.

"No."

I had the distinct impression during that phone call that Scott McGhee sounded almost *glad* to be rid of me, and Skid Row as well for that matter. He had gone on to manage acts such as Liz Phair. His heavy metal background may have been embarrassing to him at this point of time in the music industry. Which made me happy. I would not have to give him a percentage of my solo career. I could now accept these gigs. So I did.

I agreed to do some solo shows for the first time. What initially was three or four dates, turned into a two-week run of headline shows around Christmas of that year. The shows were all extremely success-ful. Lots of people came out and we had a great time. In Pittsburgh, an inebriated Vinnie Paul of Pantera came out to see the band. He jumped on the stage and proudly bellowed into the microphone.

"*This* motherfucker took Pantera *On Tour*!!! And now *Pantera* is gonna *take* this motherfucker out *On Tour*!!! RIGHT NOW!!!!"

I laughed my ass off, along with everyone else in attendance. Yeah, right.

A few short hours before, I was driving from the hotel to this "intimate" venue. Happy to play, but remembering playing a packed arena in Pittsburgh the last time I was here. Intimate venues? I will take a stadium any day over a tiny club. Who wouldn't? Any musician who is honest will admit this to be true.

Little could I have known, Vinnie Paul would be offering me an arena tour that very night, at that very club. I couldn't believe what he was saying. Surely this was just drunk talk. But, when I got home from tour the day after Pittsburgh, lo and behold, there beneath my fax machine was a list of Pantera tour dates. Much like Barbara Skydel, Vinnie Paul and Pantera had proven themselves to be a rarity in the music business. These were true friends. Paying someone back, returning a favor. With kindness, for something they did for you, long ago. Sadly, this doesn't happen much. But Vinnie Paul had made good on his word.

We were going to open up two weeks of dates for Pantera and Anthrax in the United States. We were back playing arenas.

I guess it was possible for me to have a solo band after all.

The mid-1990s were a very strange time for me. Before I started my solo band, I had been involved in a project with Kelley Deal from The Breeders and Jimmy Chamberlin of the Smashing Pumpkins called The Last Hard Men. The guitar player of this band was Jimmy Flemion of The Frogs. Kelley had contacted me in 1996 to sing for this project. I had no idea why. I had thought that the worlds of hard rock and alternative music were never the twain to meet. I thought that we were kids who hung out at the opposite ends of the playground. I found out later that my connection to Atlantic Records may have been the real reason I was contacted. We eventually recorded a self-titled album, which I funded, in its entirety, through an advance made to me directly from Atlantic Records.

The album was an experiment to see if the very disparate worlds of alternative rock and heavy metal could merge. We found out the answer was no, they cannot. Although there were some great songs, such as "The Most Powerful Man in the World," a lot of it was just filler. We recorded the album in Minnesota, where Nirvana had recorded *In Utero*. Jimmy Chamberlin recorded the drums.

I became friends with Kelley and her husband, Todd Mundt,

who became the first tour manager of my solo band. One night we decided to go see Mötley Crüe on the *Generation Swine* tour in New York City. I was invited as a special guest of the Crüe. I brought Todd, my wife, and three or four other people. In this era of grunge, nü-metal, and rap, bands like Skid Row and Mötley Crüe were decidedly out of favor. The Crüe were also playing "intimate venues," tonight at the Hammerstein Ballroom, or Roseland, if I remember correctly.

The only other guests that night were some members of the Hells Angels of New York City, along with their women. Since this was a small venue, all of Mötley's guests were watching the show in the pit, between the lip of the stage and the barricade. About fifteen of us were sandwiched in amongst the photographers and show security. It was completely packed. There was no room to move around. Most of us were drunk. I, myself, was totally hammered. This was a Mötley Crüe concert, after all.

> *Friday night and I need a fight*
> *My motorcycle and a switchblade knife*

Having a great night! Rocking my ass off. When it came time in the set for my favorite Crüe track, "Shout at the Devil," I was banging my head and whooping it up in a big way. Digging the show. At the familiar start to the song, I thrust my fist up in the air as hard as I could.

> *Shout!*
> *Shout!*
> *Shout!*
> *Shout at the Dev-al!!!!*

I punched the air as Tommy "T-bone" Lee flailed on the kit. Kept on rocking out and jacking my hand up into the air. Cocking my elbow back with just as much fury. To the beat of the song.

And then . . . one too many cock and thrusts.

One Shout Too Many Devils

Standing directly behind me was one of the heads of the New York City Local Hells Angels Chapter. In my drunken state of heavy metal worship, I thrust my fist in the air one last time and whipped my arm back as quick as I could. Unfortunately, my elbow made very solid contact with the nose on the Hells Angel standing directly behind me.

He was decidedly not amused.

This was not the typical early-twenty-something "biker guy" that you picture in your head. This was a sixty-something-year-old man, short hair, out for the evening with some ladies and his friends. This not-so-gentleman had no clue who I was or what band I was in. Getting elbowed in the face was not on his schedule that night.

"What in the *FUCK*???" he exclaimed, in shock. I turned around and faced him. He was beet red with rage. His eyes were bulging out of his skull. He didn't look too happy to see me.

Seeing how mad this guy was, I backed up quick. And uttered the immortal line:

"C'mon, dude!! It's the CRÜE!!!!!"

"*AAAAAAAAAAARRRRRRGHHHHHHH!!!!!!*"

Not following my line of reasoning, the Hells Angels' chapter leader did not seem to share in my enthusiasm for Mötley Crüe to the point where it was okay for me to bash him in the nose. I, in no way, wanted any quarrel with this guy. Who wants a quarrel with the Hells Angels? Certainly, dear reader, not I.

He rushed at me, reached up, and grabbed me by the back of the head. Pulled me down so my back was bent, my face level with his waist. *This isn't so bad*, I thought. *I'll just let him hold me down here and he'll cool out. He'll let me up in a minute.* I did not take a swing, or fight back in any way. I did not mean to elbow him. I wanted no beef with these dudes.

What happened next was really quite weird. The Hells Angels member didn't *punch* me, so much as perform a precise *surgical strike*. I felt his balled-up fist placed tight against my right nostril. Not moving. He never exactly *hit* me. Slowly, methodically, the man placed his knuckle alongside my nose and then with a soft, graceful swipe, proceeded to *move my nose over*, about an inch, to the left side of my face. It was an effective deterrent. Delivered with a brutal, yet almost *gentle* force.

It didn't really even hurt that much. But I knew he had fucked me up. I had that familiar feeling like my nose was as big as Bozo the Clown's, that sensation you get after being *bonked*. He then let me up.

The girls he was there with were pointing at us and freaking out. *"Oh my God that's Sebastian Bach! It's Sebastian Bach!! Oh my God! Leave him alone!! Oh my God! That's Sebastian Bach!!!"* over and over again. I was like, "Where were you chicks a couple of seconds ago?" The guy looked at me. Looked back at them. Behind the girls was a *massive* Hells Angels enforcer type who must've stood around six foot eight. He was far bigger than I was, and was laughing uncontrollably.

"Ha ha ha ha *haaaaa!*" he guffawed. "Hey man!! Come here!"

"Dude! You guys *punched me in the face!*"

He laughed again. "Come on, Sebastian!! Don't let that take the *wind out of your sails!*" And with that, he slapped me on the back like I was his brand-new best buddy. "Come on, man!! You can hang out with us now!" I spent the rest of the night hanging with the Hells Angels, including the guy who fucked up my face. He stood right next to me the rest of the concert, only to become *my* protector and friend, later that night. It was like a *rite of passage* to them. They thought it was funny. I thought it hurt.

After the show, I went backstage to hang out with Mötley Crüe. Tommy Lee was there with his then-girlfriend Mayte Garcia, who is one of the best dancers I have ever seen. There was a time I was in Amsterdam at a private show by Prince, at the Paradiso, and Mayte came onstage and danced like nobody I have ever seen. She was really cool and we all hung out that night. Tommy has always been a great friend and was glad to see me.

"Hey man! How are you!? Good to see you!!! How have you been doing?"

"Well, I just got kicked out of my band, dropped by my record label, and punched in the face by the Hells Angels! But other than that, *everything's great!*"

Everybody was laughing. Including me. Until I came to, the very next day.

Only the Nose Knows

We partied on through the evening with Mötley Crüe. The more I drank, the less I felt my nose throbbing and honking like a car horn. I went home and went to sleep.

Got up the next morning. Had coffee. Stood up. Went to the bathroom.

Boy, was I in for a big surprise.

I looked up into the mirror. Horrified at what I saw.

My nose had been *moved over*, to a new place, on my face.

The nose I had been looking at my whole life, was now in a different location. It was a nightmarish feeling. I flipped out, to the point where I had to take down all the mirrors in my house. I proceeded straight to the hospital.

From the emergency room, I was referred to a cosmetic surgeon. Told him what had happened. Brought along the copy of *Rolling Stone* magazine with my nose on the cover. He was like, "Okay, I get it." Scheduled surgery for me. I was told the joyous news that they were going to have to re-break my nose, and then reset it back into place. I would be confined to the air-conditioned darkness of my bedroom all summer. The skin of my nose was not to be in the sun while healing, and so I would have to stay inside for the whole month of July. *Sucks to be me*, I pondered, ruefully.

On the day of the surgery, I showed up ready to be put under. I was told it would be okay to play music during the surgery. Anything I wanted. The greatest singer of recent times, Jeff Buckley, had just died a short time before. I was extremely disturbed by his passing. His voice was the best I had heard in so many years. His album *Grace* was without a doubt my favorite record of the whole 1990s. I brought Jeff Buckley's *Grace*, by the recently deceased vocalist, along with me to have on through the speakers throughout surgery that day. As the anesthetic apparatus pumped meds into my veins, I lost consciousness to the magical, mystical sounds.

> *This is our last goodbye*
> *I hate to feel the love between us die*

I have no recollection of what happened next, after they put me out. Or to be more accurate, tried to put me out.

I awoke from the surgery, the powerful drugs still coursing through me. The next memory I have is nonsensical blabbering to the nurses in the hospital room.

About pharmaceutical cocaine.

"You guys must have the *best shit* in here! I know you do! You must have the purest blow! I know you are all holding the most *high-quality Peruvian flake up in here!! Serious pharmaceutical-grade flake!!* I know you got it!!" I blathered and cackled an insane laugh as I carried on to these poor nice ladies. About all the coke they were obviously holding.

The nurses all looked at me with a unified stare of horror upon their collective brow.

"Isn't it kind of strange that they aren't laughing along with me?"

They all looked somehow *frightened.* Skittishly, they glanced across the room at each other, then back at me.

I could somehow sense that something *weird* had gone down. I just had no idea what.

I spent the next month of my life in the upstairs bedroom of my New Jersey home. A typical humid, hot, sticky New Jersey summer. Kept the air-conditioning cranked to the max and stared out at the sun-drenched lawn. Wishing I could go outside with everybody else. Thanks a lot, Mötley Crüe.

After three long weeks of tedious healing, I was ready to go in and get the bandages off my nose. The breathing tubes extracted from my nostrils. The secretary told me to go from the waiting room into the doctor's office. As the door shut behind me, I sat down in front of a concerned-looking doctor, a nurse standing by his side.

"Sebastian. How are you?"

"Fine. How's it goin'?" I cheerily replied.

"He . . . *doesn't remember,*" intoned the doctor to the nurse. Cryptically.

"Remember what?" I queried.

The nurse's eyes looked into mine, as she spoke. "You . . . don't remember . . . *what happened?*"

"He doesn't remember," the doctor repeated.

"Sebastian. There was . . . *an incident.* While you were undergoing surgery."

"What kind of incident, sir?" Not unlike Malcolm McDowell in *A Clockwork Orange,* fresh from shock therapy, they looked at me . . . like I was insane, too.

"Sebastian. Everything was going fine. Until we put the Jeff Buckley on . . . and the anesthetic *wore off.*"

I still didn't see where he was going with this.

The nurse shifted uncomfortably from left foot to right as the doctor continued.

"You woke up. In the middle of surgery. You raised up from the operating table. You were acting as if you were *under attack.*"

I had no recollection of this.

"I ordered the anesthesiologist immediately to administer more of the gas to you. She was an older woman, only there to do her job. As she walked over to you, and attempted to put the mask over your face, to subdue you, you turned around . . . and punched *her.* You were screaming that you were *under attack.*"

I was in shock. I could not believe the story they were telling me. About me.

"After you knocked the old woman back into the wall, she cried and fled the room. You then raised up completely off the operating table. Broke through the bonds we had on you, which failed to secure you. Raised up on the operating table . . ."

"Your nose . . . *off your face* . . ."

What he was describing to me was a horror movie come to life. My life.

"We could not hold you down. It was impossible to administer any more anesthesia. You were flailing your arms."

"You got down off the operating table . . . and proceeded to *walk down the hall.*"

Who were they talking about? Who was this person? It wasn't me. Who was this man walking down the hallway of the hospital, throwing old women into the wall? With his nose not attached to his face? Surely, this could not be me.

"We had no choice. We did what we had to do."

He went on to describe the horrific scene. How he had to summon all the doctors on the floor at the very moment I was marching down the hallway of the hospital. On my way down the hall. To families. Mothers. Daughters. Children. If I were to have made my way into the waiting room, I would have scared the hell out of everyone present. And possibly done who knows what else, in my anesthetized state of mind-sleepwalk. I would imagine that staring at a man who is asleep, yet awake, with no nose, walking towards you would be enough to frighten anyone. Let alone traumatize a small child.

"We got four guys to slam you up against the wall. Got the biggest syringe, with the strongest narcs we had on hand. Jammed it deep into your upper thigh, as hard as we could go. It was the only way we could slow you down. We gave you enough meds to knock out an elephant. Which was exactly what you were acting like at that moment."

Was he talking to me?

The nurse then went on to explain that the only time they personally had seen activity such as this was with older, homeless people from the real skid row. In places such as downtown Newark, New Jersey. Coming off crack cocaine, the anesthetic, in rare cases, is not enough to put down the patient, and actually, in isolated instances, can *stimulate* the serotonin levels in the brain. Resulting in a state of complete psychosis. Perhaps the years of hard partying on the road, with Mötley Crüe, Pantera, Guns N' Roses, Aerosmith, and Bon Jovi, had made my brain more tolerant of hospital meds than most. The doctor reiterated that I was acting as if I was *under attack*.

With all that was going on in my life, being kicked out of Skid

Row, my father being diagnosed with leukemia and bone marrow cancer, the uncertainty of a future as a solo artist with a family to support, it's not surprising that my *subconscious* felt as if I were under attack. What was surprising was my subconscious *lashing out* at professionals who were only there to help me. To this day, I have zero recollection of this ever happening.

Note to self: try to *not* elbow bike gang leaders in the face anymore.

Chalk it up as another lesson learned.

Way to go, rock 'n' roll!

1993

The story of Broadway for me really goes back to the moment when my father was diagnosed with leukemia. If that wasn't rotten enough, a further diagnosis of bone marrow cancer was given at the same time. Either of those prognoses is devastating, my father having the unfortunate distinction of contracting both.

Dad called me on the phone himself to tell me the news. Upon realizing the severity of his situation, I experienced a deep, visceral sadness that I had never felt before. My anger towards my father, and family's divorce, seemed so very trite. There really is nothing to be angry at anymore when facing a beloved one's mortality. It really felt like a piece of myself was dying along with him. He had taught me so much in this world. Not only to dream, but to make dreams come true. And, along with discipline, have some fun in the process.

Everybody goes through it. There is no denying that losing a parent is one of the shittiest, god-awful moments in any person's life.

Dad's best friend, Dennis "The Twist" Tourbin, called me.

"Hey Bass. How are you doing? How are you holding up?"

"Well . . . it's my *dad* . . ." I managed to choke the words out of my throat before bursting into even more tears.

What does any of this have to do with my appearance on Broadway? Well, someday, years in the future, as David Bierk approached his final days, I would be asked to star in my first Broadway show. As the tortured Dr. Jekyll and the monstrous Mr. Hyde. The plot of the play? Henry Jekyll tries to save his dying father. Gets fucked up, and goes crazy in the process.

Not exactly a stretch.

13
FROM SKID ROW TO SAVILE ROW: BACH ON BROADWAY

2000
New York City
Theatre District

I received the call at home in New Jersey. I thought they had the wrong number.

"Uh, hey dude. I don't know if you'd be interested in this. *Jekyll & Hyde* on Broadway is looking for a new lead. I know it's hard to fathom . . . but I honestly think you'd be perfect for the role."

Were they talking to me?

Honestly, never in a million years could I have envisioned my career taking this turn. When Jason Flom called me, I listened to his reasoning.

I was intrigued.

"Sebastian. Just listen to me. The way you sing 'I Remember You.' Your clean voice. That's Dr. Jekyll. And then, your pipes on *full roar*. 'Monkey Business.' Mr. Hyde. Perfect! Would you like to go see the play and check it out for yourself?"

To be honest, after Jason's phone call, I had a feeling like this could be a new lease on life. I was being given a second chance. At something new. That was something that really excited me. But there was only one problem.

No one knew if I could pull this off.

Of course I would go check out the show. I had been playing clubs across the country in my solo band. I don't care what anybody says, not an optimum situation. You do what you have to do. A chance to be a leading man on Broadway? Instead of playing bars? Restaurants? Where the patrons are just as interested in getting ketchup for their french fries as they are in listening to the band?

I went to check out the show.

Jack Wagner, of *General Hospital* fame, was the leading man. I entered the Plymouth Theatre in New York City, enjoying even the venue itself. A beautiful, ornate building with a feeling of history and style that was breathtaking to me the first time I sat down. A shock to the system after playing bars for the last while I had been on the road. I loved the play. It was a packed house. A spring night. On Broadway.

There is nothing like it, in all of entertainment. I loved the costuming of the show. The Victorian clothing. Dark lighting. The set itself was so dramatic and cool to me. I absolutely loved the music of the play. The ballad "This Is the Moment" is one of my favorite songs of all time. The song "Confrontation," in the second act of the play, is a piece of music that is incredible to me. Dr. Jekyll singing against his evil alter ego, Mr. Hyde, line by line, remains to this day one of my favorite songs I've ever had the pleasure to sing. "The Way Back." "Alive." So much great music. But it was the actual plot of the play that had me riveted to my seat. I couldn't believe the story that was unfolding in front of my eyes and ears. Dr. Jekyll, a scientist, learns that his father is dying. He decides to try and save his father in any way he can. His only option is to invent a drug, on his own, that may or may not cure his dying father. The Board of Governors, who officiate over such matters, will not let Dr. Jekyll experiment with his drug on any humans. He is forced to administer the nascent medicine to himself. The experiment goes awry, and turns the unassuming Dr. Henry Jekyll into the menacing Mr. Edward Hyde.

Sounds like a typical night on the road in Des Moines, Iowa, playin' in a rock 'n' roll band.

The Theater division of Atlantic Records was the recording label for *Jekyll & Hyde: The Musical*. Frank Wildhorn, the composer, went to Jason Flom, the man who signed me when I was nineteen years old with Skid Row, over in the rock 'n' roll department at Atlantic. *Jekyll & Hyde* had been running on Broadway for four years, and it was time for the inevitable "stunt casting," as it's called, when a "celebrity" takes the place of a "legit" Broadway performer. Jack Wagner was the first Hollywood star to take over the role. After Jack's time was up, Frank went to Jason with one specific request in mind.

"Jason. I need a *rock star*. On Broadway. To be Dr. Jekyll. And Mr. Hyde."

"*I think I got the guy.*"

There really was no precedent for this. Fact is, I was the very first heavy metal/hard rock/whatever you want to call me, mainstream hard rock 'n' roll singer ever to be on Broadway.

It's an accomplishment that no one can ever take away from me.

Rock had flirted with Broadway in the past. *Jesus Christ Superstar* (a role I would play two years later) was the first time a heavy metal musician would be involved in a Broadway show. Ian Gillan, from Deep Purple, originated the role as Jesus on the original score recording. This was a recording project only; Gillan never performed as Jesus live.

The role of Henry Jekyll was coveted by many singers. I, along with many others, auditioned for the part. Incredibly, my hero Paul Stanley of KISS was my main competition. He tried out for the play around the same time that I did.

Ironically, Paul got to play the role of Phantom of the Opera in Toronto, my hometown. And I was chosen to play the lead in *Jekyll & Hyde* in New York, his hometown. He was decidedly nonplussed at the news.

"Dude! You're gonna play Jekyll and Hyde? On Broadway?? Are you serious? I heard Paul is PISSED!!"

Mark Weiss, my photographer friend, gave me the scoop. Paul had tried out for *Jekyll & Hyde*. He had told Frank Wildhorn he would do the play. Then Frank tried me out.

"I saw him the other day! He was like, 'Sebastian is doing *Jekyll & Hyde*? What the fuck? I told Frank I would do it!!!' "

I asked the powers that be at the play why I had been chosen. They told me that it was my Mr. Hyde that sealed the deal. They felt that I had two distinct personalities approaching the role. That my Dr. Jekyll and my Mr. Hyde were two completely different characters. None of the other actors who they considered had a Mr. Hyde as menacing or convincing as mine was on the stage.

Maybe this crazy side of me would pay off in a truly unexpected way. I received very positive reviews for my first role on Broadway. Accolades were posted in the local news, exclaiming that I was a great actor on stage. Only thing was, in the case of Dr. Jekyll and Mr. Hyde, I really wasn't acting all that much.

"Dad! You're not going to believe this! I am Jekyll and Hyde!!!!"

"I *know*," Dad harrumphed.

"No! You don't understand! I'm going to be Jekyll and Hyde! On Broadway!!!!!!!!"

Silence on the other end of the line.

Not too many people get a second chance. A second career. I have dedicated my whole life to rock 'n' roll. I had always had it in the back of my mind that it could foreseeably be possible to be successful in a rock 'n' roll band. But nobody, including myself, could have ever foreseen what was happening: Bach on Broadway. I liked the sound of that. Then reality set in.

There was *no fucking way.*

I couldn't do this!!! When I received the script, from Lachlan Buchanan, I was aghast at what I saw. The very first page was filled with dialogue . . . all from my character.

And . . . it was in *Ye Olde English.*

> Within each of us
> there are two separate natures
> two distinct personalities

The librettist, Leslie Bricusse, had written words that were so very parallel to my own life. It felt like the part had been written for me to play . . . at this exact time in my life, nearing the end of my father's life. Of course, the actor playing Dr. Jekyll's father, on stage, was named David. As was my own father.

Dad would sit in the front row of the Plymouth Theatre, with me only feet away from him, on the Broadway stage, attempting to save *his* life. We would open the show.

> I'll never desert you
> I promise you this
> till the day that I die

I fidget about in my makeshift laboratory. My assistant, Mr. Utterson, played by the amazing George Merritt, helps me in the operating room. My own father, David, dying in the front row, watching

the actor David, *playing* my father a couple of feet away. This was not acting. This was reacting. Live on the Broadway stage. For the whole world to see.

Bringing the story to life, and making it believable, was one of the most challenging, satisfying, and rewarding experiences I have ever had. When I auditioned for the role, bandleader Jason Howland sat down at the piano to run through some of the score. In the keys they were written. The Broadway vocal range of most shows is much lower, or midrange, in comparison to rock 'n' roll. Especially the heavy metal style that I am known for. Legit Broadway, on the other hand, is about natural projection—with only supplementary microphones, taped to the actor's cheekbone, singing to a live band in the orchestra pit, the challenge is to project the voice, all the way to the back row of the theater. My own voice projects the best in the high tenor range of songs such as "I Remember You." I was very relieved, and excited, when Jason uttered the following words.

"Hey Sebastian. That was a pretty good job. Sounded awesome. But hey, I have an idea. Let's try that song *up here.*"

He transposed the song up the piano. Took the melody up three keys, to be exact. Much like that day with the choirmaster back in 1976, trying out for the church choir in Peterborough, we smiled at each other as we got higher and higher up the keyboard. To where my voice sounded like it was soaring.

We tried it again.

When we got to the end of the song "This Is the Moment," the ubiquitous key change that seems almost a prerequisite of any Broadway score, I held on for dear life and went for it. The verse was quite high up in my register, pretty much at the top of my high tenor voice before I start to go up into my screaming range. But I knew I could pull it off. I took a big deep breath and belted out the words.

Damn all the odds!

Held the last word of the tune for all I was worth. Gave it all I had. Looked at Jason after the last note was sounded. We both burst into laughter. This was going to kick some *major* booty. And we both knew it.

What nobody knew was the simple question of whether or not I could *act*. I had done some acting. Played The Inspector in Tom Stoppard's *After Magritte* at PCVS high school in Peterborough. But a leading man on Broadway? Surely there was no way this could actually be happening. But it was. So now it was time for a *crash course* in acting. Which was exactly what Robin Phillips took me on.

People ask me, what is the difference of being on the rock 'n' roll stage as opposed to the Broadway stage? For me, there were two specific challenges that were unexpected and formidable to overcome. Number one, in rock 'n' roll there is no such thing as the fourth wall. When I hit stage and rock, my objective is to make eye contact with every single person in the hall at least once during the evening. All the way to the back. This is part of what being a good front man in a band is all about. Welcoming everybody to your show. Making them feel a part of the experience.

Broadway is the exact opposite of this. Since we are telling a story, none of our own personalities as cast members can get in the way of the storytelling. To make eye contact with an audience member, in theater, is strictly verboten. It took me many hours of practice to learn to not look at the crowd, to not reference anyone in the audience at all. My great friend, stage manager David Hyslop, would reprimand me on a regular basis for giving a little smirk at the end of "This Is the Moment," when I would sing my ass off, and knock 'em dead out in the crowd. He would imitate me. It was next to impossible for me to remain in character at the end of that song on certain nights. The vibes in the room were simply magical. I could not hide how much fun I was having on occasion.

My second biggest challenge was all to do with sheer *energy*. For over a decade, I had been psyching myself into delivering 100 percent the very second I hit stage. An explosion of excitement, and fun, both sonically and visually. My rock 'n' role models, as far as frontmen went, were David Lee Roth and Iggy Pop, guys that would leave every inch of blood and sweat on the stage. For me to be believable as Dr. Henry Jekyll, I could show *zero* energy. Even to be seen sweating too much would be to not pull off the role. Henry Jekyll was calm, cool, collected. From the moment I hit stage until "First Transformation," the middle of Act One where I turn into Edward Hyde, I had to be a doctor. To perform with *no energy*, to restrain my movement and mood, was one of the hardest things for me to physically and mentally learn how to do.

I would do scenes in front of the packed house where Dr. Jekyll would be required to stand completely still on the stage. The energy coursing through my veins had nowhere to go. I would develop a facial twitch or my leg would shake uncontrollably. For me to stand completely still on the stage was something my body and mind had simply never, ever done before. It's second nature, a muscle memory thing, for me to *explode* when the lights go down at 8:00 each night.

This all came to a head in one particularly intense rehearsal one day. We were running the Board of Governors scene, where Dr. Jekyll pleads his case to experiment with his drug on a human subject. I was to deliver Dr. Jekyll's soliloquy standing at the podium, with my hands on each side. Referencing my scientific notes and medical doctrines as I addressed the Board. I was to NOT move my hands during the whole speech. To move my hands would be *distracting from the dialogue.* But my hands had a mind of their own. I could simply *not stop* fidgeting on the stage. I had no idea what to do with all the energy I felt inside of me.

Robin Phillips, the director, had a unique way of teaching me how to be still.

We rehearsed the scene on the Plymouth Theatre stage, in the afternoon, with the full cast and crew present. I was wearing a Captain America shirt. I was so nervous, I had sweated the whole shirt completely out.

"Sebastian! Quit moving your hands."

Robin, incensed, directed me from the orchestra seats in front of the stage.

"Let's try it again!!"

There were so many words for me to memorize. Seventeen songs that I sang during each performance. My mind was concentrating on delivering Olde English without missing a syllable. You only got *one* shot. This wasn't a recording studio. This was not a rock concert. I couldn't hold the microphone out and ask the crowd to sing if I didn't feel like it.

No matter how hard I tried, I could not stop my hands from moving. I couldn't stop sweating. I delivered the lines as best I could, while continuing to fidget. Making Robin Phillips madder by the second.

"Sebastian!! Quit moving your FUCKING HANDS!!!" He jumped out of his seat and ran up onto the stage.

"Give me your *fucking* hand!!!!!" Robin, the elder statesman of

British Theatre, yelled in front of the shocked cast. None more so than me.

He took my hand, and placed it directly in his crotch. In front of all present. I could not understand what was going on.

Screaming at the top of his lungs, in his English accent, he jammed my outstretched palm up in between his legs.

"Every *fucking time* you feel like moving your FUCKING HANDS, I want you to think of your fucking hand RIGHT FUCKING HERE!!! These are my fucking *balls*!!! This is my fucking *asshole*!!!! Do you fucking HEAR ME?????" Yes, I heard him. Loud and clear.

I never moved my hands again.

Rehearsals were intense, detailed, and laborious. They had flown Robin, who was the play's original director, down from Ottawa, Canada, especially to teach me how to act. He was an incredible mentor, a great friend, and a wonderful man. He knew I could be molded, and would take his direction. Because I respected him. We all thought he was hilarious.

He used a word I had never heard before. When he got mad at a female actress, in rehearsal, he would call them by the affectionate term "Cunthook."

Not just Cunt.

Cunt*hook*. An astonishing word I had never heard before, nor since. I heard it a lot rehearsing for this play.

Those crazy Brits!

We rehearsed six days a week. For a month. By the time we opened the show, I was already almost *bored* of doing the show. Not bored. Just extremely well rehearsed. I knew exactly what I had to do, and nothing was going to stop me from doing it.

The night before my Broadway debut was Jason Flom's fortieth birthday party. He invited me, along with a lot of the other acts he had worked with in the music industry. Dave "The Snake" Sabo was there. It was the first time we had seen each other in years. I saw Jason in the bathroom, where we took a piss next to each other.

"Why is fucking *Snake* here???"

Jason, with his dick in his hand, looked me straight in the eye.

"Dude!! This night isn't about you. It's about me!!" So we all had a good time. Maybe *too* good of a time.

This was the first night I met Kid Rock. We hung out and had some drinks. We all ended up at Scores nightclub, getting drunk and doing blow. Mark McGrath of Sugar Ray was also there. Mark, who has since turned into a great friend of mine, turned more and more dark as we got more and more fucked up.

"What the fuck, Sebastian?? Really? When did you *give up*???" The alcohol seemed to be hitting him hard and he seemed to think I was not *rock* anymore, since I was now doing a musical. I couldn't seem to make him understand that what was important to me in music was singing. Broadway is a place for people that love to sing. I love to sing. There was no shame in doing a musical for me.

I ended up with Kid Rock and Mark McGrath in the bathroom of Scores, the night before my Broadway debut, drunk and snorting lines of coke off the back of a toilet. When I look back, it is completely shocking. Especially since I hate that stuff so much now. But I remember feeling so rehearsed, that I felt partying, like I was used to, would be a way to quell my nervousness about the situation. It worked. I woke up the next day slightly hung over, but ready to do the show. A hangover worked great for the Mr. Hyde role anyways.

Opening night was crazy. So many people came out. Jason Flom, Atlantic Records, Frank Wildhorn, Frank Barsalona, Barbara Skydel, my mom, members of the band Anthrax. My friends, family. No doubt some people came just to see me fail. I was not about to give anyone that satisfaction.

A lot of my rock 'n' roll friends cautioned me when I got the part.

"You cannot let any of the Broadway people know about your partying!!" Of course I agreed with them, and thought this would be a bad thing. Little did any of us know that these Broadway mother-truckers know how to tie one on with the best of them. Every night, after a performance, there would be some sort of get-together, a celebration, at a local establishment in the theater district. When I was rehearsing for the play, I went out with Jack Wagner, and with the leading lady of the play. We had a great time. Libations flowed. Cocaine was not unheard of in Broadway circles. I turned down Ecstasy many times. I don't enjoy that stuff. Jack's main advice to me was, "Get to the monster. Get to the monster." That's what people were paying to see.

One night Neil Patrick Harris came by to check out the play. Coleen Sexton, who played Lucy with such an incredible voice and stage presence, knocked at the door of my dressing room. My makeup artist Kevin Phillips answered.

"Dude . . . Doogie Howser is here."

It was after one of our performances and I was like, "Oh yeah, I remember that show!" I opened the door and invited in Neil for a couple of beers. Before he came in, Coleen told me, "Oh, he's a really good friend of mine. He's super cool. So be nice. Don't call him Doogie Howser, okay?" So I didn't. Incredible to see this same dude host the Oscars! It's a crazy business for sure.

There was a palpable sexual tension in the play between myself and Coleen. She was about twenty years old and sang so beautifully, it mesmerized me and everyone else in attendance. Every time she opened her mouth. When it came time in the first act for me to make out with her, I was told by the director we didn't really need to make out. But we ignored him. We made out for real, each and every time. You could set your clock to the collective gasp of the crowd. During "Dangerous Game," everything you saw on the stage was pretty much really happening between us. Broadway is a very close physical environment, on stage and off. To be believable onstage is everything. My ex-wife really did not enjoy watching this scene, and would leave the theater during this part of the show. I don't know if she ever watched it.

Near the end of my three-month contract, I received the awesome news that they were extending my run. Giving me a nice raise, as well. I was very happy to do an extra month as Jekyll and Hyde. It was around this time when the door manager came upstairs.

"Sebastian! We have a special guest this evening! Paul Stanley of KISS is coming!!"

Which was incredible for many reasons, one of them being that this was one of the nights when Dad was going to be watching the play as well. Talk about a special night!

I had adorned my dressing room with vintage KISS posters, in-

cluding a jumbo-size *Dynasty* wall mural that totally freaked out the Broadway community for the last four months that dressing room had been mine. These posters would inspire me to go out onstage and give the best show I possibly could. Like my heroes before me.

Paul was coming with Doc McGhee. Doc had been to see the show a couple of times. It meant a lot to me for him to support me, along with his wife, Wendy. The fact that Paul was coming meant everything to me. I couldn't wait to do the show for Paul with my dad watching. Afterwards, he could come back to my room, and I would blow him away with my shrine.

But this was not to be. After the show, Dad came back to the room by himself. He told me the sad news.

"Son. Great show. You're not going to believe who was sitting in front of me."

"Who, Dad?"

"Paul Stanley."

I was puzzled why nobody came back after the show to tell me he was coming. Dad told me why.

"Ummm, Sebastian, I don't really know how to say this, but . . . Paul left at the intermission."

Wow. That sucks.

This was heartbreaking to me. After Dad had put me on his shoulders in 1979 for this guy. After I had adorned my dressing room with pictures of him, on Broadway, out of respect. For dad to have to watch him get up and leave, after everything he had meant to our family, felt like a humiliating slap in the face.

Doc McGhee came back after that, along with Tommy Thayer.

"Great, great show, Sebastian. I'm serious. It was tremendous. I'm very proud of you out there. An incredible performance. Bravo!" Doc genuinely dug the play, as he had been to see it more than once.

"Hey Doc . . . How come Paul split at intermission?" I felt like a fool asking this as I stood in front of the Paul Stanley poster on my wall.

"Oh, you know . . . it wasn't this, it wasn't that," were his exact words.

I can understand sour grapes. The thing that hurt was that I am such a fan. The kid inside me was pained that I may have upset someone I had genuinely looked up to.

After this, a truly terrifying incident occurred. I was leaving the play. Signing auto-graphs for the fans at the stage door, as I did every night. The limo was set up in front of the gate for me to get inside. As I finished the autographs, I went around to the passenger side of the vehicle and got in the backseat. The left door was opened as well. Fans were shouting, "Sebastian!! Sebastian!! Great show!" As I turned to my

right, a man had gotten his head and upper body into the car with me. It was impossible for me to shut the door. As I reached over, he looked at me straight in the eye.

"Sebastian! Nice show! *We're going to whack you.*"

And with that, he slammed the door.

I was terrified.

My limo driver, Bill, turned around from the front seat and looked at me with the same ghostly expression on his face.

"Did he really just say that?"

I jumped out of the car and went after the guy. "WHAT??? You want to whack me?? What, you wanna whack off my fucking DICK??" I did this in front of people on the street. So they would see him as well. I was acting tough and crazy, but the truth was I was scared shitless. Who wouldn't be?

The mystery man whack-job just kept on walking. Never turned around. I never found out who he was, or what he wanted.

I tried, through private channels, to find out if this was something to be concerned about. I was told that if someone wanted to whack me, they would just do it. They would not bother to tell me first. Still, I was frightened enough to enlist a security team to get me in and out of the venue for a short time after this. I still wonder who that guy was, and what he wanted. Maybe his chick dug the show more than he wanted her to. It's happened more than once. Maybe this time, to the wrong guy.

In after me was "The Hoff" himself, none other than the one and only David Hasselhoff. David and his wife came and met me in the dressing room.

"Dude!" I said. "Are you doing the show?"

"I'm thinking about it," replied the Hoff, pensively.

It was my job to teach David the track of the show, as Jack had taught to me when I started. This involved David Hasselhoff running behind me as I changed clothes between set changes, ripped off my wig and put on a new hairdo, as fast as I could, to get back onstage in time for the next line. It was a lot of fun. I really miss *Jekyll & Hyde*.

I got to play the role for a second time in 2004, in North Carolina, at the Raleigh Theatre for the Performing Arts for a two-week limited Halloween run. It was fun to reunite with George Merritt and sing the songs again, but the chemistry we had on Broadway was impossible to replace. The camaraderie we had as cast members, along with the musicians in the band, the director Robin Phillips, and all of the crew, is one of my most cherished memories. We were all great friends. We all truly enjoyed being there each and every performance. David Chaney was the actor who played my father, David, in the play. His lovely wife was a stage manager. Before every time I would walk on the stage, she would stand next to me, in the wings, and whisper the words, "Sebastian . . . Shine like the star that you are."

I would walk out there with those words in my head. Those words are still in my head.

I wish every project I entered into in this business was as gratifying, fun, and memorable as was *Jekyll & Hyde: The Musical*.

It was the year 2000. I had a billboard up in Times Square. I was a bona fide Broadway Star now. Things were going so good. I walked down Broadway, saying to myself, "Things are so good. Things feel almost too good to be true." The feeling was palpable. I felt there was no way this great feeling could last forever. It was almost as if I felt something just around the corner.

Then came 9/11.

September 11, 2001
New Jersey
7:00 a.m.

The day started like any other. Meetings in New York City. VH1 offices. A beautiful, bright sunny morning. I was due in Manhattan at 9:00 a.m. to talk about some new TV show on the horizon. But on this day, there were indeed other things on the horizon. Our country, our world, was about to change. For the rest of time. Never to be the same again.

I opened up the bedroom windows and let the sun shine in on this glorious morning. Coffee. Started to get my bean on. Flicked on NewsChannel 4 New York City. All of a sudden, they showed the Twin Towers engulfed in flame and smoke.

Matt Lauer explains that an airplane had somehow *hit the North Tower.*

I sip on my coffee and watch the drama unfold. The news is disturbing, but at first seems like pilot error in the worst possible way. But then, as the morning unfolds, it becomes clear that this is not a case of pilot error. This is more serious. Something is going on. But what?

I knew one simple thing. *I want my kids.*

Paris and London had just left for school. Somehow I knew that there wouldn't be a meeting at VH1 that day. My instincts as a father kicked into high gear. As I listened to Matt Lauer on the TV, I heard in the tone of his voice that something bad was going down. I jumped in the car and went up the street to my son's school.

Got to the parking lot. Out of the car. Went to the office where school personnel were present. Everybody was nervously chattering, freaked out about what was happening.

"Hey. I want my kids right now."

The teachers explain their feelings.

"Sir. We're aware that something is happening in New York City right now. But we think it best to just let the children have a normal day at school. Let's not alarm the kids."

"Well . . . okay."

None of us knew exactly what to do. Their reasoning seemed to make sense at the time. I got a call on my cell phone right then from my ex-wife. I asked her what was going on. She told me that a *second* plane had crashed into the *second* tower in the ten minutes that I had been gone from home. I couldn't believe what she was telling me. A plane has now crashed into the second tower? It has *collapsed* into the ground below??

I told the teachers the unbelievable news.

"There are *no more Twin Towers*. The Twin Towers are *gone*."

A bunch of them burst into tears. We were more confused than ever before.

"*Oh my God.*" Panic in the school office.

Once again, I ask for my sons. Through teary eyes, the teacher again explains to me, it was probably best that I leave the boys in school so as not to alarm them. Against my better judgment, I walk back to my car. A lady walks towards me. She, too, is on her way to the office I had been just minutes before.

"*Did you get your kids???????*" she exclaims to me, her voice thick with the fear of protective motherly instinct.

"Well, no. The teachers think it best that we leave the kids here to have a normal day. Maybe this will all blow over. So I guess I'm going to just leave them here. Like any other day."

"Yeah . . . but you don't know . . . *what they're going to do next!!!!!*"

Her ominous words hit me like a ton of bricks. I turned with her, and marched back into the office. We had a common purpose.

"Give me my kids. Right now."

I didn't move till I had Paris and London with me. I took them both by the hand and got in the car. Went back to my house. Got my ex-wife.

Called my dad in Canada. "We're getting the fuck out of this country. *This is fucked up!!*"

"I know, dude. Come here right now."

"Okay, Dad. See you as soon as I can."

I pressed down on the gas, with my family in the car, and gunned it. We aimed the car towards Canada. But we didn't get that far.

Nobody in New Jersey, or New York, or the USA, or the world for that matter, knew what was happening. I myself thought that we were under nuclear attack. There were guys working on my roof that day when I returned back from school with Paris and London. "*What is going on???*" Even they knew, as they were outside working on the roof of my house. The feeling of terror was alive in New Jersey that day. I told them that we were under nuclear attack. They flipped out, jumped off the roof, and split.

Escape from New York

I drove as fast as I could. It felt like a movie. Only this wasn't a scary movie. This was *real* scary.

I listened to the radio with rapt attention. Searching for information. Trying to make any sort of sense out of the situation. I heard something on the news that I will never, ever forget. Maybe others heard it too. I remember the radio broadcast as clear as day. We were somewhere in Pennsylvania when I heard the woman broadcaster announce this insane news.

"We interrupt this broadcast for a breaking news story. This is just in: We have just learned that the U.S. government was *forced* to *take down* an airplane on approach to the White House. I repeat. The

U.S. government was forced to shoot down one of our own planes as it approached the White House. More on this story as it develops."

I left the station on the dial. But I never heard any mention of this ever again. Anywhere. Only by conspiracy theorists years later. But I have a vivid memory of this news story being reported, right around the time Flight 93 went down. This is a memory etched in my mind. Who knows what really happened that day? The day that changed the world forever.

We never made it to Dad's house in Canada. It started to get dark around 5:00. I wanted a fucking drink after this insanity. I stopped the car at a liquor store on the side of a rural road somewhere close to Stroudsburg, Pennsylvania. The small store was filled with locals staring at the news on the screen. It was deathly silent as we all collectively wondered what was happening to our country. I picked up a case of Molson Ice. We made it as far as Stroudsburg. I saw a hotel from the highway as the sun went down, and asked the front desk if they had a kick-ass suite we could stay in for the night. Yes, they did. So I brought the case of beer up to the suite and we all went to the indoor pool. I drank beers in the pool and swam with my boys. We were completely by ourselves. I thought to myself that it was cool we had turned a terrifying day into a family adventure. Which ended up with the kids swimming in the pool, and dad drinking beers.

I told this story to Dee Snider once. He said, "Well, Sebastian, that's awesome. On 9/11 you took your car and drove it straight from the World Trade Center site, right to the Flight 93 crash site. Way to go! Some pretty good family planning there, dude!!"

I laughed when I realized this.

14

JESUS CHRIST: OH THE HORROR

Let's Do the Time Warp, Again

2001
New Jersey/New York City

It was about a week after 9/11 that I was on the Jersey shore, drinking more Molson Ice. With my toes in the sand at Donovan's Reef, my favorite haunt near my New Jersey home. It was my favorite place to hang out because they would actually let you *drink beer* and *swim in the ocean* at the same time. Right in front of their bar, exclusively. A unique feature of this fine establishment. One that I utilized with great frequency.

Barbara Skydel called on the phone.

"Sebastian. Broadway is in deep, deep trouble. Everybody is scared to come to a Broadway show. The bridge-and-tunnel crowd is not coming to Broadway because everybody's scared of the bridges and tunnels blowing up. They have reached out to artists that have been successful in past shows. *The Rocky Horror Show* wants you to come in. After Joan Jett. They want you be the next rocker in the show."

There was only one problem. As much as I enjoyed Broadway, the reason I believed that *Jekyll & Hyde: The Musical* was so successful, was due to the *role itself.* It really felt like I was living my life in a more exaggerated way on the Broadway stage during the *Jekyll & Hyde* production.

The Rocky Horror Show? Ummmmm, *not so much.*

I had seen the movie, and enjoyed it. The play had wanted me to play the lead role of Frank N. Furtur. But my singing voice is in a much higher register than the main song from that character, "Sweet Transvestite." I really loved this song. But this production, unlike *Jekyll & Hyde*, was not willing to change the keys in order to suit my vocal range. There was one song in the play, however, that was in my vocal register. The character Riff Raff, originated by the show's creator, Richard O'Brien, sang the song "Time Warp." This was the role I felt I could pull off.

This was a song right in my vocal range. So, Riff Raff I was.

I have never been a fan so much of straight-up *comedy* mixed with rock 'n' roll. Other than *This Is Spinal Tap*, I really don't enjoy "comedy bands" whose main purpose is to make you laugh. If this means maybe I'm from another time, so be it. I like my performers to hit the stage serious. As a heart attack. David Lee Roth was funny as hell onstage. Dee Snider would make me laugh so hard I got tears in my eyes. Ted Nugent could cause such fits of hilarity my cheeks would hurt from smiling too hard. But all these dudes were *serious* about their humor. And cool. Diamond David Lee Roth never *made* fun of rock 'n' roll. He embodied the talent, dedication, and *spirit* of being the *best you can be* on a rock 'n' roll stage. *Jekyll & Hyde* was that for me on Broadway. I wasn't really looking forward to going on stage eight times a week trying to make people laugh.

"Sebastian. I want you to do the show. But Riff Raff really only sings one song per night."

This was another reason I wasn't excited to do the play. For all the effort it took, to get psyched up to do a show eight times a week? Doing only one song per show seemed like a lot of effort for not much payoff. For myself. And my fans.

Barbara presented me with the offer. I said, "You know what? I really don't want to do this play. I'm gonna tell them, 'No.' " But then I thought about it. I didn't want to seem ungrateful to the Broadway community itself. After all, actors would give anything to be offered the roles I was being asked to do. So I came up with a plan. I thought this was a surefire way of getting out of doing the play.

I told Barbara that I would do the play, if they would double the offer they have made, to do the show. Surely they wouldn't, no questions asked.

Barbara was a little pissed off, but said, "Okay Sebastian, I'll let them know. You have a great day at the beach."

She called back about a half hour later.

"Well, I can't believe this. Guess what? They just *doubled the offer*. You will now be appearing in *The Rocky Horror Show* on Broadway."

Dammit, I thought. *Fucking right on!* another part of my brain thought, at the same time.

This was the first time I can remember saying flat-out "No" to an offer someone had made me. I was always so excited just to sing, just to be onstage. This was a good example of learning that saying "no," first, is usually a great business tactic. One that my future manager Rick Sales, in years to come, would really illustrate for me. In many instances.

I learned really quick that no two Broadway productions are the same. The experience of doing *Jekyll & Hyde: The Musical* was completely different than doing *The Rocky Horror Show* on Broadway. I had some fun doing *The Rocky Horror Show*, worked with some very talented people. But it had none of the *gravitas*, or personal meaning, that I had experienced in the previous production.

Things were getting seriously worse with my dad around this time. A constant presence, at *Jekyll & Hyde,* only a year before, I fully expected dear old Dad to be at my debut *Rocky Horror Show.* When he couldn't make it, incredibly to me now, I felt *mad.* I could not process the seriousness, or the simple fact, that my dad was dying. I let fantasy take over from reality because it felt much better that way.

I didn't want my dad to die.

My stepmother Liz and I talked on the phone.

"What do you mean he's not coming? He seriously is not coming to my Broadway show? You guys are not coming down?"

"Dearie." As she used to call me. "Believe me, we would love nothing better in the world, than to come down to see your Broadway show right now."

It was starting to sink in. Dad's days were getting numbered.

Aunt Janine and Uncle Bob came and saw the show near the start of the run. I bitched and moaned after the performance, that my dad wasn't coming to see me. My uncle Bob just sat there, quietly shaking his head. Aunt Janine, a nurse, said this to me: "Sebastian, I don't think you realize how sick your dad really is." That shut me up quick. And made me think. If Dad wasn't even coming to see me on Broadway, this was way more serious than I ever even allowed myself to realize.

One of my best friends during *The Rocky Horror Show* was Matthew Morrison. The actor who went on to star in the TV show *Glee* was part of the cast of *Rocky Horror* when I was in the show. He was more stocky, more muscular, with more curly locks of hair than the Matthew Morrison I see on TV today. He was a super cool guy. We had a great time onstage and we hung out offstage as well.

Working with Daphne Rubin-Vega, Terrence Mann, Sally Jessy Raphael, Dick Cavett, Penn & Teller, and others in *The Rocky Horror Show* on Broadway showed more to me about stagecraft. Doing the show eight times a week for three months, I never missed a gig.

I truly felt at home on the stage.

Forever Wild

Right around this time, after *Rocky Horror*, I was given my own television show on VH1. *Forever Wild* was an hour-long heavy metal rock show that played every Friday night. We filmed ten or eleven episodes, I think. It was a completely crazy show. I got a lot of vin-

tage videos played, which made me very happy. We shot a bunch
of skits. Some better than others. But all of this came at a challenging time for me personally. My dad was in his dying days, and
it was a challenge to be *happy* and *crazy* and *wild* all the time on TV
when I was filled with anything *but that*, deep inside.

As they say, the show must go on.

Each week we would have a special guest and shoot some crazy
segments with them. Our guests included Rob Halford, Slash,
Vince Neil, Ted Nugent. We had an episode near the end of the series scheduled with Gene Simmons in Las Vegas. During this particular episode, I was scheduled to jump out of a flying plane and
parachute down to the earth below while announcing the next
Nickelback video coming up after the commercial break. They told
me the news for this while I was in Peterborough, spending time at
Dad's house, watching him die of leukemia and bone marrow cancer. I was in Dad's living room after spending all day with him. VH1
told me they had this episode set up, but they were not going to do
it. They were compassionate and knew I couldn't leave my family
at this time. I tried to keep a brave face on. Being the KISS fan that
I am, I was very excited to shoot a television show with Gene. But
I could not deny what Greg, the producer, was saying to me over the
telephone line. I was in no emotional shape to jump out of a plane,
or even shoot the show that week. It was impossible for me to argue
otherwise.

One of the last episodes of *Forever Wild* was with Vince Neil and
Tommy Lee, down in Florida. Other guests on this episode included
Meatloaf and Alice Cooper. I was drinking heavily at the time to
blot out my family situation. This worked out great shooting a television show with Vince Neil.

We stayed at the golf resort for a couple days or so, and shot the
show. Vince would call my hotel room and simply bark, like a dog.
He would not say a word. I would check my voicemail in my hotel

room, and just hear, "Ruff." "Ruff, ruff, howwwwlll" would be my sign to come out, find Vince, and get into some serious drinking.

One morning at the golf course, on a day off from shooting, the phone rang. Early.

"Ruff, ruff, ruff. Hey, you got any pot?" Vince was on the line, barking like a dog.

Yeah, of course I did.

"Because I know someone who wants some. Judd Nelson." He was talking about Judd Nelson the actor, who was looking for some weed. So Vince called me. "Hey dude, we're down at the pool. Come on down. We got beers." It was 9:45 in the morning.

I will always be a huge Mötley Crüe fan. Recently, Nikki Sixx and myself disagreed over whether I was asked to join Mötley Crüe back in 1991. No matter if Nikki is mad at me or not, I will always love the band Mötley Crüe. I was excited to hear Vince bark like a dog on my voicemail. I ran down to the pool with my weed for Judd Nelson.

When I got to the pool, Vince had already started. There was a full case of ice-cold Heinekens in between my chaise lounge and his. *This is going to be a fun day. Party with the Crüe!* I thought to myself. I cracked open a Heineken and began to get shit-faced with my hero, who was sitting next to me.

Me and Vince sat next to the pool drinking beers and getting a tan. We went out for dinner at the Fontainebleau, took a limo. By this time we've been drinking for hours. We sang along to Scorpions and Journey songs on the radio at the top of our lungs, with our buddy Bob Hewko. By the time he got to the Fontainebleau, we were pretty fucked up.

Anybody that has ever hung out with Vince will tell you that he is the nicest guy when he's not too drunk. Funny and fun to be around. But then, he has just one too many, and his personality changes, just like Mr. Hyde. This was one of those times.

Vince was making fun of me because I had done an episode of *Forever Wild* where I had my dog on it.

"Hey dude!! Did you interview your dog? That was heavy!!!! What the fuck, man??!?! You know what to do!!! You know what, dude? You DID interview your dog!! Maybe I will have to punch you out after all!!!" And he laughs.

Vince thinks it's funny to punch people out.

"Fuck *yooooooooouuuuu*!!!! Shout at the devil!!!!" Like that.

We got into a limousine and went to a VH1 party. But since we had started drinking at 9:00 a.m., we were kind of early for the opening of this particular event. We stumbled out of the limo. Vince pounded on the door of the venue. The woman handling the guest list was none other than Darius Rucker's wife. She informed us that we were early for the event and it wasn't set up yet. They were still setting up the tables. The venue wasn't even open yet. We were that early. Vince absolutely freaked out, and must not have known who she was. "Fuck you!!!! FUCK YOU!!!! What the fuck? We're coming in *RIGHT fucking now*!!!!" She would not listen, because there was nowhere set up for us to hang out. Vince let her have it as hard as he could. "Fuck you and you know what?? Fuck VH1! Fuck YOU, VH1!!!!!"

No matter how loud Vince would scream "Fuck you," they would not let us into this place. So I went back in the limousine to smoke a joint. Vince sat by himself on the curb in front of the venue. Talking to himself, over and over, repeating the words "Fuck VH1. Fuck you, VH1! Fuck you, VH1, anyhow!" he said, to nobody at all. It was hilarious.

Then we split.

We got back to the hotel and there was a party in the resort bar. Alice Cooper was there. Sober. We were there. Not.

Bad look! It's Alice Cooper. *Help.*

"Hi, Alice!!" I slurred my words.

Now, Alice can be the nicest guy in the whole world. But I will never forget the look he gave me and Vince right then and there. A look of absolute disgust. Condemnation. "Hey! How are you doing?" Alice looked at us and turned away. But in that millisecond, he let me know how grossed out he was by how drunk off our asses we were. I don't think Vince even realized, or cared. "Right on, dude!" We just kept on drinking.

I flew home the next day. Was totally furious at my ex-wife. She had been completely pissed off at me the whole time I was in Florida with Mötley Crüe. She was a huge Mötley Crüe fan and thought I was out drinking and fucking chicks with the Crüe. Yes, I was completely drunk the whole time. But I did not fuck any chicks. I came home to her, and her alone. We were fighting so much about this trip that I did not even want to go home when I got back to Newark. I called my wife on the limo ride home. "So what do you want to fucking *fight*? Or what?"

"Fuck you," was her answer. So I told the limo driver, "Fuck this. Let's go to Manhattan." I checked myself into a suite and called out some drinking buddies. To continue drinking.

[[-continue this story? i end up in jail.]]

Jesus Christ Superstar

It was after *Forever Wild* when I got the call from my stepmother.

"You're going to have to stop what you're doing and come up and say goodbye to your father. It's time."

None of us wanted to believe it. Our father seemed invincible to us growing up. Omnipresent. All-powerful. Imagining life without him was unfathomable to all eight of us children. I drove up to Peterborough with my family from New Jersey. It was obvious. It was time to say goodbye.

Seeing him in the hospital in the last days of his life was like a horror movie. He had lost the function of speech, yet did not realize this. So he would hold his hands out and try to tell us things that were obviously very, very important to him. But since he could not speak, all that came out of his mouth was gibberish. It was heartbreaking, and scary at the same time.

Dad died on August 28, 2002. I was set to start in the leading role as *Jesus Christ Superstar* in October 2002. Rehearsals started in September. This left me with around two weeks to mourn the death of my father. It also gave me a lot to sing about.

Once again, singing became my refuge. My solace. As it had always been.

The role of *Jesus Christ Superstar* is about Jesus singing to his father in heaven. He becomes wildly popular, and then is brought down to Earth and massacred on the cross as he pleads to his father in the sky to save him. The inverse of the *Jekyll & Hyde* plot. And the only possible part I could have played, only days after my own father's demise.

One thing certainly happened during the course of my run in *Jesus Christ Superstar*: I was reacquainted with the high range of my voice. During the mid-1990s, I felt like people didn't necessarily *want* to hear the clean, high tenor tone that I sang in. The style in the mid-'90s was all grunge, screaming, shouting. *Screamo* was actually a musical term at one point. I felt silly, in the mid-1990s, trying to sing *well*. The lone exception being Jeff Buckley, on his album *Grace*, I didn't feel like anybody else was even *trying* to sing good.

Jesus Christ Superstar changed all that. I learned the original score, sung by Ian Gillan of Deep Purple, on the original album by composer Andrew Lloyd Webber. Then, I learned the movie, featuring Ted Neeley as Jesus, who hit some unbelievably high Rob Halford—esque type screams during his run in the show. I had not hit notes this high in years. I had not even tried to. But now I was forced to, learning the part of Jesus.

It was really, really fun for me to scream properly once again. Not just yell as hard as I could, from the throat, like a grunge singer. To place a note, properly, on my vocal palate. Hit the note clean, and then put in a little dirty at the end after the vibrato kicks in. Place it correctly, and nail it. I started warming up again to Journey. Judas Priest. After a couple weeks, I could scream the notes as best I could. We did eight shows a week. I lasted exactly six months in the play. I did not miss one single performance.

Also in the play, as in the original 1973 movie, as Judas, was the incomparable Mr. Carl Anderson.

Carl was the type of singer I had never seen nor heard the likes of before. Carl Anderson, in one word, was all about one thing: *soul*. Carl sang with such heart and soul that he marveled anyone whoever had the pleasure of hearing him sing. His energy was completely electric. I have always been told that I have a lot of energy onstage. It took all of my thirty-two-year-old energy to keep up

with Carl Anderson's fifty-six-year-old energy. The man hit stage with everything he got. Every show. He took all of us to school.

Carl could, at times, have a giant-sized ego to match his voice and presence. That is what it takes to be successful as a singer on a stage. Carl and I had what is known as a *favored nations contract*. Whatever I got, he got, and vice versa. I was coming into the play after successful runs in *Jekyll & Hyde* and *The Rocky Horror Show*.

Carl was very much like a father figure to me thoughout the time we were doing the play. Incredibly, he was fifty-six years old when we met. My dad passed away at the age of fifty-seven. There were so many weird incidences where I felt like Dad was speaking through Carl. My father had a hilarious way of mispronouncing names. "Sebastian," he would say. "You must check out some of these new artists that are far more important than the heavy metal bullshit you like." "Who are you talking about, Dad?" "I'm talking about important artists. Music of the people. Songs that speak for the man in the street. Around the world." "Who is that, Dad?" "I'm talking about people like Bruce Springfield."

He would always mess up names like this. It was completely hilarious. "Sebastian, I'm so excited. I'm taking you to a concert. By one of my favorite artists."

"Who is that?"

"I'm talking about *David Buoy*." He pronounced *Bowie* like a water buoy. Not "Bowie" like "Zowie." What a goof!

One day, Carl and I took the escalator up to the departure terminal in the Detroit Metro Airport. Or maybe it was Minneapolis. He turned to me. With a distant look in his eye.

"Hey Sebastian. Do you like *David Buoy*?" Like the water bouy. I froze in my tracks.

This was only the second person I had met in my life that pronounced David Bowie completely wrong, and silly. Just like my dad. This must be a sign.

The tour wore on. It was during *Jesus Christ Superstar* that I developed my formidable taste for red wine. Carl was the man who introduced me to the infinite pleasures of the red grape. I had to do something.

You see, I appeared in much of *JCS* onstage in nothing more than a diaper. Bare feet, bare torso, with a white cloth nappy, I was out on the stage in my swaddling clothes. I remember looking down at what I was wearing, which was certainly not much, and saying to myself, *"I cannot believe I'm going onstage like this."* Now, this was acting.

The production of *Jesus Christ Superstar* was rife with tension from the start. The company that did the play was run by a man named Tom McCoy, who owned the rights to the touring production for the play. He had not been able to take the show on the road due to the lack of a "suitable" Jesus. Then I came along. SFX Theatrical Group had success with me in *Jekyll & Hyde*, so they thought I would be a great fit for *Jesus Christ Superstar*. But I learned one thing for sure. Like they say: it's far easier to play the bad guy than the good guy.

I had the feeling that Tom McCoy did not like me from the very start. Maybe he resented the fact that the powers that be forced me upon him as the lead in his play. But nobody could argue with the success of the play. We took *Jesus Christ Superstar* on the road in October 2002, mere weeks after my dad's passing. We sold out most performances across the country. Records show in *Variety* that we were making more than $1 million a week in ticket sales and our only competition on the road at the time was the play *The Producers*. But *Jesus Christ Superstar* did have its hilarious moments. In Act 2, there is a long extended scene where Jesus is stripped down, placed on his knees, in a diaper, and tied to the wall. The storm troopers then proceed to whip Jesus, to the soundtrack of the score, as I rise and thrash about the stage, naked and whipped under the lights to the beat of the song. When we played in San Diego, to eight sold-out shows, the Skid Row fans really got into the scene. With each crack of the whip across my back, the girls would squeal out into the night, "Get him!!! Get *him*!!" and then giggle.

The producers on the side of the stage were not amused. I didn't understand this. The businessmen were happy to take the rock 'n' roll fans' money, but they did not like the way the rock fans were watching the show. All I knew was that the chemistry and cast of *Jesus Christ Superstar* was nothing like the experience I had in *Jekyll & Hyde*. It really goes to show that an ensemble is more than the sum of its parts. Chemistry, and the relationship between performers onstage, and the band and crew, are really the deciding factors in the success of any stage performance.

Road Warp

As the months wore on, the inevitable *road warp* set in. The first couple of months were a lot of fun. We all worked very, very hard at making the show the best it could be. Around the fourth month, things started to get weird, as the road tends to do. I had my usual gaggle of rock 'n' roll fans waiting for me after every show to sign posters, but it was almost as if Carl expected the *favored nations* contract to guarantee he had as many fans as I did. It doesn't work like that.

He started to resent the fans that I had, and any extra attention that I got. It was a scenario I was unfortunately used to. Carl and I were great friends. It hurt me very deeply when resentment got in the way of a friendship that I held dear to my heart.

This fact is, the devil always gets all of the cool songs. The best songs of *Jesus Christ Superstar* are not sung by Jesus. Judas gets the best songs. Without a doubt, the song that I should've been singing in that play was "Heaven on Their Minds." The opening of the show, which is as close to a heavy metal epic as you can get on a Broadway stage. A great piece of music. I ended up having to stand at the top of the stage with my arms outstretched, motionless, while Carl sang the song. He did an incredible job. But a lot of the fans coming to see me sing felt ripped off that for over $100 a ticket I didn't really sing that much in the play.

The ending of the show, the curtain call, became the straw that broke Jesus's camel's back. The cast members would come out to the refrain, the *coda* of the song "Jesus Christ Superstar," and naturally Judas would be the second last on stage, and then Jesus would come out last. Night after night, the crowd would save their biggest response for when Jesus came on the stage. Which was kind of appropriate, being that the name of the play was *Jesus Christ Superstar*. Not *Judas Priest Superstar*.

One day, on the way to the show in Indianapolis, Carl and I were following each other to the theater for the matinee performance. It was a crisp, bright winter day. Being that we were *favored nations*, Carl and I drove our rental cars in tandem to the venue. All of a sudden, I looked in my rearview mirror and Carl was no longer following me. "*That's weird,*" I thought. My cell phone rang. It was Carl.

"Sebastian!! I just got in a fender bender!! I'm not going to be able to do the show!!!" This was the very first time that Carl didn't play the role of Judas, and an understudy would be onstage that day with me.

As I drove on, I actually passed Carl somehow. He must have passed before without me realizing it. I looked to my left, and there was Carl on the side of the road. Regaling the police and other people in the area where the accident was, various passersby. I can see it clearly now. That was his personality. He was a very big presence. Spiritually, vocally, physically. I smiled to myself as I looked at him. Entertaining everybody around him, even at the scene of a car accident. He couldn't help it. To be entertaining simply was the man's nature.

Carl had a birthday coming up. Natalie Toro, who played Mary Magdalene in the show, suggested to me that we have a surprise birthday party for Carl, in my hotel suite. I was totally excited and into the idea to throw a birthday party for my friend. Little did any of us realize this would be the last birthday Carl Anderson would ever have.

Cleveland, Ohio
February 27, 2003

The suite was packed with party guests. Cast and crew members from the show, friends, family, local theater enthusiasts from the Cleveland area. I had a two-story suite with a circular staircase that was perfect for entertaining. This was Carl's birthday, and Jesus was going to give Judas a great time tonight. The wine flowed and we were all laughing. It was a very fun party in honor of Carl's birthday. I really loved the guy. We all did.

By this time, after six months on the road, the tension was undeniable. Carl and the "legit" theater crowd had come to resent the rock 'n' roll fans that I brought to the show. But nobody resented the attendance figures, or the box office receipts. Of course, I began to *resent* them for resenting *this*.

It became mind-numbingly depressing and repetitive to do the role eight times a week. I myself ended up doing the show for exactly six months. Eight performances a week. And I never missed the show. No matter what the drama or backstage tension was, and there was a lot.

We hit Columbus, Ohio, around the first week of April. My birthday. A meeting was called for the full cast and crew. We were to have an afternoon "rehearsal" on one of the days of the show. *Are you kidding me?* we all thought. We had been doing the show for six months now. We were completely "rehearsed" beyond belief. There was no reason to do this. There had to be ulterior motives of some kind. The whole tour was sold out across America. You couldn't even get a ticket. We knew what we were doing.

As it turned out, when it came time for the rehearsal, I couldn't believe what we were there to accomplish. At the end of the show, I would come out last and get the crowd going. Get everyone clapping to the beat of the theme song. After being on the cross and dying, with everyone in the venue crying, it felt good to have people wipe the tears from their eyes and smile. Laugh. Feel good as they exited the show. Every night, the object of that performance was to have the cast, crew, and audience in tears at the end of the piece. It became quite a lot to bear, month after month after month. If we didn't feel that everybody was crying at the end of the show, we felt like we had not done a good job that night. "Hey man, we kicked ass tonight." The big road crew dudes would high-five me coming off the cross. "Yeah man, that was really kick-ass." We would blubber to each other with tears running down our faces.

God, I wanted to rock. That's all I could think about. I want to have *fun* onstage again.

The director of the play, a pasty-faced short little white New Yorker dude, was certainly no Robin Phillips, in any way whatsoever. The purpose of the rehearsal in Columbus was to eliminate me from clapping at the end of the curtain call. It had nothing to do with the show itself. The producers had grown tired of the audience response that I was receiving at the end of the show. So, in front of the whole cast and crew, I was told to simply walk on the stage and not clap. "Jesus wouldn't do that."

How would you know? Were you there?

Starting now, Jesus would come out *before* Judas. Judas would come out at the very end of the curtain call, from this day forward. I was being demoted for no reason whatsoever other than I was getting the crowd too excited, and that didn't fit into the *favored nations* contract, I guess. So their only choice was to have Jesus not come out last, in Jesus's play. And to not let Jesus clap at the end of the show.

I couldn't believe this. Natalie Toro, and other cast members, came up to me in the rehearsal and were high-fiving me with a look in their eyes that said, "Wow. I'm sorry, dude. *This really sucks.*" I had had enough. I marched up to my dressing room. Took my ghetto blaster and my KISS posters off the wall. I called Jo Jo, one of the roadies I had in Madam X back in 1985. He came down to the theater to help me pack my shit. *Fuck this. I'm out.*

Carl Anderson met me in the stairwell on the way down in the street. He wanted to fight. Judas versus Jesus. For real.

"You really *piss me off*."

"Oh well. I'm sorry, Carl. I don't mean to piss you off. Look. We all know. You guys just got the wrong Jesus."

This remark only incensed him more. We squared off in the stairwell. There was no way I was going to physically fight this man that I loved. He was mad as hell. I wasn't going to take it anymore.

Ladies and gentlemen . . . Jesus has left the building.

The last place I want to be is somewhere I am not wanted to be. My Madam X roadie drove me to the airport to get a Hertz rental car. I put my stuff in the back of the car and aimed it towards New Jersey. Towards home. A place I had not been in six months now. I missed my children. I missed having fun. I guess it was true what the placard said. *Jesus is not a rock star.* At least not this one.

I drove through the snow for a day or two. When I got home, I was incredibly sad. All I really needed was a couple of days off. Pretty much every person in the cast had missed a show, or partaken in a day or two off. I had taken *no* shows off. After six straight months, I needed a rest. I got home, and people were very mad that I did not return to the play. They sent me my last paycheck on April 3, 2003, my thirty-fifth birthday. I had spent my thirty-fourth year as Jesus.

A couple of weeks later, I received incredibly shocking news. Natalie Toro called me. "Sebastian. You're not going to believe this. Carl Anderson has leukemia."

It turned out that when Carl got in the fender bender, on our way to the performance in Indianapolis, he had experienced pain in his knee when he hit the dashboard upon contact with the other vehicle. He went to the doctor about his knee, only to receive the following news.

"Carl, I hate to inform you of this. But you have leukemia."

I couldn't believe what I was hearing. *This* man? So strong, so vibrant, so alive? With as much energy, talent, and presence than anyone I had ever been on the stage with before? How could *this* guy be sick? How could *this* guy have the same disease *as my dad*? At the same exact age? Made no logical sense whatsoever.

Fuck you, cancer.

I had spent Thanksgiving with Carl Anderson. With his beautiful wife, Veronica, his stepdaughter Laila Ali, and her husband at their house in Las Vegas. Laila Ali lived in the same development as Vince Neil. We spent half the day at Vince's house, looking at Mötley Crüe memorabilia. Vince then drove us over to Laila's house, where we spent Thanksgiving dinner. I had remarked to Veronica Ali, Muhammad Ali's ex-wife who was also Carl's ex-wife, "Wow, these colored greens sure are delicious!" The house erupted into laughter. "*Colored* greens? I like that one." Carl, Veronica, and Leila all laughed at my Canadianism.

I thought that's what they were called.

I had a great friend in Carl Anderson. I had learned so much from him about singing. About performance. About hard work. About red wine. And now he had the same disease, at the same age, that I was singing to my father about, every night, during the show. I couldn't believe the odds of this.

Months later, I got another phone call from Natalie.

"Carl died."

That was it. Since his birthday in Cleveland in February, since I had been fired on my birthday in April, less than a year later, Carl passed on. From the same accursed disease as my own dad. A father figure to me, Carl also left us at the same age as my father. And my father's father before him.

I will miss you, Carl. Thank you so much for the inspiration, friendship, and talent you shared with us so generously. You were one of the greatest singers I have ever known, and were a great friend to me, and everyone else you worked with. All I know is this. When I reach the age of fifty-eight?

I will think of you both.

Gilmore Girls

After Broadway, I got yet another surprising telephone call. From Barbara Skydel, again.

Telling me about a TV show called *Gilmore Girls*. My first response was, "What is that?"

She explained to me the premise of the show. A mother (played by Lauren Graham) and daughter (played by Alexis Bledel) struggle to make it on their own, in their hometown of Stars Hollow. Alexis puts together a band with her friend (played by Keiko Agena). I was to play the "hunky guitar player" of Lane's band (played by Keiko Agena). Thus "Gil," on guitar, was born.

Gilmore Girls is a big TV show that continues to play around the world to this day. It's funny how I get recognized in different areas of the public. In certain parts of town, rock 'n' roll bars, music stores, etcetera, I will get recognized for Skid Row. In Canada, I will get recognized for *Trailer Park Boys*. But in shopping malls across America? Museums in Italy, walking the streets of Europe or South America? If it's a little girl, with her mom, I will invariably hear the following words: "*Oh my God, it's that guy from Gilmore Girls.*" I was on the show for seven seasons, and very much enjoyed my time interacting with such a fun and talented cast and crew.

One of the actresses on the show was none other than Sally Struthers, who played Gloria on one of my all-time favorite TV programs, *All in the Family*. We had a wild night at her house, with me and my stand-in on the show, Kerry. Stoned out of my mind, I was staring at all the Emmy awards from her decades in the business. I remember Sally was laughing the whole time and it was really fun to party with Gloria. I almost felt like a Meathead myself that night.

One of my favorite memories of the show was the day when Geddy Lee of Rush came to visit on set, with his daughter, who was a very big fan of the show. Kerry called me in my hotel room at the Sheraton Universal.

"Hey dude! You're not going to be believe who's here to watch us today!"

"Who is that?"

"Geddy Lee of RUSH is here!!!"

I was like, "*What?*"

Gives you an idea as to the scope of the show. I went down to the set, and there he was. The Voice of the Holy Triumvirate Himself. A Canadian Deity. He told us all that he and his daughter enjoyed *Gilmore Girls* very much, and he complimented me on my transition from rock 'n' roll to television. "Seamless," he told me. I beamed with pride. We had such a great time that day. Around dinnertime, I said to Geddy, "Hey man!!! Why don't you and your daughter *be in the show?"* He started laughing, and said, "Oh, I don't know, Sebastian. Let me think about it." I ran over to Helen Pai, producer (whose name was an anagram for our band, Hep Alien). I said, "Oh my God, we *have* to have Geddy Lee on the show!!" I knew that Daniel Palladino, and Amy Sherman-Palladino, series creators and writers, would love it. (I had spent a booze-fueled night at the Rainbow with Daniel, talking about the day he first saw Rush, on their first-ever tour playing in the Los Angeles area, back in the '70s.) She said, "Okay," and we filmed a scene in which Geddy and I sang and played guitar. Sadly, when it came time to watch the episode, Geddy was barely noticeable in the scene. Which was a real shame. But it was so much fun hanging out with them that day and working together for an hour or two. It felt amazing to be on a television set with Gloria from *All in the Family* and the *lead singer of Rush*, all at the same time. Was this a dream I was living? Or what?

SuperGroup.
Well, It's a Group . . .

2006
Las Vegas, Nevada

A far more silly television venture presented itself as an opportunity from VH1. A reality-tv show (#redflag) called *SuperGroup.* I was to be paired in a house in Las Vegas with none other than Ted Nugent, Scott Ian, Evan Seinfeld, and Jason Bonham. We were to perform a concert at the end of the two-week filming, where we lived together at the house of notorious Las Vegas character Nico Santucci.

Perhaps the most ironic thing about this television show was that our group was to be managed by none other than Doc McGhee. The guy who had signed me to a management contract when I was a teenager. None of us knew who the other cast members of the show were before we got to Las Vegas. When I entered the rehearsal room, and found out that I was going to be in a band with Ted Nugent, on a TV show, I couldn't even fathom my own life.

My dad had given me the album *Weekend Warriors* on the exact same Christmas day that he gave me the KISS album *Alive!* back in the '70s. I had stared at that cover painting of Ted, shooting bullets out of his guitar, for untold hours. Brought it with me to All Saints Church Choir practice, to wave around the room and show it to my friends. Ted Nugent was one of my all-time musical and personal heroes. He was without a doubt the funniest, wildest front man in rock. But even more than that, one of the most talented guitar players the world will ever hear. I could not have had more love in my heart for Ted Nugent. Before we shot the show.

This was after my dad, grandfather, and Carl Anderson all died near the age of fifty-seven. Ted, when we began the show, was exactly fifty-seven years old. So he obviously assumed the role of my father on *SuperGroup*. The fact that Ted was this age while we shot the show was not lost on me. I definitely looked up to him as a fatherly figure, a mentor, a confidant. Ted played the role well, and was very nice, even showing compassion towards me about losing my dad. Since they were the same age, when I was with Ted, that my dad died, it was easy to relate to him. And he to me. The fact that Dad had bought *Weekend Warriors* for me at Christmastime endeared Uncle Ted to my dad, without a doubt.

After my experience in *Jesus Christ Superstar*, I had started to drink wine every single night. Carl Anderson turned me onto it, and I had subsequently developed a taste for grapes bordering on the voracious. I learned on the show *SuperGroup* that a little alcohol goes a long way while shooting a television show. After watching the show, I vowed to myself I would *never* drink on television, ever again. And I haven't.

Ted has always viewed himself as a strong campaigner against drinking and drug use. I was drinking wine and smoking during the making of *SuperGroup* and he knew it. Ted's admonishment of me became a part of the show. The climax of the last episode, in concert, where I pretend to drink Jack Daniel's onstage, drove Ted nuts and was actually quite a funny part of the show.

One incident sticks out in my mind from *SuperGroup*. I knew that Ted had racist tendencies, or at least I myself had heard him use reprehensible words such as the n-word. I had known this from the time I shot an episode of *Forever Wild* at Ted's house, in upstate Michigan. After a day of shooting, we had a barbecue on his deck with his friends. Once the cameras were turned off, I was shocked at the language of these guys. It was all n-word this, *black* this, talking about the Detroit riots in the late '60s and other stuff that nobody else I knew was talking about decades later. It broke my heart that this guy I looked up to musically so much came off as so backward in his attitude towards race. Coupled with his happy-go-lucky attitude towards killing animals, I've always thought it a shame that Ted's lifestyle and political leanings in his later years undoubtedly overshadow his incredible *music*.

One day we were shooting *SuperGroup* in the Las Vegas house. Ted was on the couch, and I was next to him. We were discussing band names and I ended up thinking up the name Damnocracy, which was no doubt a crap name, but the best that we could do, under the gun.

Out of nowhere, Ted burst into a rant to no one, and everyone.

"You want to know something, Mr. Bach????"

"What's that, Uncle Ted????" I was laughing. Ted was so funny he made my cheeks hurt when he talked. I always had to rub my face after hanging out with him, he was so hilarious.

"Let me tell you something right now, Sebastian. I am as BLACK as a black coal miner in the black of a black night! I am a *nigger*. I tell you what, Sebastian! Uncle Ted *don't lie!* I'm as *black* as a *black cold night* under the *black moon!* I'm a black *knight!* I'm as black as James Brown pullin' a black train of black coal into his black *town!*" The smile had disappeared from my face.

I couldn't stand the way Ted talked like this. It made me sick to my stomach. Coming from the Bahamas, going to school at Mary Star of the Sea School in Freeport, the only white boy in a class of forty black children, I have never been able to understand racism in any way. It makes me angry and nauseous.

Not everyone in the room was Caucasian. As I looked up, to my shock and horror, I saw the men behind the cameras. The cameramen who had been filming this exchange with the Nuge were African American gentlemen. They were repulsed and horrified at Ted Nugent's words. I got up from the couch, embarrassed. I was ashamed as I walked past the cameramen and out of the room. Disgusted, I did not want to be filmed next to this archaic exchange of words that was horrible for *all* to hear. I certainly did not want what was just filmed to ever end up on TV, or anywhere.

I called the producer Rick Krim, the man behind SuperGroup. Who was also responsible for first airing Skid Row videos in the late '80s. He had a conversation with Ed Luftglass on the set, and together they summoned the balls to *confront Ted Nugent.*

"I can't fucking do this, dude."

"What?"

"I can't be on TV next to Ted Nugent using the n-word. Telling everybody he's black. He's actually a white, middle-age man. He's not black. He's not James Brown. I thought the cameramen were going to start crying, for fuck sakes. That's enough."

"Okay. I'll talk to Ted."

The next time I saw Ted, he was storming around the house, yelling at anybody and everybody.

"What the *fuck*? I can't say what I want to say? I can't use the words I want to use? Whoever is any of these producers to tell me what to say?"

It was completely lost on the Motor City Madman how his insensitive words, from another time, had hurt actual, real people in the room with him in the year 2004. I would not be a part of a hurtful campaign of bigotry right in the room with crew members he did not even seem to acknowledge. He certainly did not seem to have any sort of remorse for the *pain* of his words, that hurt these guys, who were only there doing their job. Which was to try and make Ted Nugent look good.

Celebrity Fat Club

2007
Southern California

A year or so later, I would film another show on VH1 called *Celebrity Fit Club*. Along with Bobby Brown, Kevin Federline, Nicole Eggert, Jay McCarroll, and others, we got through the show. As cringeworthy as the title is, I actually did lose a lot of weight and learned a lot about eating healthier and fitness. One day I was walking across the military boot camp set complete with Drill Sergeant Harvey Walden. Producer Keith Geller came up to me and said, "Hey man, these dudes want to talk to you."

"Who?" I asked.

He led me over to these two African American dudes. I did not know who they were. Or, more accurately, I did not *remember* who they were. But I had indeed encountered them before.

"Hey, Sebastian. We were the two cameramen that were filming you and Ted Nugent that day on *SuperGroup*. The time when you stopped the shoot and stomped off the set. We want you to know something right now."

"We will never forget what you did that day."

I laughed at first, and then got a little emotional. They got emotional as well. They shook my hand and looked me straight in the eye. They proceeded to explain to me how much it meant to them that I stormed off the set, and how they dug it how I had the balls to tell the producers to tell Ted Nugent to shut the fuck up. They explained to me that they would never forget me standing up to The Nuge in front of them, and that they would always have my back, in any way, as well.

If you could've told me, when I was ten years old, that the words of two strangers would mean more to me than the respect of the almighty Ted Nugent, I would have not have believed you. But racism is simply abhorrent to me. I do not understand it. Yes, I love the guitar solos. The hair. The loincloth. "Cat Scratch Fever." I really love the song "Smokescreen." But if that same smoke screen is used to cover up something as stupid as racism, then I'm sorry, I'm out. I did not mean to make any sort of statement that day while shooting *SuperGroup*. I just could not be in the same room as any fool who uses those words. I don't give a fuck who you are. But my actions meant something to these two cameramen.

And that meant something to me.

Once again, standing up for something I believed in, made a difference to a stranger that I did not know. Just like rock 'n' roll.

Don't ever be afraid to stand up for what you believe in.

Even to your heroes.

Sometimes you should leave people on a pedestal. Where maybe, they should remain.

Because sometimes, if you pick them up, they can easily drop.

And break.

Trailer Park Boys

As I've said, depending where I am, I get recognized for different things. When I go to a rock 'n' roll bar, it's Skid Row of course. When I go to a shopping mall packed with twelve-year-old girls, worldwide it's "Aren't you that guy from *Gilmore Girls*? But when I walk the streets of Canada, my home country, there is one thing that I get noticed for, above all else.

"Hey!!!! Who out here likes *model fucking trains*?" comes the rallying cry.

The funniest TV show I have ever seen in my life is called *Trailer Park Boys*. Starring Bubbles, Ricky, and Julian, along with Mr. Lahey, JRock, and who can forget Cyrus. "You don't even fucking *know* that nobody even fucking *likes* bullies!!!" I wrote that line. They kept it in. Memes we made out of this. I mean, that Cyrus is a *dick*.

When I first saw the show, I was more than a bit confused. I actually thought, *Is this a real show?* After about fifteen minutes, I realized it was, in fact, *a comedy*. Go back to the beginning of this book. Doing acid, jumping off the bridge? Into the waters of Peterborough, Ontario? Getting high playing Asteroids in the arcade? Collapsing into the fetal position at the variety store? We kind of lived just like this, in the late '70s/early '80s, in Canada. At least we did in my town.

I have since become great friends with the lads. To the point where, in 2006 on the road with Guns N' Roses in Canada, we invited the Trailer Park Boys to go on tour with us. They came on the bus, and traveled the snowy Canadian highways and byways, all across the country, partying and rocking with us. When I showed Axl Rose the show for the first time, he erupted with such hilarity we all took notice. The show resonated with him as much as with me. Or maybe Indiana was a lot like Ontario back then. Maybe that was the way pretty much everywhere. Regardless, Bubbles in particular became very close friends with Axl. To the point where I was on tour in 2010 with GNR in Australia, I open my hotel room door, and there is Bubbles with his glasses on, looking for some dope.

I look forward to much more meaningful acting with the Trailer Park Boys, well into my elderly years. As long as I don't have to pay for that bee on the honey oil as well, eh?

15

BACH IN THE SADDLE

The Return of the Redheaded Stranger

2006

I received a mysterious phone call. Actually it was a text. It just said, "Hey. It's Axl."

I was like, *"Which one of my friends is playing a stupid joke on me?"*

There was no way this was Axl Rose. That didn't even enter my mind. I thought for sure this must be a friend of mine playing some sort of trick.

Then I looked at the area code for whoever sent the message. It said 310. Southern California. Could it really be? So, on a whim, I just pressed "call number." A deep voice answered the phone. "Hello?" There was no mistaking the tone. The intensity. It was indeed my friend from the past . . . Mr. Axl Rose. "I figured thirteen years was enough," he deadpanned.

True. It had been thirteen years since we last spoke.

We began texting each other. A lot. It was really cool. It made me feel important. Because nobody had any idea what Axl had been up to for well over a decade now.

I always have wondered, *what does that say about me*? I guess it's a testament to our friendship years before. Maybe he could relate to what I do, the way I can relate to what he does. Maybe it's because I just treat him like a normal guy. Which not many people seem to be capable of doing.

I was doing promotions for the *SuperGroup* television show and was making an appearance on the Q104 FM Friday Night Rock show. Also in attendance were Chris Jericho and Scott Ian. We were doing a standard interview. I was texting Axl while we were on the air. Everybody was blown away. Especially Eddie Trunk.

Axl texts to me, "What you doing?" I told him I was on the radio right there and then. I started getting texts from Beta and her son Fernando, Axl's assistants. "Yeah? Is it cool?" I told them, "Yeah. We're just shooting the shit live on the air. Getting ready to wrap it up. Having a couple of drinks. Come on down!!" Incredibly, Axl said, "Maybe I will." I thought nothing of it. I told everyone there that he was saying he was going to come down, but even I myself did not believe that to be true. There was no way he was going to show up at the station. It was one in the morning. We had been on the air for hours. We were getting ready to split.

Just before we were about to all go home, I looked up at the security cameras which were focused on the lobby down below. There was a sudden burst of activity on the street level. I saw the security guards and other people rustling around a couple of other, unseen people. Three or four figures burst out of the melee and walked with intent towards the elevator.

Could it really be?

And then, through the door, there he was. For the first time in well over a decade, I saw my friend again. He had come to be part of an interview that is now the stuff of legend. It was incredible to see him again, for the first time in so long.

Thus began a rekindling of our friendship that proved to be extremely helpful to my solo career. Axl does not let many people into his world. But when he does, he treats you like family and is as generous and giving as can be. He began inviting me to cities around the globe, to jam with him onstage at the end of Guns N' Roses shows. I would get a call and it would say: "Baz, get to JFK. You have a First Class ticket to Dortmund, Germany. You're going to be on stage with Guns N' Roses in 12 hours at Rock AM Ring in front of 70,000 people. Get your ass to the airport." The expense and effort he would go to, just to have me sing one song with him in a foreign country, was astonishing to me.

One night, at Castle Donington in England, the insanity was palpable in the air. Axl had been late going to some of his shows and his then-manager, Merck Mercuriadis, pleaded with me in any attempt, however vain, to somehow get him to the stage on time. Axl's vocal warm-up, even in 2006, was on a *cassette*. Even with the advent of recordable CDs, and by that time digital music players, the biggest rock star in the world was warming up his voice to a cassette. There was no cassette player in the hotel room that day. Merck and Fernando were frantically scouring the local area around the hotel for an analog cassette player, to no avail.

Somehow a tape player was located and the show went on. We all took a helicopter to the concert site. We were late for the show and the crowd was restless.

Axl's friend, a girl named Diane from New York, was on the side of the stage. Her fun, happy demeanor changed when she, along with everyone else, felt the crowd turn a black mood. Axl came onstage, only to stop the show after a couple of songs due to the stage being slippery. He refused to go back on until it was made "safe," and he would not slip, while performing. Diane burst into tears as the crowd started to boo. I told her this was all part of rock 'n' roll. She did not understand how heavy this shit could get. Having been on the road with Axl Rose for decades now, I fully understood the volatility and intensity of how the situation could get. Diane didn't understand that Guns N' Roses fans *expected* danger.

The band went back onstage and finished the show. Near the end of the set, bass player Tommy Stinson took his instrument off and proceeded to smash a cameraman over the head who got too close to him near the front of the stage. The cameraman was part of the GNR crew and did not understand why he was being attacked for simply doing his job. Tommy was so drunk, I bet he didn't even know he was attacking his own employee.

The show finished. Axl was in a rotten mood. "Come on. With me. Right now." He demanded that I get on the helicopter with him and Diane. He was so mad at Merck, that he refused to let him on the helicopter ride back home. Merck was completely incensed that Axl would take me on the helicopter, instead of him. He was left to drive hours back in a car, along with the 70,000 or so concertgoers, the considerable distance back to London from the Donington festival site.

We took off in the helicopter back to London. Axl was in foul spirits and refused to put his seat belt on. I had been drinking and I had a pretty good buzz on by now. Axl was despondent about the show, and kept talking about how bummed out he was and what a shit mood he was in. His hand fidgeted nervously on the door handle of the helicopter. I looked at him, thinking to myself, *Oh my God. He is going to open up the door and jump right the fuck out of here. To his death. It's up to me to save him.* I spent the rest of the flight with my eyes affixed to his every movement. Like a laser beam. I was not going to let my friend die. Axl was just crazy enough to make me think this was a possibility.

We got back to the hotel, which happened to be the Mandarin Oriental, on London's prestigious West End. Sat down at the bar downstairs and started inhaling bottles of red wine. Axl started getting into a good mood. The waitress approached us. "Hi! Axl! Sebastian! *Do you know who is sitting over there?*" she whispered to us. We both shook our heads. *"Jon Bon Jovi."* I couldn't believe it.

Jon and I had had a falling-out about Skid Row royalties back in 1990. We traded barbs in the press. I said some extremely immature things that I had regretted years later. Jon took a chance on me, and our band. I had achieved the impossible, which was to make a living playing the music I love. At the end of the day, I will always be indebted to him for that.

Fuck it, I thought. I stood up and walked over to Jon. He looked up from his glass of wine and stared at me. What was I gonna do? He was trying to read me. Was I going to be cool? Was I going to be a dick? The ball was in my court.

Maybe it was the wine talking. I had no desire to quarrel with him, or anybody at that moment. I stretched out my arm and we shook hands. Jon stood up. "Hey man!" We hugged each other like old friends. Which we were.

I invited him over to Axl's table and we all sat down. The Italian wine flowing, we discussed the business of rock 'n' roll, what we were all doing. Axl had told me he admired Jon's business acumen. We talked about the tour and had a great conversation. At one point, I congratulated Jon on his latest single, which was a country cross-over track called "Who Says You Can't Go Home." It was a hit, and based on that, I congratulated Jon on his success. Jon said "thanks a lot" and looked over at Axl. Axl did not say a word.

The next day, I was with Axl. "Hey man! That was really cool of you to congratulate Jon on the success of his song!!" Axl turned to me and snapped. "I never fucking *congratulated* him on the success of his *fucking song*! That was *you*! I never said *anything*! I never said that!!" Evidently, Axl wasn't a fan of the song.

One night we went out to dinner. Italy, I think it was. Axl had invited the whole band and the whole crew to a posh Italian eatery. I was very excited to be there. He was seated at the head of the table. I was in the middle. Of everybody else.

"Hey Axl! I'm on this TV show, man! It's fucking crazy!" This was after *SuperGroup* had finished filming, but before it aired. The show was a lot more fun to film than it was to watch.

I excitedly blabbered on to Axl. "You know what dude? I got paid X amount of money. For only two weeks' work!! You know what?? I *guarantee*, if they would pay *me* that much, they would *definitely* pay you, I dunno, like a *million* dollars!!!" Axl looked at me with a steely glare. Rolled his eyes. He was not impressed. "Sebastian. You don't understand. I will pay VH1 1.5 million dollars . . . to *leave me the fuck alone*."

You could hear a pin drop in the restaurant.

I don't think you'll be seeing the Axl Rose VH1 reality show anytime soon.

One night at the Hammerstein Ballroom, in New York City, Kid Rock and myself are jamming with Guns N' Roses. Jimmy Fallon was there, along with cast members from *The Sopranos*. It was on this night where I met the second manager of my career, Mr. Rick Sales.

Making Metal Dreams Come True

There he was, backstage with us. Looking like a heavy metal Jack Nicholson, hanging out and watching the GNR show. I had only ever had one manager in my life, Doc McGhee. Along with Doc's brother Scott, they were the only guidance I had ever had in the music industry, up until the time I met Rick Sales. I have been working with Rick ever since that day. Rick Sales and his team have put me to work consistently since then. My co-manager Ernie Gonzalez helps Rick navigate the madness. I had already started recording the album *Angel Down* when Rick became my manager. He started guiding my career right as I was recording *Angel Down* and right before the show *SuperGroup* started airing on TV.

It's absolutely essential to have a manager in the entertainment industry. With rock 'n' roll, Broadway, television, recording, and touring, it became impossible for me to manage my career by myself in any way. Rick also taught me one valuable lesson . . . about saying "no." No more tribute records for $700 on a Saturday afternoon. I was amazed that people rarely accept no for an answer. Much like the time I turned down *Rocky Horror* on Broadway, I learned that saying "no" is one of the most important parts of this industry.

We continued recording the album with producer Roy Z, at the legendary Sound City Studios in North Hollywood. The same Sound City that Dave Grohl made that movie about. I had never been in a studio like this. Basically the biggest difference about Sound City was its lack of automation. Even on the first Skid Row album, back in 1989, when we wanted to hear a song playback, producer Michael Wagener could program the faders for a rough mix each time we listened back. Volume levels, EQ levels, would all change in real time, on the fly, via the computer-automated system. Sound City had no such automation. Every time we would record a song, I would ask Roy Z to hear it back, and he would say, "Dude, this isn't a mixing studio." We were there *just* for recording, not mixing or even playback. We had to go to another studio for that.

I must admit listening back, you can feel the power and the vibe of Sound City on the album *Angel Down*. After my first solo record, *Bring 'Em Bach Alive!* on Atlantic Records, this was a big deal to me. My very first all-studio solo record. With Steve DiGiorgio, Bobby

Jarzombek, Metal Mike, and Johnny Chromatic, my live band, we went in there and knocked out a record that has lasted the test of time along with the classic Skid Row CDs from years ago.

On a whim, I asked Axl Rose to sing on the record with me. I had sung the song "Sorry" on the Guns N' Roses record *Chinese Democracy* in New York City at Electric Lady. So, kind of joking around, I said, "Hey! Axl! When are you gonna sing on *my* record?"

"Where? When?" I couldn't believe his reply.

Neither could the record company. After all was said and done, they wanted to release two versions of *Angel Down*. One with just me singing on the record, and one with Axl and me both. I told them politely to *go fuck themselves*. This was my record. Take it or leave it. Yes, Axl is my friend. But Axl Rose's voice is one of the most defining, intense, and badass-sounding instruments in the whole world of rock 'n' roll. To have the sound of his voice, alongside mine, on my record, would be incredible to listen to for me and the fans.

The first song we cut was a cover of the Aerosmith track "Back in the Saddle." The screams that Steven Tyler hits, with such range and force, on the original *Rocks* album recording has always set the bar for any heavy metal screamer. It was a complete gas to scream as high and as loud as we could. Axl said he had always wanted to sing that song. I did too. Roy Z came up with the idea, and we created a heavy metal–blues scream jam that kicks ass along with the best of 'em. Joey Kramer told me he heard our version, and that he loved it. If the drummer from Aerosmith digs the track, that's good enough for me. Thank you, Joey!

The second track we cut was the first single from the album *(Love Is) A Bitch Slap*. A mean riff, over a fun, cowbell-driven rhythm, the track got a really cool write-up in *Rolling Stone* magazine: *"refreshing to hear Axl Rose with a band and a song as lean and as mean as this."* You're welcome, *Rolling Stone* and Planet Earth.

But my favorite collaboration between me and Axl on the *An-*

gel Down record is the song "Stuck Inside." This riff and monstrous groove contrast perfectly with the verses, which are clean and cool. The harmonies in the choruses are challenging. The middle of the song, where Axl comes in and wails, is possibly the most heavy metal moment I have ever heard Axl Rose sing since "My Michelle" back on *Appetite for Destruction.* The final chorus of the song builds into Axl hitting the top of his vocal range and beyond. I love this track and still play it live to this day.

The night Axl came down to record was legendary. I still really didn't believe he was going to sing on my record. Sure enough, at about midnight, he pulls up in a sports car outside the dingy little recording studio we had rented out for vocal overdubs. This was in a rough part of North Hollywood, and we actually got orange traffic pylons to surround his car so nobody stole it while we were session.

After "Back in the Saddle" and "(Love Is) A Bitch Slap," we had been rocking a couple hours. We had some Francis Ford Coppola Red wine floating around. We're smoking some pretty good weed. He was about to split after "Bitch Slap," but I was dying to hear him scream over the "Stuck Inside" riff. "Axl. Can you please just do *one* more?"

"What the fuck? I've been screaming all fucking night."

"Dude, come on. Just one more?"

He looked at me and said, "All right, fuck it," came into the studio, and asked for my silver briefcase. Sat down, wrote some words. Got up, went back behind the mike, and proceeded to kick some holy motherfucking ass on the track.

The fan favorite from the album *Angel Down* has got to be the song "American Metalhead." An extremely challenging song to sing, along with the song immediately following it, called "Live and Die." Along with "Negative Light," these are the most heavy metal songs I feel I've ever recorded. "American Metalhead" remains in the live set almost a decade later. The riff is immediate. The groove, punishing. We change the name of the song to suit whatever country we're playing that night. The place goes nuts when we rip into "Polynesian Metalhead." Or "Norwegian Metalhead." "Brazilian Metalhead." What have you.

One song on the record is called "By Your Side." A ballad that I wrote with Roy Z about the death of my father, the song has become a fan favorite, especially in South America, where it receives substantial airplay on the radio. Another song, called "Falling into You," is my only recorded piano ballad. I wrote this song with Desmond Child, at the behest of Jason Flom years ago, the song finally making it to the recording studio during the *Angel Down* sessions.

Despite the incredible production by Roy Z, amazing mastering by Tom Baker, and the legendary Axl Rose on three songs, the album did not sell as many copies as I thought it was going to during the first week of release. In my delusional mind, I just figured it would be a number-one record like *Slave to the Grind* was. I truly believe that the solo records I put out sound just as good in every way as the original Skid Row records. But we live in a different time. The advent of the Internet, streaming services, torrents, and downloads have completely changed what it means to be in a rock 'n' roll band today. But at the time of the *Angel Down* release, I still did not fully realize how different things worked. Call it a very rude awakening.

I was on the road on a radio tour across the country, promoting the record. In a car, traveling from morning radio station to morning radio station. In my mind, I figured if I do an interview on the morning show, the station will add my single into rotation. Of course, this never once happened. I was brought onto the morning radio station shows *as a celebrity*. Could've been Pauly Shore. Could've been Mr. T. Making an appearance on a morning radio station does nothing for a music career anymore. Yes, they will play Skid Row songs all day. But much like Nikki Sixx has said, and Ian Astbury,

Joe Perry, Steven Tyler, we're all in the same boat. Radio will not play any *new* song by any band that actually helped *build* the radio station. It's boring and it makes no sense whatsoever. But it's out of my control. All I can do is keep my head down and rock.

Being a guest on a morning radio show can be humiliating. Sure it can be fun, but a lot of the time you get the old "here's the dude from the *hair band* with the *hairspray*, it's back to the *eighties*, the spandex, get out the *Aqua Net*, get out your *hair dryers* and *lipstick*." I wanted to fucking smack idiot DJs who talked to me in this way. When I pull up to a gig, and I see on the marquee that I'm playing at the *World Series of Hair or SpandexFest,* it makes me want to physically vomit. It's so easy to just call something *rock 'n' roll*. The term *hair band* was invented in the late '90s for an infomercial record, I think it was *Freedom Rock*, dude. The term *hair band* did not exist when we were in Skid Row. If it did, I wouldn't have ever wanted to be in a hair band. All I have ever considered myself is rock 'n' roll, and that's all I ever will be.

After pointless morning radio show interviews talking about the old days and hair spray, not getting my song added into rotation, it became evident to me I was there for comic relief as much as anything else. That's not the reason I was traveling around the country. I started drinking *very* heavily the week when I found out *Angel Down* wasn't the number-one smash hit I expected it to be. After my morning radio press, I would go to the nearest bar and start drinking at about noon. Then we would drive to the next town. I feel sorry for Kyle, the record company guy who accompanied me that week. I was most definitely not fun to be around.

The record company that released *Angel Down* was simply not equipped in any way to deliver a Top 10 record. The unpronounceable name of Merovingian Music, run by by buddy Jack Ponti from New Jersey, put the album out. Distributed by Caroline Records, I should have known that this was not Universal, or Atlantic, or Geffen. This was MRV Records and I was lucky to be putting CDs out.

The fact was that MRV and Caroline Records could not compete with major labels and their distributors.

In my drunken, deluded mind, I began to lash out. "You mother-fuckers!! I gave you all *the return of Axl Rose*! I give you this incredible album on a silver platter!! And you *fuck it all up*!! What the *fuck*?" I would drunkenly yell at anybody who would listen. On one drive to a town on the radio station tour, I played the song "If You Want Me to Stay," by Sly & The Family Stone, on repeat for at least three hours. While I sat in the backseat, drinking myself into a stupor.

> *If you want me to stay*
> *I'll be around today*
> *to be available for you to see.*
> *But I'm about to go*
> *And then you'll know*
> *For me to stay here I got to be me.*

I looked up into the rearview mirror. Kyle, the record company guy, was looking back at me. Literally frightened at my sadness. I felt sorry for him. I can't stop playing the song. I just wanted the pain to stop.

We got to my last interview, at The Bone radio station in Houston. I entered the control booth where the two DJs were seated. There was an empty seat for me in front of the microphone. The video camera was placed to film me while I did the interview. For the whole Internet to see, they had placed a giant Skid Row poster so I would be surrounded by my old bandmates who had kicked me out of their band years before. This did not excite me in any way. As I walked into the radio station, I walked over and picked up the poster, and turned it around so that it was a blank sheet of cardboard.

This pissed off the DJs. "Why did you do that?"

"Because I'm not here to talk about the old days. Talking about the old days is fucking boring to me."

"What do you mean? You don't want to be associated with a platinum-selling band? That's Skid Row?"

"The only time they were ever a fucking platinum-selling fucking band was when I was singing the fucking songs. I have a new record out and that's why I flew here. You want to fucking talk about that?"

Gee, this interview is off to a great start.

Flew back to New Jersey after the Houston interview. I got completely shit-faced drunk the whole plane ride there.

Not an Anomaly

2009
Garden State Parkway, New Jersey

Drivin' down the road doing 95 miles per hour.

Oh yeah.

Making my weekly jaunt to the local record store to pick up some new music. I'm all excited, because today is the day the brand-new Ace Frehley CD is out. I can't wait to pick it up. I've never missed any release by a KISS member, and this is no different. I can't wait to check it out! I'm really hoping this will be a worthwhile, cool addition to my KISS collection. Ever since I was a little boy, I've looked forward to a day like this. Going to the record store, buying the latest album by my favorite band. Cracking open the release with my thumbnail. Opening it up. Looking at the packaging. Putting it on the stereo, cranking the shit out of it. Checking out what is the scene now with my favorite artist. The new Ace album is out! It should be a national fucking holiday.

I'm driving my IROC, the one that I took to The Ace's house so many moons ago. I even had him autograph the dashboard.

To Sebastian,
Rock on
Ace Frehley

In silver paint pen, on the vehicle. With KISS stickers on the side, as seen on *MTV Cribs*. After I sold my house, in 2015, the guy who bought it actually took my car, because it was on the property, and tried to *charge* me eight grand to get it back. *Fuck you, motherfucker. You can fucking have the fucking car. The memories mean nothing to me now. Drive it up your fucking asshole. Oh wait. It doesn't work. Ooops! How did that work out for you?*

But I digress. I'm wheeling around in the IROC, up and down the parkway. Crack open the new Ace CD. Put it in the player. The one with the flexible, bendy arm that I bought in 1990, when having a CD player in your car was like a new kind of space-age like technology. The bendable flexing arm let the IROC careen at extreme, fast speeds. With its little-to-no suspension, I could crank tunes without skipping. Let's check out the Ace.

Rock 'n' roll is a vicious game.

From the first chord of the first number, I cannot believe what I'm hearing. This is, without a doubt, the best Ace Frehley CD I have heard in years. Holy shit. I can't fucking *believe* how heavy this music is. Cranking it down the highway, I'm going, *Why is this so good?* The power, aggression, attitude, playing was like nothing I had ever heard on an Ace record before.

And then it hit me.

Oh.

My.

God.

This is it!!!!!!!

THIS IS THE SONG I WROTE WITH ACE FREHLEY!!!!!!!!!!
FINALLY!!!! OH MY GOD!!! You can't be serious.

"You Make It Hard for ME"!!!!! Holy FUCK!!! Anton was right!! The song sounds incredible. I cannot believe it!!! And there it is!!! My melody line. The main guitar riff, the music in the chorus, even the cowbell on Anton Fig's drums. The power chords. The down strokes I told him to do, just like Johnny Ramone. Everything is there. The only difference, fifteen years later, was that "You Make It Hard for Me" had now been changed to "Foxy and Free." Other than that, it was the same song I have on my microcassette from the Acement back in the mid-'90s. And here we are fifteen years later. The song had *finally* made it onto a CD. The *opening* song on the new record, no less! I could not believe the world was to hear what we had created, so many years before.

I shout screams of joy into the air as I was driving down the road. It sounds so *great*. Just the way I had intended it. Especially the riff in the chorus. It felt like it could have been off the album *Slave to the Grind*. The song had the feel of *Slave*, especially "Creepshow," with the cowbell behind the beat of the chorus. It kicked *total fucking ass*, even in the car, fifteen years down the line.

With my right hand, I grab the CD packaging from the passenger seat of the car. Excited to see my name, along with Ace Frehley's. This song was going to show the whole world The Ace was *back*. I couldn't wait to show my friends!

I open the CD packaging excitedly. Go to the first song. Look at the credits.

Song written by: Ace Frehley.

My name is nowhere to be found.

What? How can this be? There's no way.

And yet there it is. *Song written by Ace Frehley*. And Ace Frehley alone.

My name appears nowhere on the packaging.

Two songs later is a cover of a Sweet song, with the guys from

Sweet's names prominently displayed in the credits. The album is dedicated to Dimebag Darrell, the Pantera guitarist Snake had introduced him to. I had written the opening song to the record together with Ace, and yet my name was nowhere to be found.

I pull the car over. Pressed stop on the CD player. And cry.

I held my head in my hands and cried for a while. I shook in rage later, but crying was the first response. It was a childhood reaction. Based on childhood feelings. Staring at the wall of the KISS posters, imagining what it would be like to be in the band myself. Getting to not only meet my heroes, but make music with them as well. To be left off for my songwriting, and my publishing, was unfortunately not something new to me. Other guys like to paint themselves as songwriters, while painting me as the ubiquitous front man, only there to prance around the stage and do interviews and photos and talk between the songs. While they take care of all the *serious* work. But this has never, ever been *reality*. You can hear it for yourself. My records can all pretty much be identified by the way they sound. Can other musicians honestly say the same? If you listen to the first song on *Anomaly*, you will have no doubt that what I am saying is true.

When I tell this story to my friends, they say, "Well, why don't you solve this in court?" Because it's like taking Santa Claus to court. I love Ace Frehley. I have all my life. And I always will. So I've never even brought it up with Ace. And as disappointing as this is, I will not let it take away my love for Ace and KISS and rock 'n' roll. I never expected to make it in rock 'n' roll. I never expected rock 'n' roll to be *easy*. Or kind. This situation just reiterated what I already knew. Rock 'n' roll is, and always will be, a vicious game. As I wept in my car, I had to laugh at the same time. This is all Ace ever knew. To get screwed around by the music industry. This is all he *knew*. Bad contracts. Shitty deals. Getting ripped off. Underpaid. *It's a long way to the top, if you want to rock 'n' roll.* Rock 'n' roll will chew you up and spit you out. Rock 'n' roll is not for the weak. Rock 'n' roll is not for the faint of fucking heart, either. So get the fuck over it.

Why would I write about this in the book? The story is already out there on some KISS fan sites, and now I want my fans to know the actual truth of the situation. I love KISS and rock 'n' roll, but that is my song. As much as it is Ace's. I wrote it with my heart and my soul. For the guitar player that I loved. And always will love. I will not let the rock 'n' roll "music business" take away my actual love for rock 'n' roll *music*.

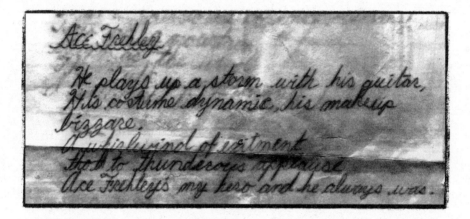

I Lost My Home in a Fucking Hurricane

Yes, that's right. It's true. Think of the fucking irony. Most musicians/entertainers who make it big eventually are forced to move from the big mansions they bought when they first "made it." It's the nature of the business. Usually, they say, a typical life span for an entertainer is somewhere around seven years. People get into you, they dig your whole scene, then they get tired of you, and move on to the next thing.

Never had that problem.

When I got kicked out of Skid Row in 1996, I was like a fish out of water. I did not know what to do. I had been in the band since 1987, so Skid Row was, is, and always will be, the "best" years of my life. My "prime" years. Ages twenty to twenty-seven or something. When I was no longer in the group, I literally had no idea what to do with myself.

But through my solo band, more television shows than I can remember, and Broadway, I was indeed able to support myself quite well, thank you very much. While my bandmates from Skid Row all moved out of their New Jersey mansions that we each bought, in 1990, I had been happily ensconced in my home for over twenty years. My real home. The only real home I ever really knew. Since my family moved to three different countries by the time I was eight, I made a promise to myself as a little boy that when I grew up, I would move as little as possible. I kept that promise to myself.

Fate had other plans.

In the summer of 2011, I was playing concerts. One of these shows was the Colorado Rock Jam, with Godsmack and Twisted Sister.

I knew there was supposed to be a storm hitting New Jersey that day. No big deal, I thought. I had lived in the same house for over twenty years. We had never had a drop of water, nary a trace of moisture, in the basement. The whole time we had lived there. My basement was beautiful. After *Jesus Christ Superstar*, I had earned enough money to completely finish the basement into the ultimate rock 'n' roll man cave. I called it "the Basement that Jesus Bought." The whole basement had hardwood floors. A full rehearsal studio, with full PA and monitors. A full recording studio. A guest bedroom. Soundproofed walls. A media center. All of my rock 'n' roll memorabilia, one-of-a-kind KISS and of course Skid Row items that only I possessed. We wrote and rehearsed the Skid Row album *Slave to the Grind* in this very basement.

Then Hurricane Irene happened. She took everything away. From me. From my family. From my past.

I have not healed from this whole experience yet. At all. My home was crucial to me. It's where I could shut everything out. Where the noise of the crowd, the glare of the spotlight, the stares of strangers all ceased to exist. I remember back in the early '90s, I wanted to move to Hollywood. I have always wanted to live in California, ever since I was a little boy and my dad would fly me and my sister to visit our grandma in Walnut Creek. Years later, I told Slash that I wanted to move to LA, and he said, "Baz, that's a bad idea. You can't move to LA. You belong on the East Coast. That's what grounds you." Part of me was hurt when he said that. It was like he didn't want to hang out with me or something. But, after thinking about it, I knew what he was saying was exactly true.

[[-Axl shipping me out of LA story?]]

Biblical in Proportions

2010-2014
Adventures in Couch Surfing
Los Angeles

Getting divorced, in 2010, was a trauma that I do not wish upon anyone. After I swore to myself when I was ten years old that I would never do that to a child of my own, to have my family break up was soul crushing.

There are so many reasons why this happened. I don't really feel like writing about it this book, because it's so much of a bummer.

After having three kids, and having been married for almost twenty years, I was faced with an uncertain future to be sure. My wife was divorcing me and Dad would not be there for the kids anymore. Just like my dad before me, and his dad before him.

All of this happened just a couple of months before our home was destroyed by Hurricane Irene. It's overwhelming to contemplate. The ramifications of all these occurrences, happening sequentially, were for my life truly biblical in proportions.

I had to run. I had to get away from New Jersey. I tried to have another house there. To be there for my kids, an hour or two after school, a couple of days a week. Most days I would sit in this little house, completely alone. I have never been a suicidal person. I'm too good at having fun for that. But sitting alone, in an empty house, in New Jersey, with no family, and no future that I was aware of, was the closest I have ever been to having no hope whatsoever. I simply had no idea what to do. I just wanted to spend time with my daughter, be there for her as she grew up. I was so ready for that. After all the mayhem and the craziness of my life, I finally had a beautiful little girl to call my own.

Then she was gone, too.

During the show *Celebrity Fit Club*, we all got prizes and extravagant rewards when our team won the challenge. Each one of us got no less than five trips, vacations at various exotic resorts around the world. My ex-wife and I were divorcing when I was rewarded these trips. To Cancún, different resorts in California, Puerto Vallarta, Aruba. How ironic that I could not find a girl to go with me to any of these. I was stuck with all these tickets and passes to resorts around the world. *With nobody to go with.* I said, "Fuck it, I'll go by myself." What did I have to lose?

Got on a plane. Went out to LA. Lined up three resorts in a row to go to. San Diego, Ojai, another one. When I got to LAX by myself, I rented a car by myself. Got in it by myself. Started driving down the highway to San Diego by myself. More alone than I had ever been in my life. *What the fuck was I doing?* I started crying so hard, it was almost impossible to drive. *I was driving by myself to an empty hotel room? For what? This was fucking insane. Was this what my life had come to? Why?*

I checked into a hotel on the beach. Went immediately to the bar. Started drinking. Of course people were like, "What in the fuck is Sebastian Bach doing here?"

I met a bunch of people and we partied. Big surprise. After goofing off in downtown San Diego that night, me and a bunch of other people I had just met went to the beach after the bars closed. I told this guy Jordan that my wife left me, and my kids were gone, and I would never see my daughter grow up. I was inconsolable.

"Well," he said, "I don't give a fuck what anybody says. Nobody in the world should ever be this *hurt*." I listened to what this dude said. He was right. Nobody should feel the way I was feeling. I had to figure out a way for me to even *want* to keep going.

California had always been the happiest place in the world to me. Whereas I had moved from country to country as a little boy, I had always gone to California on vacation. So in a way, California was the one *constant* in my home life. It never changed. It was always there. It was always beautiful. I always had a smile on my face when I was in California.

If there was one thing I needed desperately, it was a smile on my face. So I really had no other option. If I was going to start over, after losing my family, my home, my band, my dog, even my bird, California was the place to be. Beverly Hills. Swimming pools. Movie stars. Always dug that theme song.

My manager, Rick Sales, helped me immeasurably in this time period. He was always there for me. As a friend, talking as if he were family himself. The popular image of a rock 'n' roll manager is the cigar-chomping, big-wheel, head honcho. The unfeeling, uncaring megalomaniac. But I can say that Rick Sales honestly cares about the musicians he works with. He talks to you as a family member as well as a business associate. Which is just what I needed, going through all of this crazy crap. Rick knew what I was going through from life experience. I did not. All of this rotten life stuff was new to me.

I had nowhere to live. I had miles saved, from decades of travel. I cashed them all in for hotel rooms in LA, car rentals, and the like. I would have to send money back to my ex-wife in Jersey, which made it even harder to start over again. Stay in hotels, fly back to Jersey, come back here, back to Jersey again. Trying to stay in Jersey to see my kids. But I would never get to see them. They would rarely come over to the house and see me. There was literally zero point to me being there.

My last night in New Jersey was spent with my daughter at a restaurant. Just me and her, by ourselves, as it always was when I lived there. We went to eat dinner. I stared at my phone for a text that would never come. Absentmindedly watch the TV on the wall. I love my daughter so much. But a kid needs a mom *and* a dad to feel right. I don't know what to do to be happy. Us having dinner together two or three times a week does not make me happy. It's just not enough.

I needed to make a change. For myself. For her, too. I needed my daughter to know her father as a happy man. Not the sad dude she was talking to now.

Once again, rock 'n' roll comes along and saves my world. My friend Rita Haney, Dimebag Darrell's love of his life. We had been through so much together with Pantera. Taking them on tour. Them taking *me* on tour in my solo band. I made a Facebook post saying, "Hey. I'm looking for a place to stay in California." Rita read this and messaged me right away, saying, "Hey dude. You can stay at my house!!" I couldn't believe what I was reading. How rare is that in rock 'n' roll? Lots of people can talk the talk. But very few in show business actually Walk the Walk.

> *Re*
>
> *spect*
>
> *Are you talking to me?*

Me and Rita had fun living together. Although I was drinking heavily at this time. I stained her bedsheets with red wine. I also left the stovetop on, after I made coffee. I am sorry, Rita. I did not mean to do either of those things. I can never thank you enough for giving me a chance at a new life.

Alas, all good things must come to an end, and after a month or so, I needed to find another place to live. I had been jamming with the band Camp Freddy, whose members included Dave Navarro, Donovan Leitch, Chris Chaney, Mark McGrath, and on drums, Matt Sorum. I had been friends with Matt since the *Use Your Illusion* tour and it was fun to play with him again in Camp Freddy. "Hey Baz, come stay here with us. Until you can get back on your feet." I was so blown away. I had a great time staying at Matt's. Although he was sober, along with his awesome wife Ace, he would pour wine for me at night. Cooked breakfast for me in the morning. We went running a couple times, and genuinely got along great. He's a very nice guy and extremely professional musician.

After about two weeks, Matt came in the room and said, "Hey Baz. Me and Ace got to *get our vibe back*." He explained to me that his wife felt inhibited having loud sex, with me in the very next room. I told them to go for it! Fine with me.

I needed my own place to live.

Matt said, "Hey dude, let's just go walking around and look for a place." He loved to walk his dogs on the streets around their house.

We went on a walk. I took down phone numbers of available apartments. We strolled on down the street together, and saw there was a vacancy. Knocked on the door. A nice lady opened it up, and greeted us cordially. We explained to her that I was looking for a place to live, and she unbelievably said, "Well hey, you can stay here. I have an extra room." I could not believe what I was hearing. We were just walking around, and found a place without even trying. How does this even happen? I moved into Betsy's spare room. It was only a block or two away from Matt's. Betsy explained that when she saw me and Matt walking the dogs, coming towards her house, she thought that we were a gay couple. I laughed my ass off. She thought that Matt and I were a romantic couple, taking a stroll, walking our doggies, looking for cute apartments to check out. I explained to her that this was not the case. We laughed. I thank Betsy for her hospitality and generosity.

16

THE LAST FRONTIER

For my third studio record, *Kicking & Screaming*, my manager Rick Sales hooked me up with an incredible producer by the name of Bob Marlette. I have been working with Bob since then, due to the fact that he really helps me put together music I want to hear. And that I want you to hear.

Bob, in turn, hooked me up with the incomparable John 5. The guy that has literally reinvented rock 'n' roll guitar playing in recent years. The first time I had any contact with John 5 was years before there was a John 5. When he was just called John Lowery, he was a rock fan who waited in line all day to be part of the Skid Row "Piece of Me" video. You can see him jumping off the stage doing a stage dive, plain as day. If you can recognize him, that is.

John sent me a song called "Tunnelvision" that we still play live to this day. I played with other people on *Kicking & Screaming*. It was very much a snapshot of my life at that time. A confusing time for me, going through a divorce and losing my home. When I listen to *Kicking & Screaming* I'm very proud of the music on it. It's so much of a snapshot in time that it's hard for me to listen to these days. But

I stand by the album as a quality piece of music. The songwriting, musicianship, production, and attitude of the record all kick ass. I think the title track and also the last song of the record, the ballad "Wishin' " (which I dedicate to my children), are among the best songs I have ever recorded.

For my next studio record, *Give 'Em Hell*, I was fortunate enough to have the best of the best in the business beside me. Again, I had John 5, for the song "Temptation," which became the first single off the record. Even more incredibly, I had my longtime buddy Duff McKagan on bass guitar and also rhythm guitar for the first half of the record. I had played in Australia with Matt Sorum's all-star band, Kings of Chaos, with Duff as well. We played on that day with Van Halen and Aerosmith both. A once-in-a-lifetime bill, I still pinch myself when I think about it.

On the way to the gig, I asked Duff, "Would you would be interested in collaborating on some music?"

"Sure! When? Where?"

And that was pretty much it! He brought in a song that ended up being called "Harmony" that I think turned out perfect. A great combination of tough riffs and melody, all at the same time. He introduced me to the guitar player Devin Bronson, who cowrote "All My Friends Are Dead," "Taking Back Tomorrow," and lots more on the record. He ended up doing some gigs with us and is a great friend. I have Duff to thank for this collaboration.

To make the album even more memorable, to me as a rock fan, the incomparable Steve Stevens from the Billy Idol Band came in on guitar, and wrote some songs as well. One song in particular, called "Push Away," I think is very unique in both of our repertoires. We have done that song live a couple times, and got a great response. It's quite haunting, as is the rest of the record. Lyrically, this album is quite dark, to the point where I refused the record company permission to put lyrics on the sleeve. It is very much a snapshot of a dark time in my life that hits me right between the eyes. Which is exactly what I want my music to do.

In between these two albums, I released an all-live package called *A Bachalypse Now*. I was originally approached to do a live DVD only, to which I said "sure," as a commemorative collectible for the tour we had done in that period. Then halfway through the project, I was told the record company wanted it to come out on CD as well. So, I went in the studio and made the CD part perfect audio-wise. On the third DVD disc, there is a show from Graspop, which we left completely untouched in every way. It is very funny to watch, and is my favorite part of *A Bachalypse Now*.

I have been with the record label Frontiers for a couple years now. I miss the old days of record companies. Going to radio stations, playing the latest song, talking about recording it. These days, we put the video up on YouTube and that's pretty much the extent of promotion. Different days for sure. But the cream always rises to the top. When we play the new songs live, they go over huge. Because we play with conviction. That's what rock 'n' roll is all about. We carry on.

I'm so lucky to have managers Rick Sales and Ernie Gonzalez by my side. Navigating me through this crazy business. They help me with the Internet, being a book writer, an actor, musician—all of these things. I could not do it without these guys. Rick Sales and his whole team allow me to do what I do, and get the music out to the world.

I am very lucky to have the legendary agent Troy Blakely on the team. Every since the passing of my friend Barbara Skydel, Troy has kept me busy working stages around the world. I am always on tour. I am always busy. I can't do this without Troy Blakely and APA. I thank them very much for putting me to work!

My longtime band and crew members are integral to my continued success in rock 'n' roll. My drummer, Bobby Jarzombek, was the best man at my wedding, and has been behind the kit for ten years now.

My tour manager, Dave Hart, is a great friend and gets us through the madness no matter what. Believe me, I could write a whole other book on the trials and tribulations just of being on tour in a rock 'n' roll band. Dave also does sound for the band and makes following us a challenge for some bands. I'm happy to have him running the show. My guitar players, Brent Woods, Rob DeLuca, Jeff Kollman, Kevin Chown—I am so very lucky to play with these cats. Chris Miller and Bryan Laffin do monitors and save my ears so I can keep rocking into the next decade and beyond. Being on a bus with real friends is essential, and makes going on the road so much fun. The road is impossible if you hate the dudes you're with. And I love the dudes I'm with. So that makes it easy.

It was right around this time my album *Kicking & Screaming* was released. After the chart disappointment of *Angel Down*, I was elated when *K&S* debuted at number 72 on the *Billboard* chart. Of course this is not number one. But compared to my previous release, I was very excited to see the album come in at such a higher place.

One night I went to Chateau Marmont with my friend Justin Murdock, of the Dole Pineapple dynasty. He's been a friend since I met him with Axl, years ago. We have kept in touch somewhat over the years. He invited me to Chateau for dinner and cocktails. When I got there, he was seated at the table with a man by the name of Art Davis. Who has given us Billboard Live and The Voyeur, among many other LA establishments. He told me a story at dinner that night about how Janis Joplin gave him a blow job in the early '70s, when he was in his early twenties. I was very impressed by this. We laughed and had a great time that night.

I was hanging out at the Rainbow a lot. It felt like my home away from home. Ever since 1987, the Rainbow has been so nice to me. Always welcoming. Accommodating. Treating me incredibly. One night I went and there was Art Davis again. He was with his wife

Cheryl. I had known Cheryl Rixon as a *Penthouse* Pet of the Year in the early '80s. Even more than that, she was *Creem* magazine's model with Judas Priest, in an iconic photo session with Rob Halford. She was on the back of Rob's motorbike, in a bikini, being led by a leash. This created an indelible stamp on my mind. I couldn't believe I was hanging out with the chick from *Creem* magazine.

I mentioned to Art, like I did to anyone within earshot, "Hey! I am looking for a place to live in LA!" He said, "Hey! Maybe you could come live at our place!" I had absolutely no idea what they did for a living. I did not know that Art had started many clubs and restaurants in the LA area. Was completely unaware that Cheryl had her own line of jewelry stores called Royal Order, with eighty-something stores in Japan alone. For all I knew, I was going over to check out a room in the valley above a garage or something. I was out of Matt Sorum's place, out of Betsy's apartment, and using my frequent flyer miles to bounce around from hotel room to hotel room in the Southern California area. This was getting to be really, really old. I had been living out of a suitcase ever since the divorce. I used to dream of unpacking my suitcase and hanging up my clothes and leaving them there, like I used to do before the hurricane. I was tired. I was just looking to start anew in this place that I always wanted to be in. Art said, "Come on over!"

I was late of course, looking for it. It was somewhere in Beverly Hills I had never been before. When I got there, I almost fell down. It was so incredibly beautiful.

They opened the doors, and I was let inside a house the likes of which I had never seen before.

Aaaahhhhhhhhhhhhhhhhhhh.

Here were the rock 'n' roll gods smiling upon me, yet again. *Yes, this'll do,* is what I thought. But more than just a room to live in, I was getting a new *family.* I lived with Art and Cheryl for about two years. Got to know their sons Luke and Dylan to the point they felt like little brothers. We had so many great holidays, dinners, and fun together and we continue to do so. When my daughter Sebastiana would fly out from New Jersey, Cheryl and Art treated her like their own daughter. It meant so much to her and to me.

When we go on tour in Australia, I am lucky enough to go to Cheryl's mom's house for family dinner. In Perth. On the other end of the planet. How lucky am I? I am so very proud to call Art and Cheryl, and their whole family, my great friends.

October 6, 2012
Lake Geneva, Wisconsin

I am playing a corporate show tonight, somewhere outside of Chicago. I have been doing quite a few of these over the last couple of years. People these days seem to want to take my picture as much as hear me sing. I think it has to do with tagging me on their Facebook page or something. That sure is important to a whole lot of people. Corporate gigs are weird for any musician. It's somewhat strange to play in front of a bunch of wealthy businessmen and their women, as opposed to throngs of sweaty, denim- and leather-clad rock 'n' rollers. But the pay that you get from these gigs makes it, literally, an offer that many of us can't refuse. Lots of musicians, from Elton John to Billy Joel to Paul McCartney, do these kinds of shows nowadays. "All You Need Is Love" . . . but love doesn't pay the mortgage.

I get to the beautiful resort and check into my room. I have no idea where I am. I assume that I am at some resort outside of Chicago. Nothing more important than that. I go to sleep and wake up around 7:30 in the morning. I go out onto the balcony of my suite to smoke a joint, which always puts me right back to bed. As I go out onto the balcony, I shut the door behind me so the hotel room doesn't soon reek of pot and I don't get kicked out of the hotel, which happened to me once in Anchorage, Alaska. It's no fun getting kicked out of the hotel in the snow in Alaska, not knowing where else to go. Not to mention it certainly did not make me very popular among the road crew and band members that day.

As I puff the last remnants of my joint, it's absolutely freezing outside. I'm wearing a leather jacket but no shoes or socks. My feet are bare. I am cold.

To my surprise, the balcony door is locked. I cannot open it. I cannot get back into my hotel room. I am three stories high up in the air, not to mention being actually high myself. I am stranded out on the balcony of my hotel room with no way to get back inside the building. My feet are freezing. I am stoned and my teeth are chattering. This sucks. I want to go back to bed.

I try repeatedly, with force, to open the sliding glass door and get back inside. The powerful marijuana kicks in and I become paranoid and start to freak out. What the fuck am I going to do? How am I going to get back inside? It's fucking freezing out here.

After realization sets in, I consider my choices. Let's see. I could jump off the balcony and probably break my ankle. Or, I could try to climb onto the roof of the resort and see if I can find somebody on the other side of the building. Not wanting to break my ankle from the fall, I decide to try and get on the roof somehow.

I place myself over the railing of my balcony and onto the gutters of the rain sewers below. I am adjacent to the hotel rooms next to me. I shimmy myself from hotel room to hotel room, hanging onto the balconies of each guest room. I am hanging on for dear life. It is very cold. I am trying to get to the building across from me. This is fucking crazy. I feel like Spider-Man. Did I mention, it's cold?

I hold on to the railings of each balcony one after the other, trying not to wake the guests within. I finally reach the other side of the hotel. The gutter drain that I am standing upon is placed precipitously over a courtyard that seems somehow familiar to me. I don't know why.

I finally reach the roof of the other side. I reach out as far as I can and pull myself up, with all my might. I straighten my arms out to hoist myself up onto the roof above. The roof is covered with gravel. It is sharp, and cuts into the bottom flesh of my freezing-cold feet. I walk across the rooftop, ignoring the pain of the gravel digging into my soles. I look up at the sky and I have to laugh at what in the hell is going on. I reach the end of the rooftop and look down into a crowd of stunned security guards below. One of them looks up, points out, and utters the familiar refrain, "Holy fuck, it's Sebastian Bach! You fucking rock dude!" He starts to laugh.

I stand in the cold, in bare feet, on the roof of the building, by myself, in the morning sun.

"I'm locked out of my fucking room, brother!" The guards look up and know who I am, probably by my long-ass hair flailing about in the wind. They start to laugh, too.

"What's going on, man?"

"I locked myself out of my room," ha ha. Now, everybody starts to laugh.

"I'll meet you over there!" says the security guard.

I walk across the hotel rooftop again and this time it hurts more. Because I know I'm alright. Because I don't have to get there. I finally shimmy back down the roof to the eaves trough and get myself back over to my balcony. The security guard lets me in the room, and tells me that a bunch of hotel guests had called wondering why a long-haired man in a black leather jacket was hanging off the side of their third-story hotel balcony at 7:30 in the morning.

Where I am looks strangely familiar. A certain palpability. Like the memories of a distant past. Still, can't quite place it, though.

The security guard makes sure I am secure, and after we share a laugh, we start to shoot the shit. "Well, that was quite the way to start the day."

"Hey man, how does it feel to be back?"

"What?"

Then it begins to dawn on me. I think to myself, *Could it be?*

I go back out on the balcony. This time, making doubly sure not to close the door behind me. I look down into the courtyard below.

I am staying in Lake Geneva, Wisconsin. Where we recorded the first Skid Row album. All those decades ago.

It all starts to come back to me now. Incredibly, in this sprawling, mega-resort, with thousands of hotel rooms and separate buildings, my room is directly across from Royal Recorders. The exact studio where I sang every song on the first Skid Row album back in the summer of 1988. Before I was a "famous person." I look from my hotel room balcony, in 2012, straight into the back window of the studio. Straight into another time. I remember this exact window. This was where Michael Wagener made his collection of all the Coca-Colas he drank during the session. By the end of the album, the window was completely blacked out by empty Coke cans, with the odd can of Budweiser thrown in by one of us for good measure. I remember the courtyard vividly, where we would play Frisbee or toss the football around between takes. Where we would have BBQs and get drunk. Where we would dream together of becoming rock stars. The courtyard is also where we had the "end of album" party, where the band and producer and engineers and management and crew all got shit hammered together and had a blast. The band Enuff Z'Nuff was at this party too. Doc and Scott had bought us bottles of Dom Perignon as a gift. I walked into the studio kitchen and saw Donnie Vie, the lead singer of Enuff Z'Nuff, popping open Skid Row's champagne and guzzling our suds straight from the bottle. *Enuff Z'Nuff of that*, I thought. I walked Donnie out of the kitchen into this very courtyard and explained to him, in quite emphatic terms I'm sure, that he needed to stop guzzling my champagne, posthaste. I remember wanting to whoop his ass for doing this. But why spoil a good party? That kind of behavior would come later. The last time I gazed upon this courtyard, no strangers at all knew who in the fuck I was.

I start to think about what had just happened to me. Cosmic, dude. How is it that my room is here, all these years later? How is it that for the first time in my life, I am locked out onto a third-floor balcony and cannot open the door to get back inside? How is it that I have no other option but to crawl and claw my way back over to this studio, pull myself on top, twenty-four years later, only to find myself standing in bare feet on the other side of the ceiling that echoed the sound of me singing "18 and Life"? With my hands raised to the sky, laughing my ass off? You really can't make this up. This is some trippy shit.

Or is it? As I look back upon my life, is this yet another case of my life and music being so closely parallel? From "Youth Gone Wild" in the studio, to "Kicking and Screaming" on the roof where it all began, it all seems to make perfect sense. Perfectly crazy. Perfectly impossible.

Maybe there was something going on that night in the Bahamas . . . so many moons ago . . .

Bach to the Future: Thank My Lucky Stars

2015
Studio City, California

I am in love.

What John Lennon said was indeed true. At the end of the day, at the end of your *life*, at the end of this book . . . love *is* all you need.

After a lifetime of volume and craziness, I enjoy peace and quiet just as much now. I am almost fifty years old. Halfway through this wild ride. If I'm lucky.

Thank God I met her.

Thank God she saved my life.

I am fortunate that my voice can still hit the high notes, even higher than I used to. I am very happy in the studio making records. Listening back to *Give 'Em Hell*, there is no doubt in my mind what I will be doing into my sixties, and hopefully beyond. Lord willing.

If I make it that far.

I thank Don Lawrence for teaching me the proper techniques I need to sing for a living. I thank Bon Jovi for introducing me to Don Lawrence at such a young age. It is undoubtedly the bel canto vocal style of scales that keeps my voice powerful and strong throughout the decades. I don't just go up there and *wing it*. There is a process, a system, of getting my voice to do what it has to do. When I play live now, the music takes over. I rock as hard as I can. Our band gets better the more we play. I don't feel any different now when I'm *onstage* than when I was in my twenties. But when I get *off* stage, my body is like, *What the fuck are you doing, dude?*

The industry has changed so much since I started. These days it's really important to have the VIP package. Everybody wants to meet the band. Get a picture for their Facebook profile. When I was a kid, we just went to the show, got fucked up, and then split. That was good enough for us. We could not have imagined meeting our rock 'n' roll heroes. Nobody had ultra-HD cameras on their phones, at all times, ready to videotape you eating lunch, going to Home Depot, coming out of the bathroom. A couple of years ago at a Roky Erickson show, I had to smash some dude's camera who was taking a picture of me taking a piss. This is extremely annoying. Sorry to the dude with the broken camera. Actually, I'm not.

Now that the book is done, I will begin on my next record. I am so lucky to have a record deal. I don't know what kind of sound this album will take. I would love to do an album that has the same feel as the '70s albums I listen to constantly. The analog sound of those records is precious.

I met my wife Suzanne about a year ago. And it's safe to say that this year has been the best year of my life.

How fortunate we are. To meet another human being that you're beyond attracted to, that is your greatest friend, is truly the rarest thing of all. Nobody is perfect. Everybody has their faults. Certainly I do, dear reader. The relationship I have with the love of my life, my happy wife, is all I could ever ask for. For so many reasons. She accepts me for who I am. Good and bad. She doesn't try to change me. I never understood that. Meeting somebody, and being attracted to them for certain qualities they have. Then becoming annoyed with those same exact qualities. It's happened to me. The manic energy can be tough to live with and a challenge to deal with. But we complement each other in so many ways. We are very much Yin and Yang. We are inseparable. We cannot stand to be apart. I am now married again and living in a beautiful home in Southern California as I write this. I have a new family, with four beautiful boys, and our beautiful daughter, that I am proud to call my own.

Never in my life could I have envisioned meeting the love of my life, along with two boys who are so nice and fun to be around. I love my new sons so much. They make every day fun. I never understood the concept of being *tied down* by a *family*. Nobody will ever tie me down. I'd like to see you try.

Suzanne is so good for me in so many ways. When we're on the road, at a restaurant, and I look across the room and people are filming us eat, I can turn into a real prick. Again, I am sorry for this. I just don't particularly want to take a picture with my mouth open, a fork held up to my face, as pancakes and syrup drip down onto the plate. This is not a good look for me. Or for you either. Nothing personal.

Suzanne has known me longer than I've known her. In Arkansas, when she was a little girl, she had a Skid Row poster over her light switch on the wall. Suzanne would literally turn my switch

on and *off* whenever she went into her bedroom. Her mom would do the same. Suzanne still switches me on and off, nightly. Sometimes in the morning, too.

When I blow up and throw a hissy little bitch fit, it's Suzanne who says, "Hey dude. Chill the fuck out. These people are paying for those pancakes and syrup. They love you. You're a lucky dude. You should be nice to everybody, no matter what." I try to explain to her that I don't like being filmed while we eat. Then, I give up. Because you know what?

She's right.

My friend Fred Coury says, "There's something about Sebastian. He can go through all sorts of crazy shit, be shot out of a cannon, and end up landing on his feet. With his hands in the air. Saying, 'Hey!! What the fuck is *up*!?!?!?!' " When Fred came over to our new house, and he met my wife, his words to me were "FUCK YOU with this house, man!!!" All in good fun. But I do thank my lucky stars, and God above, or whatever it is that does see me through. Somehow. I have the most beautiful wife in the world, who loves me, a new family, a new home, and a new future. I am happy. Again. For the first time in a long, long time. What would I say is the biggest lesson I've learned in life? When you find true love, you better hold on to that. Don't let go. There is no worse feeling than when love goes wrong. When your heart is broken. Because there is no better feeling in the world than being loved. Loving another. Having a partner in life. Someone to share experiences with.

We have as much fun as possible.

To me, that's what life is all about.

You Are the Rock Star

After all the craziness, after all the mayhem, after all is said and done, I'm pretty sure I have this "Life" thing figured out now. My buddy Duff said recently, I've spent a lot of time walking into walls. Maybe it's time for me to learn to walk *around* the wall.

Recently Scott Weiland died. On his tour bus. From cocaine. Cardiac arrest. Like Shannon Hoon, and so many before him. When I read back this book, I realize just how lucky I truly am. Just to be here to write this book. Just to be here *at all*.

I was with Scott Weiland not too long before he died, at my friend Donovan's wedding. We sat down, and without speaking, for some reason burst into the song "Out of Time" by The Rolling Stones. *That's really weird we're singing this song,* I thought.

Baby baby baby you're out of time . . .

And then he was.

I had recorded this song years ago, with Joey Ramone, for the Ramones' album *Acid Eaters.* What led me and Scott Weiland to sing

411

this song impromptu, out of nowhere, in the middle of a wedding, was something that struck me as odd when he passed away. I didn't know him that well, but his death made me very sad. We are the same age.

Having adulation and attention from the public is what many people believe will make them happy inside. I certainly did, dreaming of being a rock star as a kid. However, being almost fifty years old now, it's times with my wife and daughter, family times with my sons, Netflixing and chilling, that are among the activities that soothe me the most. The laughter of a child. If you have true love, trust, family, a beautiful partner to share your life with, then *you* are a rock star too.

The term *rock star* has changed so very much from when I was a teenager. Now, guys with computer programs, hedge fund managers, athletes, even presidents are called rock stars. "He was certainly the rock star in that debate," you hear bandied about on FOX News. The term is actually the highest compliment one can give to another. To bestow the title of rock star, upon a football player for example, is the ultimate accolade one can give. How ironic it is, that real rock stars find it ironic to call *themselves* rock stars. "When I hear the term 'one of the last remaining rock stars' I think 'one of the last remaining *assholes*,' " I've heard Dave Grohl (one of the last remaining rock stars) say. Well, it bugs me when a fucking *dentist* gets called a rock star. It bugs me when Kris Jenner calls Kim Kardashian a rock star. And it bugs me even more when Kanye West calls *himself* a rock star. Please. Perhaps you should learn how to sing or play an instrument before you give yourself the ultimate compliment that one can give.

This is all I have been told, pretty much my whole life. I hope this book explains a journey from childhood, to rock stardom, and back to family again. Yes, I have had a lot of fun. But at the end of the day, it's the melodies, songs, music onstage, and in studio that

lasts. Not the stories, not the self-destruction, not the fighting with other band members. When we are all dead and gone, none of that will matter. Yet, the music will live on. The music will play forever and ever. And that's the thing. Music is so important to all of us. Music has been my life. Chances are, if you are reading this book, music plays a central part in your life as well. Music was central to my parents' life. It's my wife's life. Our children are so enamored with music that it surrounds me at all times now. Our family likes to rock 'n' roll all night, and party every day. And nobody can ever take that away from me.

Peace Amongst the Chaos

After a lifetime of touring the planet, with a bunch of sweaty, smelly dudes, nowadays I look at touring as a *family activity*. I like to have my wife and children with me as much as possible. That means, on the road, too. It's called human nature. If the man loves a woman, and the man's job is to play music around the world, I have realized the only way to keep the relationship going is to be together as much as possible. I really love touring the world with my wife by my side. We are so lucky to do this.

When I hear the audience go nuts and crazy for rock 'n' roll, I still get chills on my arms, and go nuts and crazy along with them. The difference now is, after almost fifty years of volume and craziness, I enjoy just as much the peace, silence, and tranquility of a sultry summer night. I even listen to music at a *quieter volume* now. My doctor told me I need to do this at my age. And you know what's amazing? I have discovered that I can hear even *more* in the music when I just *turn it down* a little. Wow! Turning it down? So I can hear it? Who knew?

An evening by the fire. As nuts as rock 'n' roll is, I enjoy the quiet times equally now. I need to recharge my batteries after this crazy life. The energy you see onstage is real. When I'm done with the show, I have found I need *balance* in my life in order to continue.

I need peace amongst the chaos.

I need to rest my ears before I crank heavy metal. I need to rest my voice before I scream. I need to rest my body before I go on tour. I need to rest my mind before I go to sleep.

I love to make records. I am excited to make a new one. Writing this book has been cathartic, and has given me time away from the studio . . . to make me want to go back into the studio. I thank you for that.

I thank my children, Paris, London, Sebastiana, Presley, and Trace. We have been through so very much.

> *I wish I could be everything to you*
> *but wishin' won't make it true*

Now it's time for good times. Love, smiles, and laughter. After everything we've been through, to see my kids smiling again, on the other end of the mayhem? Nobody is smiling more than me.

Most of all, I thank Suzanne. I have found true love. I have found the love of my life . . . and she has given me a life that I love. And I love her for that. She is my best friend. She is my companion in this world. Not to mention, she is pretty easy on the eyes. I love you, Suzanne!!!!

She gives me the foundation and grounding I need. To do what I was put here to do.

To rock.

To scream.

To go wild.

She gives me the energy I need to bring the rock around the world . . . to you.

I thank every one of you for over thirty years of rock 'n' roll. It's all I ever wanted to do.

I needed to get some things off my chest.

April 14, 2016
Las Vegas, Nevada
T-Mobile Arena

Guns N' Roses got back together again last night. Yes, I wrote and you read that correctly. Guns N' Fucking Roses. The title of their tour is Not in This Lifetime and I can't think of a better name. We were sitting at dinner at around 9:30 p.m., relaxing, after playing a show on our own the night before in Vegas. Talking at the dinner table, "Oh, this is so great!! I can't believe, that for once, we just get to *watch* a show, be entertained, instead of entertaining everybody else!" Sometimes it feels too good to be lazy. And then, the text comes in.

"Stay alert! My Michelle. After Slash's solo."

Oh my God! We get to the gig, and sure enough, right before "My Michelle," I am welcomed onto the stage by Axl, Duff, and Slash. Guns N' Roses. Guns N' Roses *Reunion*. To be part of this experience is hard to put into words. The only way I can think to describe it is two words.

Time travel.

What a concept. Who really gets to *travel* through *time?* Just the week before, we filmed a new episode of *Gilmore Girls*, for the first time in twelve years. *Twelve years?* What an incredible experience that was, as well. To go back on the set, and see all my friends—all the crew, the producers, directors, lighting guys, cameramen, they were all there. And when we shot the scene, it felt as if our legendary band, the mighty Hep Alien, had never even broken up.

What an amazing opportunity to have. Just to show up, all in the same room as individuals with whom you know you have chemistry. It's almost as if time never passed.

HEY DUDE? WHEN ARE YOU GETTING THE BAND BACK TOGETHER?

2009

Bungalow 8, New York City

A hot New York City street night. Hanging out with Axl, after touring with GNR all over the place. He introduces me to this hangout called Bungalow 8 in the city. This fine establishment is named after the exact bungalow at Chateau Marmount that John Belushi died in, of a cocaine overdose, in 1982. It's quite the hang. Full of models, actors, musicians all out looking for a good time.

One night, some mid-level executive from VH1 is present. I'm there with Axl just hanging out. Everybody wants to meet him. They think.

"Hey Axl, this is the Vice President of VH1!!!" He looks over at the VP, straight in the eye, who reaches out to shake his hand. Axl declines the handshake. Looking around the room, then directly back into the man's eyes, he utters the immortal phrase:

"VH1? You guys have been *fucking me around for a long time.*" Then the executive's face turns a pallid shade of white, as he looks as if he's been kicked directly in the nuts. It was hilarious. I think he cried.

Another night at the Bungalow, I run into my old good buddy Dave Bryan from Bon Jovi. I had not seen him in decades. We were hanging out, catching up, laughing and having a great time. I went over to his table, where he was sitting in a booth, with some other people. One guy in the middle of the table had a baseball hat on. With his head down, in the dark club, I did not recognize this person. But he recognized me. Dave Bryan noticed me coming up to the table.

"How's it going, man?"

The guy next to him kept his head down as he started to talk. "Sebastian? Bach?" The man goes through a brief list of my dubious accomplishments—punching this person, insulting this person, breaking this person's jaw, breaking this law in this state, etcetera. He keeps on referencing some of my more dubious offenses, some described in this very book, to the hilarity of all present at the table. Then all of a sudden, at the end of this humorous tirade, he looks up at me, finally, and says, "So! I got one question for you, and one question only, Mr. Sebastian Bach.

"WHY IN THE HELL AREN'T YOU IN JAIL RIGHT NOW??????"

Everybody laughs, and finally I recognize this man. One of my favorite actors of all time. Mr. Sean Penn. The reason I say Sean Penn is one of my all-time favorite actors is because in every role I ever see him in, never do I see Sean Penn. I see the role he is on the screen to play. He is so convincing in every movie I've seen him in that the characters he plays are 100 percent completely believable.

"Oh my God!! I just saw that movie you did, *Milk*!?!?! I really loved it, man!!! I couldn't believe it! You kissed a *dude*!! That was *heavy*! Wow!!"

Everybody laughs. "Oh c'mon, admit it, Sebastian!! I made you uncomfortable because you *liked it*!!!!!" Everybody laughed some more. We decided to get a bottle of booze and go up to the private room upstairs, to hang out and shoot the shit.

As an actor who I constantly respected, I asked Sean how he knew everything he was saying at the table. Obviously a very serious rock 'n' roll fan, he told me that he had followed my career since we first came onto the scene. We talked about our mutual love and respect for Axl Rose and Guns N' Roses. "Yes, Sebastian. I have followed your career since you started. Getting into trouble . . . always with *that face*." I just started to laugh. I could've said the exact same thing about him.

He asked me what I was up to and I had to go into the usual story of the breakup of Skid Row. I don't even know if he knew Skid Row had even broken up. I tell him about Broadway, which was cool, and my solo career, which I thought was impressive. With his intense commitment, and belief in his acting roles, I thought he would understand and respect my situation in the music business. Which was being kicked out of the band I had helped make successful, and in some ways being *forced* into a solo career. I would not be the first one to try to get back with a band that had kicked me out. I had often used the analogy in the press. "If you got fired from your job at Pizza Hut, would you go begging for it back???" I thought he would laugh at this. His response was the opposite of what I was expecting.

Sean just shook his head.

"Why?"

"Why what?"

"Well, why would you *not* want to get the band back together?"

I explained to him, because of musical differences, personalities, he said this, I said that, blah blah blah blah. He just looked at me like he didn't understand what I was saying. "I need to make the music I need to make. I need to make art that I believe in."

"But Sebastian. You're not understanding one simple thing."

"What?"

"If all of you, the five original musicians in the original band, got back together on a stage? *That* would be the art . . . *in and of itself.*"

Now, it was *my* turn to not understand what *he* was saying. I thought it was all about the *content.* Not the *form.* Shouldn't the music itself be more important than who I make the music *with*?

"The music you made with Skid Row was the music that touched the world. If you five got together again? *I* have been waiting for that. I would buy a ticket for *that.* I would come and see that."

I was floored. I respected this actor more than I could put into words. And here he was, like the rest of the planet, all the press, pretty much everywhere I go, uttering the same familiar refrain.

"Hey dude? When are you getting the band back together?"

It will never cease to amaze me how much music means to all of us. In the fabric of our lives. It is without a doubt the most visceral art form. You can see a movie or television show and feel nostalgic and fuzzy and remember how you felt when you first watched it. But there is nothing like music to reactivate the feelings and memories of days gone by. When you hear a song from your childhood, it's astonishing how much do you feel inside just how you felt when you first heard it. It is an amazing mystery that we will never solve. And it *never wears off.* I go through periods of listening to different artists. When The Eagles' documentary came out, I watched it over and over again. I was transfixed by the unbelievably kick-ass Mr. Joe Walsh. So what do I do? I go out and buy every single record he ever did. Without question. That's how I listen to music. I can't get enough of it. It's always been like that.

I know our fans of Skid Row feel the same way I do. How could they not? So there is a goal for the future. How fun would it be someday to get together again? For the sake of rock 'n' roll even. It's not like there's a lot of us left.

What would it take to get together again? First of all, we would need to be able to get together in the same room. Which we have not done in over twenty years. I know it's crazy. That's rock 'n' roll.

I think this is the key to success. I think that if we could all stop insulting each other on the Internet, realize what our music actually *means* to the people's lives who enjoy it, then maybe we could get back in the same room and see if there is a chance for this. To get the band back together, dude.

I completely understand why people want us to get together again. They are classic albums.

Do I want a reunion myself? None of us are getting any younger. I look at The Eagles and how they reunited. Only now to have Glenn Frey leave us, too soon. Dio. Lemmy. Philthy Animal Taylor. Scott Weiland. Keith Emerson. David Bowie. Prince. These are all very big inspirations for Skid Row to get back together. I look at the fact that we are all still healthy, and collectively have a lot of good years left. I would love to feel the excitement of being in a band together again. Being in a solo band is a lot of pressure and responsibility. It would be a good experience for us to *share* responsibility again, instead of making all of the decisions, good and bad, on my own.

As I get older, I don't have to have everything my way *all* of the time. I realize that collaborating with other people results in more than the sum of its parts. When I see my favorite bands reunite, I understand what people are saying to us. That a team of players is different than watching one solo player. The songs that we made in Skid Row were made by five people. Yes, I would like to hear those songs, one more time, played by those exact five people who played them on the records, in my lifetime.

Will it happen? Who knows?

They say that being in a band is like a marriage. I can attest to that. I was married for twenty years, broke up, only to find love again. When I did not know true love even existed. Yes, it is possible to find love again.

My love for singing rock 'n' roll, and my love for singing Skid Row songs, will never, ever end. As this book ends, I can see new beginnings. On the horizon.

What I can see is based on what I can feel. What I sing is based on what is in my heart. I believe that positive energy comes back to you.

I believe that rock 'n' roll is forever. I *believe*.

SELECTED BACHOGRAPHY

(with release dates)

Attic Records:
Maple Metal (1985)

Atlantic Records:
Skid Row (January 24, 1989)
Slave to the Grind (June, 1991)
BSide Ourselves (1992)
sUBHUMAN rACE (March 7, 1995)
40 Seasons: The Best of Skid Row (1998)
Bring 'Em Bach Alive! (November 2, 1999)

Atlantic / AVISION Entertainment:
Oh Say, Can You Scream? VHS/LASERDISC (1990)
Roadkill 3D VHS (1993)
No Frills Video (1993)

Spitfire / Eagle Rock:
The Last Hard Men (2001)
Forever Wild DVD (June 15, 2004)

ProgRock:
Frameshift 2: An Absence of Empathy (April 12, 2005)

MRV / Caroline / Get Off My Bach:

Angel Down (November 20, 2007)

Angel Down Limited Edition Featuring *RoadRage*, a Film by Sebastian
    Bach (July 21, 2008)

Astralwerks:

Battle with the Bottle (2008)

Frontiers Records:

Kicking & Screaming (September 21, 2011)

Kicking & Screaming Deluxe Edition Featuring "As Long As I Got the
    Music" DVD (September 27, 2011)

A Bachalypse Now DVD/CD (March 26, 2013)

Give 'Em Hell (April 22, 2014)

PM:AM Recordings:

Dada Life Featuring Sebastian Bach: "Born to Rage" (2015)

PHOTO CREDITS

ACKNOWLEDGMENTS

This book would not be possible without the guidance, attention to detail, and extreme patience of Carrie Thornton and Ernie Gonzalez. Carrie, thank you so much for your belief in my writing. It means more to me than you could ever know. Ernie, I need to thank you so very much for your professionalism. The way you work with me soothes the savage beast inside. I just can't do it without you man.

To my manager Rick Sales, thank you for being the one guy that I know who truly read this whole thing all the way through from page 1 to page 448. Your input and opinions mean everything to me. Thanks for literally being on the same page as me!

I would also like to acknowledge the following people:

Kenny Fox, Brian Cruikshank, Bill Sax, Dave Aplin, Andy Rytch, Bobby Jarzombek, Brent Woods, Rob DeLuca, "Metal" Mike Chlauschek, Johnny Chromatic, Steve DiGiorgio, Brent Woods, Devin Bronson, Beta, Fernando, Bascha and family, Mark and Sabrina, Del James, Tommy Mayhue, Sherid, Shayla, Dylan McGhee, Larry "Ratso" Sloman for thinking I could do this before anyone else, David Hyslop, Joe Godwin, Kevin Phillips, Jim Byk and Jason Howland for turning me into a Broadway Star, Jimmy VanZino, Mr. and Mrs. Mulvehill, Masai, Marshall, Bobby Buckelew, Dave Feld, Scott Trusler, Todd Goldstein, Ian Osborne, Toby Anderson RIP and family, Joe Stable, Alan Tubi, Amy Bailey, Monique Frehley, Rick Krim, Dana Marshall, Wayne Isham, Curt Mavis, Jean Pellerin, Barb Sparkman, Nancy Moore.

ACKNOWLEDGMENTS

God Bless the Roadies. We make it Rock. But you guys make it Roll:

Chris "Mohr'shead" Mohr, Double Live "Ronzo," Terry Sasser, Todd Mackler, Steve Pritchengast, "Big" Jim King RIP, Bob "Burly" Elkins, James "Midge" Villasvic, Dave Hart, Bryan Laffin, Chris Miller, Richard Diaz De Leon, Randy, Toby Francis, Jimmy Duncan, Said, Bobby Buckaloo, "Jersey" Jay Jeffreys RIP, Larry "Love" Walsh and family, Michael Walsh RIP.

To my Family: Tiana, Presley, Trace, London, Reece, Loc and Lo (rhymes with rock 'n' roll!), Heather, Warren, Marley, Bless, Izzy, Zac, Liz, Kevin, Stacey, Jackson, Alyson, Steve, David and Sara, Hunter and Emma, Michelle and Dave, Max and Nicole, Charlie, Nikki, Alex, and Jeff, Mike and Caity Bierk, Davy Bierk.

To the Perry County Missouri Historical Society.

To Dave Draiman: Thank you from the bottom of my heart for introducing me to the love of my life, Suzanne. I truly never knew life could be so great. I will always love you for that. I wish you all the best and I can never thank you enough. Abby and Brett, Jen and JB, BL Dave, Jeff Fioretti, Jeff Adams, Melissa Correales, Stacey, Mary Hooton, Charrie Foglio, Sergio Perafino, Drew Masters, Lenny Stoute, Mike "Moon" Taveroff, Kevin McCallion and family, Joe Stable, Mr. Embury, Alan Fullerton, Meredith Usher, Greg Alfred, Scott Carter, Steve Hunter, Judd Smoke, David Wild, Ian O'Malley, "Fingers" from BAB, Gary "The Byrd" Kempf, Mr. Affuso RIP, Mrs. Affuso.

To the crew at Dey Street Books—Lynn Grady, Michael Barrs, Heidi Richter, Julie Paulauski, David Palmer, Suet Chong, and Sean Newcott. For my awesome cover, thanks to the dudes at Meat and Potatoes, and Mark Seliger.

To Mr. and Mrs. Southworth: I will never forget the night (or early morning) you drove me to Newark so I could be there for the birth of my first son. Thank you for opening your house and garage to your son's band and allowing the band Skid Row to happen. Could never have happened without you guys.

To Mama Snake, from "Legs": thank you for opening your home to the craziness of the band Skid Row. No one loved Skid Row more than you did. And we all loved you just as much back! We were your biggest fans. Thank you Mama Snake for allowing the band Skid Row to happen. In your living room, no less!

Note to your Self: If I forgot your name, I am truly sorry. I feel like I just played three countries in three days. Oh wait, I did! OK so you got to excuse me, I have to go warm up now tonight for the show TONIGHT in San Juan Capistrano!!

I believe, mother truckers!!

See you at the show!

They're coming to take me away, haha . . .

ABOUT THE AUTHOR

SEBASTIAN BACH has sold in excess of twenty million records worldwide as lead singer of his former band, Skid Row, and as a solo artist. Far from just being a multi-platinum recording artist, he has expanded his career over the past decade to include a five-season recurring role on the hit series *Gilmore Girls;* voice-over work on *SpongeBob Square Pants* and *Robot Chicken;* starring roles on Broadway in *Jekyll & Hyde, The Rocky Horror Show,* and *Jesus Christ Superstar;* and appearances on ABC's *Sing Your Face Off,* the comedy series *Trailer Park Boys,* MTV, and VH1.